Selling Out

Setting Out

Selling Out

Culture, Commerce and Popular Music

Bethany Klein

BLOOMSBURY ACADEMIC
NEW YORK · LONDON · OXFORD · NEW DELHI · SYDNEY

BLOOMSBURY ACADEMIC
Bloomsbury Publishing Inc
1385 Broadway, New York, NY 10018, USA
50 Bedford Square, London, WC1B 3DP, UK

BLOOMSBURY, BLOOMSBURY ACADEMIC and the Diana logo are trademarks of
Bloomsbury Publishing Plc

First published in the United States of America 2020

Copyright © Bethany Klein, 2020

For legal purposes the Acknowledgments on p. vi constitute an
extension of this copyright page.

Cover design by Rebecca Heselton

All rights reserved. No part of this publication may be reproduced or transmitted
in any form or by any means, electronic or mechanical, including photocopying,
recording, or any information storage or retrieval system, without prior permission
in writing from the publishers.

Bloomsbury Publishing Inc does not have any control over, or responsibility for, any
third-party websites referred to or in this book. All internet addresses given in this
book were correct at the time of going to press. The author and publisher regret any
inconvenience caused if addresses have changed or sites have ceased to
exist, but can accept no responsibility for any such changes.

A catalog record of this book is available from the Library of Congress.

ISBN: HB: 978-1-5013-3930-1
PB: 978-1-5013-3931-8
ePDF: 978-1-5013-3933-2
eBook: 978-1-5013-3932-5

Typeset by RefineCatch Limited, Bungay, Suffolk
Printed and bound in the United States of America

To find out more about our authors and books visit www.bloomsbury.com
and sign up for our newsletters.

Contents

Acknowledgements	vi
Introduction	1
1 Popular music for art's sake	17
2 Popular music as big money	39
3 Alternative goes mainstream	61
4 A different kind of selling out	85
5 Popular music in advertising	111
6 Promotion in popular music	127
7 Popular music and beyond	153
References	165
Index	185

Acknowledgements

Thanks to Leslie Meier and Devon Powers for the conversations and collaborations that led to the development of this book. The article we published in *Popular Music and Society* in 2017 ('Selling Out: Musicians, Autonomy, and Compromise in the Digital Age') was an especially important springboard. I've been lucky to collaborate with two of the cleverest scholars of popular music and commerce, and even luckier to count them as good friends.

The School of Media and Communication at the University of Leeds is home to many researchers whose work I both enjoy and respect: special thanks to Leslie Meier (again), Stephen Coleman and Dave Hesmondhalgh for their valuable comments on the manuscript, to Nancy Thumim and Matthias Revers for allowing me to incorporate book chat into social calls, and to loads of other enthusiastic friends and colleagues for spirited discussions and links to relevant examples. I'm also thankful to my brother, Josh Klein, who applied his experience as a music journalist and extensive knowledge of popular music to draft chapters.

Thanks to Leah Babb-Rosenfeld and Amy Martin at Bloomsbury for their support, and the reviewers of the proposal and manuscript for their thoughtful feedback. An earlier version of Chapter 5 appears in *The Oxford Handbook of Music and Advertising* (2020).

Finally, I'm grateful to Jonah and Sid, who together ensure that every day includes singing, dancing and listening to music. But please turn the volume down: I'm trying to think.

Introduction

'Selling out' accusations have long been wielded against individuals and organizations across a range of sectors perceived to have compromised their values for financial gain or the pursuit of power. The politician who goes back on a promise in order to seemingly maintain or increase their influence, the journalist whose investigative curiosity ends when it comes to companies that are relied on for advertising revenue, the small business owner who accepts a takeover offer from a multinational: each may expect the 'sellout' label. The language of 'selling out' has played a particularly central and persistent role within popular music culture, connecting to long-standing tensions between art and capitalism, and allowing ordinary fans as well as professional commentators to police the porous boundary between culture and commerce and to highlight wider promotional trends in society. At a time when commercial and private interests exert growing influence, normalizing private control over everything from arts to healthcare (Philips and Whannel 2013, McGoey 2015), discussions of culture versus commerce, independence and creative freedom take on grave importance. What, then, are we to make of claims that there is 'no such thing as selling out' (McCourt 2005, Berkmann 2010, Corr 2012, Eshun 2012, Molotkow 2012, England-Nelson 2015) and that 'selling out no longer exists' (Fiorletta 2011, Richards 2011)?

It can seem as though there is little left to sell that hasn't been sold: the aggressive spread of promotional culture (Wernick 1991, Davis 2013) has enabled branding to extend into nearly every nook and cranny of everyday life (Aronczyk and Powers 2010, McAllister and West 2013). Authenticity and creativity are resources to be mined and exploited in the service of selling (Banet-Weiser 2012, Klein 2009) – especially as digitalization has cast traditional sources of revenue for cultural producers into uncertainty. The relationship between art and capitalism once critiqued by artists espousing values of Romanticism has given way to an age when it is perfectly normal for big brands to sponsor art galleries, awards, creative workshops and festivals.

The commercialization of culture has been aided rather than resisted by cultural policy that has privileged measurable financial benefits over more difficult to evaluate social benefits of investments into art and culture, including music. Considerations of cultural value outside the purely economic realm help us to imagine an alternative universe, where there are lines that should not be crossed, some things are sacred and the public good is revived. Exploring the nuances and changing contours of selling out debates allows for the re-animation of a discussion that many musicians, fans and commentators have consigned to history.

This book explores the history, meaning and unsteady path of selling out in popular music culture as a reflection of the global embrace of commercialization across a range of sectors, in order to address the following questions: what role and purpose has the concept of selling out served in popular music culture over time and across genres? How have political, economic, technological and cultural changes challenged the basis of selling out debates? What do we lose when we lose the ability to make judgements about selling out? What can we learn from the case of popular music and apply to other arenas (for example, journalism, education and healthcare) where similar debates have been dismissed as irrelevant? In this chapter, I explore the history of the phrase 'selling out' within popular music culture and argue for the work the phrase performs as discourse. I consider classic and recent work on art and capitalism, the commercialization of culture and the value of music, laying out the reasons for using popular music as a case study and selling out as an exploratory lens.

What is 'selling out'?

The phrase 'selling out' describes the act of abandoning 'previously held political and aesthetic commitments for financial gain' (Hesmondhalgh 1999: 36). While popular music may be the setting in which the phrase has been most commonly applied, the OED dates the usage of 'sell-out' as 'a sacrifice of principle or betrayal' to the 1860s, with examples hailing from the political arena. Randall Kennedy (2008) examines the history of the term as a label for African-Americans viewed as acting against the interests of the black community for their own advancement, from slaves who alerted plantation owners to planned rebellions to recent prominent politicians, leaders and intellectuals. While Kennedy points to the negative consequences of widespread racial indictments, he also sees the term as serving a purpose for maintaining communities and policing boundaries. Art and, later, popular music required certain conditions rooted in Romanticism (the embedding of notions of autonomy and individual genius) and capitalism (the replacement of a patronage system with a market, and the linking of creators and products through copyright) to be met in order to earn a seat at the selling out table (Pillsbury 2006). Once adopted, the term here similarly worked to maintain (music) communities and to police boundaries (between art and commerce).

The phrase eventually became such an ordinary part of popular music debates that we may be inclined to dismiss it as a cliché, but this would be a mistake:

> What can seem like a cliché to an academic scholar also functions for music fans as an important means for making sense of the world; better to inquire as to what is at stake to make such ideas attractive and important than to dismiss them forthwith. From there we can begin to understand the cultural tensions informing the selling out argument: because it matters.
>
> Pillsbury 2006: 136

The inclination to wave away selling out as a fan construction that fails to capture the complex reality of the music industries ignores the value of the phrase in communicating how we experience the world, including the boundaries we hold up as meaningful. It also leaves unexplored the role the idea plays in policing and maintaining the line, however permeable, between culture and commerce in popular music culture.

While recognizing the many different ways of delineating 'popular music' as an object of study, following Roy Shuker, I use the term 'popular music' to include 'the diverse range of popular music genres produced in commodity form, largely, but no longer exclusively for a youth market, primarily Anglo-American in origin (or imitative of its forms), since the early 1950s, and now global in scope' (Shuker 2016: 6). The activities of popular musicians have been scrutinized by fans and critics for signs of 'going commercial' even before Beatlemania revealed avenues of capitalizing on success previously unimagined (perhaps best captured by the empty cans of 'Beatle Breath' sold to fans). Various dimensions of music-making, from the sound of the music itself to a musician's association with a commercial company, are vulnerable to perceived transgressions.

The most common dimension to attract charges of selling out in popular music is the sound of the music itself. In such cases, artists who are perceived to have changed their sound or musical style in order to achieve commercial success are viewed as having sold out. The change may involve straying from the conventions of a genre, using different instruments or using instruments differently, or breaking with musical principles associated with a particular music tradition. Simon Frith offers a useful interpretation of this version of selling out when he asks, 'Why Does Music Make People So Cross?' (2004). As he notes, the pursuit of 'crowd-pleasing' can provoke anger that 'performers or composers are *betraying their talent*' and the 'most familiar version of this argument is the rock cultural concept of "selling out"' (Frith 2004: 66, emphasis in original). Anger directed towards the music itself may stand in for anger about a perceived 'betrayal of identity', especially for fans who view musical taste as differentiating them from mainstream consumers (Frith 2004: 67). Accusations of selling out are often expressed with reference to the music, even if used as an indicator of other transgressions or to convey the concern that commercialization drains subculture of its power (Moore 2005).

Musicians who adopt a more commercial sound may attract mainstream and larger audiences, but risk alienating early fans. Choices that are perceived to have been cynically made with the goal of reaching as wide an audience as possible are open to charges of selling out: the Rolling Stones and Blondie were among those groups on the receiving end of such accusations when they flirted with disco at the height of the style's popularity. While the adoption of commercially friendly elements – from trendy instrumentation or more polished production, to more mainstream content or delivery of lyrics (e.g. in language or accent) – is often the focus, it is not music alone which is under the microscope. Non-musical choices, including appearance (John Lennon described the Beatles' adoption of mohair suits as selling out (Williams 1969)), stage show and collaborations (from tour mate to producer), can similarly be scrutinized for signs of compromise for financial gain. Of course, such examples rely on a certain amount of mind-reading to support an interpretation of 'selling out' or 'going commercial', with artists able to justify their choices as driven by and part of an artistic vision, rather than monetary gain. Like many, if not most, charges of selling out, whether the artist's intention is artistic expression or cashing in is unknowable and ultimately superseded by public perception.

Moving outside the content of music and performance to the context of making and promoting music, artists must confront another set of choices and possible missteps in the form of the companies with which they associate. Selling out debates in the 1980s and 90s often revolved around independent bands 'signing' to major labels: the mainstream success of bands like Nirvana and

Green Day led to an explosion of independent bands being offered major label contracts, and to cries of 'sellout' when they accepted (see accounts in Azerrad 2001, O'Connor 2008). Whether an artist is perceived to maintain creative control can mitigate the charges, while excessive merchandising, exorbitant ticket prices and a too-cosy relationship with the press can aggravate them. Even television appearances have been deemed too commercial for some: the Clash and Arctic Monkeys are among those who refused to appear on British music chart programme *Top of the Pops* and others have declined, at least temporarily, to make or appear in music videos (for example, George Michael for *Listen Without Prejudice, Volume 1*, Radiohead for *Kid A* and Pearl Jam after their success with *Ten*).

Across the range of activities, selling out in popular music is a charge levelled when an artist is perceived as pursuing *commercial* gain at the expense of *cultural autonomy*. The phrase 'cultural autonomy' is used here 'to capture activities that may be understood as creative and/or artistic, and that likely relate to economic security, but also activities that do not clearly fit these categories, including choices of distribution or affiliation informed by ethos or ethics' (Klein, Meier and Powers 2017: 222). The use of music in advertising represents an example of commercial affiliation and has served as an illustration of the culture/commerce tension in action. Criticism of artists who have partnered with corporate brands is not new: in 1988, Neil Young's 'This Note's for You' satirized the growing trend of corporate sponsorship and advertising featuring popular music and musicians. However, by the turn of the twenty-first century, with the indie-vs-major argument essentially exhausted through co-optation of indie by the mainstream (Hesmondhalgh and Meier 2014), the use of popular music in advertising became a prominent focus of selling out debates.

The most recent shift in selling out debates can be located in the proliferation of claims over the last decade declaring the concept's irrelevance. In an excellent piece that ties together many of the issues that have prompted and challenged the utility of the selling out concept within popular music culture, music journalist Dorian Lynskey questions whether 'the old tyranny of the purist' has 'given way to the tyranny of the realist', and whether we are 'seeing the last days of the sellout' (Lynskey 2011).

In fact, the concept's irrelevance to popular music has been declared in every decade since it entered the popular music lexicon: songs and albums have satirized the concept (we witnessed the Who *Sell Out* in 1967 and Supergrass was *In It for the Money* thirty years later in 1997); music journalists and musicians have challenged the tendency of some accusers to equate commercial success with selling out; and artists have provocatively and enthusiastically embraced activities critiqued as selling out. At the same time, as this book will demonstrate, selling out has been regularly invoked in heated debates about artists developing more commercial sounds, independent bands signing to major labels and the use of popular music in advertising.

What is different now is that charges of selling out are rare sightings and reports of the demise of selling out are almost blasé. In the *New York Times Magazine*, Alexandra Molotkow avers, 'If you can be popular on your own terms – if you can be Arcade Fire or Bon Iver and still win a Grammy – there is really no such thing as "selling out" anymore' (Molotkow 2012). Of licensing popular music to advertising, Jessica Hopper writes in *Buzzfeed*, 'what was once considered to be the lowest form of selling out, of betraying fans and compromising principles, is now regarded as a crucial cornerstone of success' (Hopper 2013).

Scholars, too, have identified a shifting landscape that no longer accommodates selling out. In his historical account of music used in advertising, Timothy Taylor argues, 'there is no longer a meaningful distinction to be made between "popular music" and "advertising music"' and 'selling out is no longer an issue' (2012: 229), given the regular movement of musicians and messages between the worlds of music and advertising. In a piece on *Medium*, danah boyd (2014) questions 'whether or not the underlying concept is meaningful in contemporary youth culture'. As well as identifying the term's flexible connotations, boyd suggests that, in the context of the music industries, the 'notion of selling out requires that there is one reigning empire. That really isn't the case anymore' (boyd 2014). Justin Lewis links the loss of the phrase with the triumph of consumerism: 'At one time we associated the idea of "selling out" with artists—writers, actors, musicians and so on—who compromised their craft for commercial ends. The triumph of consumerism is such that the phrase is rarely used anymore. As George Gerbner observed, our culture is manifestly *about* selling, if not selling out' (2013: 69, emphasis in original).

One strand of the triumph of consumerism involves cases of ever closer relationships between musicians and consumer brands, through licensing, sponsorship, endorsement deals and product placement. Increasingly, such relationships are relied on to replace volatile or threatened revenue streams in the global music industries: the global recorded music market has been growing since 2015, thanks largely to paid streaming subscriptions (IFPI 2019), but overall revenues are only two-thirds of what they were in 1999 (Savage 2018a). In this context, consumer brands are positioned as supporters of popular music culture, and activities once dismissed as selling out are seized upon by artists looking for diminishing sources of funding for their creative efforts. In 2009, I wondered if the charge of selling out was a 'distraction from how the use of music in advertising constrains, highlights, or suppresses meanings that audiences have the ability to create' (Klein 2009: 99). I still feel that accusations against individual artists fail to see the forest for the trees (artist decisions are, after all, a response to the conditions they find themselves in), but I've come to view the discourse of selling out as an incredibly important focus for the work that it does.

Selling out, discourse and debates

Its declared irrelevance provided the catalyst for exploring the cultural history of selling out in this book, but there are other good reasons to focus on the concept of selling out in popular music culture. First, it is an evocative and ordinary example of language used to police profit-driven activities and their potential consequences. Journalism, education, healthcare and music are components of all our lives but, whereas few people might feel confident discussing the commercialization of journalism, the marketization of education or the privatization of healthcare, many have experienced and discussed issues related to selling out and popular music – as when a favourite artist is perceived to have gone mainstream or when a much loved song is used in a television commercial. Second, selling out in popular music culture has its roots in non-music examples, as per the historical use of the phrase in politics and around race (as noted above). This is a useful reminder of the stakes of the selling out debates *beyond* music: selling out points to the values of autonomy and integrity we expect of actors in whom we invest our trust, to support democracy, to support community. Third, the concept of selling out offers an entry to key debates about art and capitalism, the commercialization of culture and the cultural value of popular music for musicians and fans. Finally, selling out is a productive focus because it is not simply a phrase that has waxed and waned in popularity, but a discursive barometer of the relationship between culture and commerce. In this section, I explore how selling out functions as a discourse and how it provides a bridge between ordinary, everyday music chat and important debates about art, capitalism, commerce and value.

This book traces selling out as a discourse, defined, following Norman Fairclough (1992), as spoken or written language use as a form of social practice, which is both shaped by social structures and socially constitutive. 'Discourse is a practice not just of representing the world, but of signifying the world, constituting and constructing the world in meaning' (Fairclough 1992: 64): it constitutes social identities, social relationships and systems of knowledge and belief.

Fairclough employs discourse analysis, a combination of linguistics and social theory, as both a systematic method of approaching texts and a critical contextualization which takes into account ideology and power. The approach often explores discourse and social change in relation to how marketing shapes language, and how language shapes social practice – in this way, discourse is not just a valuable lens for examining selling out, it is also thematically linked. Relatedly, renewed sociological interest in capitalism in the 1990s (Sennett 1998, Boltanski and Chiapello 2005) homed in on the detrimental social consequences of new working and management cultures. Fairclough's collaboration with Eve Chiapello to understand how the 'new spirit of capitalism' socially structures management texts (Chiapello and Fairclough 2002) is driven by 'the belief that texts have social, political, cognitive, moral and material consequences and effects, and that it is vital to understand these consequences and effects if we are to raise moral and political questions about contemporary societies, and about the transformations of "new capitalism" in particular' (2002: 14).

In considering the importance of language in social and cultural change, Fairclough notes that 'in many countries there has recently been an upsurge in the extension of the market to new areas of social life' (1992: 6), with education, healthcare and the arts among the sectors forced to understand their services as commodities and their users as consumers. He cites educational discourse as an example of the commodification of discourse, where the use of marketing language leads to wordings that 'effect a metaphorical transfer of the vocabulary of commodities and markets into the educational order of discourse' (1992: 208). Fairclough characterizes this change as 'more than just a rhetorical flourish: it is a discursive dimension of an attempt to restructure the practices of education on a market model' (1992: 208). In popular music culture, we have witnessed a similar transfer, reflected in the declared irrelevance of selling out, and related shifts in wording, from musicians as artists to artists as brands, from fans as communities to fans as consumers, from music and commerce as linked but separate, or as one.

By looking back at when selling out entered the vocabulary of popular music culture, and by tracing its travels over time and across genre, we revive the boundaries between culture and commerce that restructured practices of music making deny. Along the way, we encounter related terms, like authenticity, going commercial and independence, that can help us understand what the concept of selling out has sought to communicate and protect – sometimes problematically, when its use excludes by race and gender, and sometimes constructively, when its use challenges corporate power. Authenticity, in particular, is a term so malleable that it travels to different genres, eras and contexts with relative ease, hiding the work of division it performs. The following chapters demonstrate how discourse shapes debates, and opens and closes possibilities for understanding popular music's relationship to culture and commerce.

In order to track the use of 'selling out' in popular music culture, I located the phrase and its other tenses (sell out, sold out) across more than 10,000 popular and trade press articles from the 1960s to the present. I used the open source document mining platform Overview to search and organize the articles. Most of the sources, and the majority of the artists profiled or interviewed, are based in the US and the UK: I therefore cannot argue that the story I tell captures international variation, but it is also the case that the US and the UK have been and remain global centres of the music industries, thus setting the discursive tone. The artists featured in the press coverage, and consequently in my analysis, tend to be located in genres that have experienced significant commercial success (even if some of the artists mentioned have not), that have recognized the notion of selling out as meaningful and that have been of interest to advertisers. While Fairclough's perspective on discourse influenced my view of selling out as doing, not simply saying, I stop short of analysing texts in terms of genre and style: I've identified the dominant discourses of selling out at work in press coverage to structure the book chronologically and thematically. While a sense of compromise and commercial intent has remained inherent to notions of selling out over the time period covered, debates have clustered around era-specific activities and tendencies.

The concept of selling out in popular music culture is one manifestation of the long and complex set of links between art and capitalism. Glenn Pillsbury (2006) explains the emergence of selling out in the mid-nineteenth century as reflecting key changes to the relationship between creativity and commerce. Romanticism and the notion of 'original genius' acted to protect the status of art and artists at a time when 'the decline and large-scale disappearance of the aristocratic patronage system (which had been in place for centuries) and the concomitant rise of industrial capitalism necessitated that artists of all types operate according to some kind of marketplace economics' (Pillsbury 2006: 137). The pressure to balance commercial appeal with 'inspired' art challenged fine artists from the late eighteenth century. In contrast, for many critics, the popular culture enabled by mass production and mass media in the twentieth century reflected a complete embrace of commercialism and distance from the sort of elevation high arts sought to achieve.

Theodor Adorno and Max Horkheimer's 1944 critique of the 'culture industry' has become the extreme archetype of this perspective: like factories, the culture industries produce standardized cultural goods, which only appear different through pseudo-individualization, and which represent a collapse of important distinctions, including those between art and advertising. It's easy to dismiss the critique as elitist and as painting all of popular culture with the same brush, but their account is also amazingly prescient of some of the worst trends of commercialism in media and music. Aeron Davis (2013: 100) locates the centrality of promotion in the music industries as linked to the financial unpredictability of cultural products: he suggests that reliance on the work of promotional intermediaries can constrain creativity – a tension which he links back to the Frankfurt School's cultural industry thesis – even as the decentralization of activity in cultural industries translates to a high degree of autonomy for some producers. In her analysis of the promotional role of popular music, Leslie Meier (2017) too looks back to the culture industry thesis as an early critique of the relationship of culture to capitalism, though she notes that it doesn't account for artistic achievements that emerge from a commercial system, which other schools of thought (e.g. the Birmingham School, later cultural industries approaches) have more successfully explained.

The concept of selling out has been used to monitor the relationship of popular music culture to capitalism, and the potential strings attached to economic investment in musicians. Changes to the funding of popular music have limited opportunities for artists to follow their inspiration, distanced from commercial pressure: record labels no longer throw money at artists, as they did through the 1990s, and what state funding exists is increasingly driven by neoliberal and entrepreneurial ideologies (Hesmondhalgh et al. 2015, Hogan 2017). Musicians have had to adapt to music's transformation into a commercial product and to negotiate their relationship to capitalist values as they try to make a living without reducing their work to making money (Baym 2018). In

Chapter 1, I explore how values associated with art served to legitimate popular music and to import the selling out concept into popular music culture.

Providing a backdrop to the relationship between art and capitalism, and music and capitalism, is the commercialization of culture more broadly. Commercialism, or the focus on profit-making over all else, came to define American culture in the twentieth century, despite a history of frequent and organized critiques of consumerism (Cross 2000). The unending desire for more consumer goods has sanctioned the presence of advertising across nearly every space that can accommodate it (which is to say, nearly every space) (McAllister 1996), and the internet has enabled customizability that masks its data-based power and social control with the promise of a personalized consumer experience (Turow 2011, Einstein 2016). The rampant commercialization once associated with American stereotypes has spread around the world, tucked inside the global superpower's popular exports, including its 'cool' advertising.

The 'creative revolution' within the US advertising industry of the 1960s offered a striking challenge to previously held distinctions between culture and commerce, with popular music a common creative tool (Frank 1997). As Thomas Frank describes, 'Admen in the 1960s loved rock'n'roll, or at least claimed they did' (1997: 113), and the hip consumerism promoted by the advertising industry drew on the images and sounds of the counterculture, including rock music. Jim McGuigan extends Frank's historical account of the conquest of cool in advertising to argue how, more recently, neoliberal capitalism has become attached to the value of cool as a way of discouraging disaffection and driving global consumerism: 'Cool capitalism is largely defined by the incorporation, and thereby neutralisation, of cultural criticism and anti-capitalism into the theory and practice of capitalism itself' (2009: 38).

The movement of the market into every aspect of life, labelled 'promotional culture' by Andrew Wernick (1991), has resulted in the adoption of promotional practices in a range of sectors, not just the promotional industries, and has normalized promotion as a mode that individuals both encounter and reproduce daily (Davis 2013). Promotional culture's reach has little respect for boundaries, whether geopolitical, social or ethical (see Aronczyk and Powers 2010, McAllister and West 2013). Misdeeds of companies (Klein 2000) and nations alike (Aronczyk 2013) are erased by quality branding, and authenticity is a resource to be mined to that end (Banet-Weiser 2012). For popular music, promotion has expanded from a set of activities that took place after the product was completed to encompass all dimensions of music's production, distribution and consumption (as, for example, through the treatment of an artist as a brand) (Powers 2013a, Meier 2017). Promotional culture has simultaneously multiplied the opportunities available to musicians to sell out and challenged the relevance of the concept, given the ubiquity of such activities. This book looks at the expansion of promotional activities in popular music culture from the 1960s to the present, with Chapter 6 focusing on the recent intensification of promotional activities as a revenue stream positioned to replace demolished music sales and complement modest streaming royalties.

Finally, my focus on the discourse of selling out, the work it does in policing the boundary between culture and commerce, and what we lose if we dismiss the concept as no longer relevant, connects to current debates about why the value of music cannot and should not be reduced to economic impact. In the UK, the notion of 'cultural value' has offered terrain on which scholars have challenged economic reductionism and highlighted the social benefits of arts and culture, including music. While the phrase elides precision, given the long-standing academic debates about the meaning of its two constituent parts (see O'Brien 2010, Crossick and Kaszynska 2016), attempts 'to understand the value of the arts and culture' in terms of 'the difference that they make to individuals and to society' (Crossick and Kaszynska 2016) resist the tendency for definitions and measurements of cultural value (particularly in the policy realm) to fall back on the quantifiable and economic (O'Brien 2010, Belfiore 2015).

Research into the cultural value of music – how it might help us to understand ourselves and others, or encourage us to be engaged citizens – joins a tradition in the sociology of music and popular music studies of celebrating the benefits of taking part in music activities (or, to use Small's word, 'musicking' (1998)). Music can culturally enable flourishing, as deftly explored by David Hesmondhalgh (2013a) to make the case for 'why music matters'. Research which has interrogated the concept of cultural value itself often makes a pitch for why and how cultural policy might move beyond the purely economic: for example, Adam Behr, Matt Brennan and Martin Cloonan explore how audiences and artists value the live music experience, noting that assessments in terms of cost or value for money 'do not necessarily apply to a live music experience in ways they might to other commodities' (2016: 414). However, despite a declared interest by politicians and funders in cultural value, it remains difficult for non-economic assessments of cultural value to influence cultural policy or public funding without economic, or at least quantifiable, measures being re-introduced:

'the dominance of the economic frame for the discussion of value in a policy context has remained unchallenged' (Belfiore 2015: 102).

Trying to separate out the non-economic from the economic value of mass-produced culture such as popular music can prove especially difficult, given the circulation of popular music as a commodity and the commercial success of the global popular music industries. While positive economic impact can co-exist with negative social impact (Belfiore 2018), as it happens, many examples of popular music that have brought meaning to individuals and communities have also achieved great commercial success. Instead, we might consider how an economic lens can accommodate ethical dimensions. The moral economy approach has proven fruitful for understanding benefits of cultural production and consumption in this way.

The study of moral economy demands that 'any adequate understanding of culture and economy and the relationship between them requires a recognition of the extent to which they contain and are shaped by norms and values, including moral-political values' (Sayer 1999: 54–55). The moral economy approach evaluates 'economic systems, actions and motives in terms of their effect on peoples' lives' (Sayer 2000: 80–81) and takes into account the ethical dimensions of economic arrangements and their effect on well-being (Sayer 2007). Mark Banks (2006) applies the concept to the work of cultural entrepreneurs: he identifies how moral purpose and social outcomes motivate cultural entrepreneurs, countering assumptions about such work being led by self-interest or profit-making. For Banks (2017), one way to do justice to creative work is to focus on its ethical dimensions within a moral economy, which can help us understand what conditions support flourishing and well-being – he uses the example of professional (jazz) musicians and the internal goods and satisfactions that drive them. Hesmondhalgh brings together moral economy perspectives with the capabilities approach he drew on in *Why Music Matters* (2013a) to explore how the latter 'in the realm of media might help form a richer sense of the value of knowledge and aesthetic–artistic experience, in terms of their ability to contribute to human flourishing' (2017: 14). The capabilities approach, as developed by Amartya Sen and Martha Nussbaum, focuses on the importance of what people are able to do (what they are capable of) to achieve well-being, and moral economy can highlight how capitalism might not support those cultural goods that offer potential benefits (Hesmondhalgh 2017). Keith Negus's invocation of 'the moral economy of artistic worth' (2019: 375) in his analysis of the value of recorded music under the dominance of digital conglomerates suggests the market shift to music as content undermines the experience of music as artistic expression. What is shared across these studies is the belief that the potential benefits of musical participation, in the form of enhanced well-being or human flourishing, is both vitally important and easily neglected by a narrow economic approach.

This book contributes to these ongoing attempts to make sense of what music does for us, individually and collectively, by examining the role of commercialism and consumer brands in mediating our relationship to popular music. The discourse of selling out has driven debates in popular music culture that highlight fundamental values perceived as under threat, such as artistic integrity, cultural autonomy and community, when the value of culture is defined through commercial success. By exploring more closely debates around selling out, we can better understand what the loss of the phrase reflects and what is at stake when consumer brands exert greater power over the production, distribution and consumption of popular music.

How this book is organized

To understand the role of selling out in popular music culture, in Chapter 1 I explore how popular music made the transition from mere entertainment to art, thus inheriting concepts like authenticity and autonomy from the art world, and gaining access to the notion of selling out. The Beatles, Bob Dylan and the Who each redefined the relationship between art and commerce in the context of rock. The 1960s demonstrated the potential value of selling out discourse for monitoring and maintaining boundaries between culture and commerce, but also highlighted the exclusionary nature of selling out discourse in popular music, where the threat of commercialism is framed as a white, male rock concern. Chapter 1 considers both roles of selling out discourse.

Unprecedented business growth in the music industries meant that by the 1970s popular music was big money, with a broader set of commercial opportunities available to musicians. Arena rock, and its focus on big spaces and audiences, arguably to the detriment of sound, became a symbol of the bloat associated with 'going commercial'. Bruce Springsteen offers an interesting example of an artist who managed to achieve large scale success while simultaneously maintaining fans' perception of the artist as an authentic everyman – in part through his (seeming) lack of engagement with the business side of music. Other artists, like Blondie, challenged the very basis of selling out debates by playing with concepts like authenticity through musical pastiche and a declared desire for commercial success. Chapter 2 looks at how tensions between commercial success and selling out have been navigated by artists.

For a period in the late 1980s and early 1990s, charges of selling out were focused on previously independent artists signing contracts with major labels. The idea of cultural autonomy had particular significance for those artists whose independence was a choice born from the anti-corporate stance associated with punk. Chapter 3 explores the development and politicization of independent record labels in the US and UK: while the emergence and growth of punk and its descendants share similarities, differences between the two national contexts meant that independent music was more easily assimilated into the UK mainstream whereas, in the US, attempts by major labels to exploit the popularity of 'alternative' music were met with resistance by fans whose anti-corporate ideology extended to corporations in the music industries. Bands like rock group Hüsker Dü and, later, Nirvana and Green Day had to weigh the benefits of major label support against inevitable accusations of selling out.

Early rap offers some notable parallels with punk and indie music: much of the early support for rap was through small, independent labels, with mainstream popular music industries hesitant to invest and promote rap until its popularity and endurance were inarguable. Unlike independent rock artists, however, rap artists have enjoyed a more positive relationship to consumer brands and commercial opportunities from the start. In Chapter 4, I explore partnerships between rap artists and consumer brands, from Run-DMC and Adidas in the mid-1980s to the ongoing position of colas as sponsors for hip-hop stars. A history of mistreatment of black artists by the mainstream music industries and the role of entrepreneurialism for African-American communities begin to contextualize the relatively relaxed relationship that many rappers have to consumer brands. At the same time, rap is no stranger to selling out, with the phrase's racial connotations critical to judgements of artists perceived to have betrayed the community that supported them. I consider the potential consequences of rap – now the most popular genre in the US – supplying a template for popular music's relationship to consumer brands.

The increasing use of popular music in television commercials became the focus of selling out debates from the late 1990s. Perhaps the most direct and visible example of a relationship between an artist and a brand, the use of music in advertising hit music fans where it hurt (their emotional connection to songs) and became a stand-in for the expansion of commercialism and branding into areas of life that had previously been seen as sacred, even if their own commodified nature denied such clear boundaries. In Chapter 5, I look at how licensing music to television commercials went from a stigmatized, but often well-paid, choice for artists to a desirable, but often not well-paid, revenue stream, following the precipitous decline of music sales triggered by illegal downloading and maintained by streaming. I argue that acceptance of the use of popular music in advertising ushered in the era of 'no such thing as selling out'.

Today, no single category or activity will automatically or necessarily be regarded as selling out. The consequences of digitalization, the rise of promotional culture and market-driven cultural policies together shape the activities and perspectives of artists, who are pressured to contort and present themselves as brands. Partnerships with consumer brands extend the strategies described in previous chapters, with sync licensing, sponsorships, endorsements and product placement forming a portion of the revenue streams pursued by artists. I consider some of the new spaces for brand relationships and new challenges for achieving profits through them. The artists who tend to reap significant financial benefits from brand partnerships of all kinds are typically music superstars, drawing attention to the true beneficiaries: the brands themselves, the remaining big players in the music industries and, increasingly, digital conglomerates with only a passing interest in music. Chapter 6 ends with a discussion of the 'promotional fatigue' that has led major artists like Ed Sheeran and Lady Gaga to step back from social media or consumer brand partnerships: do these examples represent a challenge to commercialism?

Although the book takes popular music as its focus to understand how culture-commerce battles have waxed, waned and shifted, similar dynamics and claims to undermine boundaries intended to protect cultural, political or social output from commercial influence and control are at work in other areas of our everyday lives. Chapter 7 draws on examples from journalism, education and healthcare, and asks what we might learn from the case of popular music about the danger of inviting unabashed commercialism, with its neutral (or worse) aesthetic and political values, inside our house. I argue for why the construct of culture versus commerce, and its attendant notion of selling out, still matters: debates about selling out in popular music culture allow citizens to contribute to broader discussions of commercialism through expressing their views about the meaning of culture in their lives and the values that matter to them.

1

Popular music for art's sake

Popular music culture inherited and adapted long-standing debates about art and capitalism, grappling with the slippery notions of authenticity and autonomy that had sought expression through Romanticism in the early nineteenth century. Music movements and scenes of the 1960s that imbued certain genres of popular music with the values and meanings of art also opened the door to the policing of commercial affiliation in ways that would have seemed inappropriate to apply to 'mere entertainment'. Within this context, the concept of selling out gained purchase for some popular music cultures, as demonstrated by various events and activities, including the controversy around Dylan going electric in 1965 and the Who's pop art reflection on commercialism, 1967's *The Who Sell Out*. This chapter explores how popular music earned the right to selling out discourse by mapping popular music's course towards art and by exploring some early disputes around and cogitations on commercialism.

The concept of selling out was not an obvious or natural fit for popular music produced as a commodity form and circulated within a commercial market. Popular music's access to the selling out concept depends on the understanding and treatment of certain types of popular music as art, rather than mere entertainment, and on the increasing centrality of the notion of authenticity in assessments of performers and products. This chapter traces the legitimation of popular music as art through the relationship of early rock to art and its treatment as such. It considers claims to authenticity and classed, raced and gendered differences with respect to selling out. Famous cases of selling out in the 1960s – both charged and self-confessed – can be understood as setting a pattern about what it means to sell out and who can sell out under what circumstances that continues to resonate through subsequent decades. Finally, it seeks to shed light on the complex and at times contradictory relationship that popular music has to commercialism – one that echoes long-standing dimensions of traditional art worlds while presenting particular issues relating to scale and popularity.

Through key examples – the Beatles, Bob Dylan, the Who – I explore how links to one form of art or another, and appeals to one notion of authenticity or another, reside at the foundation of and are necessary for entry to selling out debates. Popular music, like more traditional forms of art, has a relationship to commercialism that is not straightforward. Selling out debates distinguish acceptable commercialism (commodity form, financial success) from unacceptable commercialism (compromising values, deserting communities). On the one hand, selling out discourse pursues the valiant goal of protecting communities from the perceived influence of the mainstream market. On the other, it delineates insiders and outsiders in ways that reveal its construction: the badge of art, the version of authenticity promoted within rock culture and access to selling out debates are only available to some musicians and genres, some of the time. The potential value of selling out for policing important boundaries between culture and commerce must be weighed against its tendency to make distinctions that privilege existing power relations and hierarchies around class, race and gender.

Movement from entertainment to art

The movement of popular music from entertainment to art did not take place at one moment, across all genres, for all listeners. Nor indeed would we contend that popular music as a category is universally treated as art today. There are many historical instances that could be classified as evidence of people applying artistic criteria of one kind or another to forms of popular music. For example, in his analysis of jazz criticism, John Gennari (2006) traces the canonization of jazz as art. He explores the growth of anti-commercial critical discourse in jazz criticism through the 1930s and 1940s, noting that one of the most significant early jazz critics, John Hammond, 'was among the first to popularize the word "commercial" as an epithet' (Gennari 2006: 36). Yet it is around rock culture that such a treatment of popular music becomes entrenched. As Keir Keightley writes, 'Taking popular music seriously, as something "more" than mere entertainment or distraction, has been a crucial feature of rock culture since its emergence' (2001: 110) and while 'some listeners did take mainstream popular music seriously prior to the advent of rock', 'it is within rock culture that this activity is at its most intense' (2001: 111). For this reason, and because rock provides the model on which subsequent cases of artistic legitimation and denial are often based, I focus primarily on rock for this discussion. However, I begin with a consideration of folk music, in the context of the American folk music revival of the 1950s and 1960s, because of its link to folk art and because of the role played by Bob Dylan in crystallizing notions of authenticity within both folk and rock music, as explored more fully below.

The folk tradition in art and music

Thomas Crow (2014) locates the folk music and art revival of the 1930s and 1940s as laying the groundwork for what would become known as Pop Art, noting links in the development of popular music along the way. I pick up the links between Pop Art and popular music later in the chapter, but give a brief overview of the role folk revivals played in the legitimation of popular music as art here.

The path of folk or outsider traditions within the visual arts was an unsteady one. While a few influential individuals championed American folk traditions from the 1930s, their place in established art spaces was rare (Crow 2014). By the 1960s, folk art's status was formalized by the founding of the Museum of American Folk Art in 1963, and the 'increasing number of contemporary folk art exhibitions, especially throughout the 1970s, suggests the establishment of an identifiable artistic field' (Ardery 1997). Over the same period, American folk music also experienced varying degrees of attention and popularity, including from art world inhabitants whose 'impulse to link leftist politics with native voices from below ... shifted away from the visual arts toward the more receptive sphere of music, where it engendered an enduring idea of American folksong' (Crow 2014: 10–11). The American folk music revival gained in popularity in the 1940s, with Pete Seeger's the Weavers at the forefront, and developing by the early 1960s into a movement set to go mainstream.

Crow's (2014) skilled and fascinating exploration of the interlinking folk art and folk music traditions demonstrates the art world's role in changing the way folk traditions, including folk music traditions, were viewed and appreciated. The parallels between the folk art and folk music worlds are not exact, of course, but there is a dimension that is particularly helpful in thinking about popular music's journey from entertainment to art. The folk art tradition was and remains marked by two distinct categories of art and artist: elevation and placement of the work of outsiders within formal art institutions (e.g. Grandma Moses), on the one hand, and the adoption of similar styles by traditionally trained artists drawing on folk traditions (early Pop Artists like Jasper Johns), on the other. Similarly, the folk music revival included musicians performing in the traditional style of the communities from which they came and musicians from outside those communities – often equipped with privileges of race, class and education – drawing on the same traditions. For some revivalists, like Pete Seeger, the role of the latter was first and foremost to draw attention and audiences to the former. From this perspective, and as with self-taught artists (Fine 2003), authenticity for folk revivalists placed great importance on the performer's identity, as much as on the material performed. For folk music, authenticity is defined by that which is 'musically pure, genuine and organically connected to the community that produced them' (Keightley 2001: 121). Musicians not from those communities, but supportive of the folk traditions, could not re-write their biographical histories (though some, like Dylan, tried), but could seek a version of folk authenticity by staying true to the material and community. If folk authenticity relies on staying true, however, then shifts away from traditional styles or traditional material must draw on a different sense of the term. The emergence of folk rock, marked by original material and non-traditional instrumentation, was thus crucial in producing rock ideology. While influenced by folk ideology, the 'authentic' in folk rock, and later rock, was instead rooted, alongside related notions of autonomy and authorship, in Romantic and Modernist concepts imported from the art world (Keightley 2001).

Both movements contribute to rock's conception of authenticity but in different ways: 'While Romanticism locates authenticity principally in the direct communication between artist and audience, Modernism manifests its concern with authenticity more indirectly, at the aesthetic level, so that the authentic artist is one who is true to the Modernist credos of experimentation, innovation, development, change' (Keightley 2001: 136). There are shared ideals too, however: 'Both Romantics and Modernists are anxious to avoid corruption through involvement with commerce and oppose the alienation they see as rooted in industrial capitalism' (Keightley 2001: 136). The evolution of folk music to folk rock through to rock demonstrates how appeals to authenticity shifted from a definition applied to folk art to values associated with fine art, including notions of originality, autonomy and genius. At the same time, certain values from folk, particularly around community, were maintained: 'When the folk-rockers individualized the folk concept of authenticity, they changed the political principles of their performances, but they continued to offer an experience of community' (Frith 1981a: 164).

Authenticity and popular music as art

The above example itself suggests the slipperiness of authenticity, which takes different shapes for different genres and at different times: as David Shumway notes, 'authenticity is an indispensable value but one that is historically and culturally relative' (2007: 527). Authenticity is a messy business, but requires unpacking before I move on to examples of musicians being affirmed as artists or accused of selling out, because it is so intimately tied to such affirmations and accusations. Agreeing a definition that captures the meaning of authenticity with respect to popular music generally is near impossible. Keightley's definition offers a persuasive combination of precision and generalizability:

> 'Authentic' designates those music, musicians, and musical experiences seen to be direct and honest, uncorrupted by commerce, trendiness, derivativeness, a lack of inspiration and so on. 'Authentic' is a term affixed to music which offers sincere expressions of genuine feeling, original creativity, or an organic sense of community. Authenticity is not something 'in' the music, though it is frequently experienced as such, believed to be actually audible, and taken to have a material form. Rather, authenticity is a value, a quality we ascribe to perceived relationships between music, socio-industrial practices, and listeners or audiences.
>
> Keightley 2001: 131

Such a flexible definition captures the adaptability of the term in various contexts, depending on the version of authenticity appealed to by artists and often cohering around genres. And yet for all this variability, the understanding and application of authenticity within a genre tends to still follow either the trajectory of the folk art ideology linked to the blues and hillbilly traditions central to the folk music revival, or the trajectory of fine art, reflecting the Modernist and Romantic values associated with the rock tradition.

Connection to the community that produced them remains a central tenet for country musicians, whose roots lie in the hillbilly music promoted by folk revivalists. Elements that matter for country music include 'signifiers of group membership' in order to make claim to the country identity (Peterson 1997: 218), and 'being able to show a family heritage in country music' (Peterson 1997: 219). Similarly, today's blues musicians continue to grapple with a perceived link of authenticity to race, with blues clubs pressured to conform to what tourists associate with authenticity, including blackness (Grazian 2003). That same emphasis on the performer's identity and background has a legacy in hip-hop: thus, selling out in hip-hop is often not about commercial success per se, but turning your back on the community while presenting an inauthentic picture of that community (Quinn 2005). Conversely, rock and its sub-genres rely on a perception of autonomy and original expression, unencumbered by commercial influence: the centrality of commerce to the rock version of authenticity is one reason why this version dominates selling out debates.

In terms of being 'uncorrupted by commerce' (Keightley 2001: 131), popular music, particularly from the development of rock onwards, may seem to sit uneasily with authenticity. Unlike folk, 'rock was born *within* the popular mainstream as an *exclusively* youth-oriented music. These differences crucially affected the way rock culture played out its folk-influenced world view, because they allowed rock to emerge in the simultaneous embrace of anti-mass ideology *and* mass commercial success' (Keightley 2001: 122, emphasis in original). 'Authenticity in rock & roll', writes Shumway, 'is more complicated because it, in contradistinction to folk music, is defined by the institution of stardom' (2007: 530). In other words, commercialism is inherent to rock and its offshoots, while anti-commercialism is inherent to the notion of authenticity that informs its value system.

This is not to say that commercialism is irrelevant in genres that align more closely with a folk art sense of authenticity. The examples of country and hip-hop noted above both demonstrate complex relationships between commercialism and authenticity even if they do not necessarily exclude commercial success or relationships to consumer brands. (In this way, popular music departs from folk art, where the appearance of marketing savvy or commercial influence can challenge the construction of authenticity valued by curators and collectors (Fine 2003).)

As Sarah Banet-Weiser describes, 'the authentic has never accurately defined the relationship of art and commerce' since 'artists have always been involved in collaborations with those industries and organizations that finance, distribute, and sell their work' (2012: 99). 'Yet, the idea that commercialization corrupts the authenticity of art appears to continue to structure tastes, policy decisions about funding federal artwork, and cultural boundaries' (Banet-Weiser 2012: 99). Monitoring of commercialism of one form or another is a key aspect of evaluating authenticity across genres. But it is also the case that the presence of commercialism in popular music (and in arts generally) creates the tension that motivates appeals to authenticity.

So where does that leave us with authenticity? There are two consistent themes that should make us wary of authenticity's central role in the legitimation of popular music as art and in the selling out debates. The first is its resistance to definition and subsequent flexibility. As Alan Moore concludes, 'Siting authenticity within the ascription carries the corollary that every music, and every example, can conceivably be found authentic by a particular group of perceivers' (2002: 221) – though, in practice, the value holds more sway among some genres and audiences than others. The second theme is that authenticity is both constructed and constructive: as a descriptor it tells us less about the object and more about the social and cultural attitudes informing the evaluation. Richard Peterson uses the phrase 'fabricating authenticity' to 'highlight the fact that authenticity is not inherent in the object or event that is designated authentic' (1997: 3). Like its use in other forms of commercial popular culture, authenticity is 'continuously negotiated in an ongoing interplay between performers, diverse commercial interests, fans, and the evolving image' (Peterson 1997: 4).

Authenticity is both crucial to understanding popular music as art and popular music as able to access selling out debates, and flexible and constructed/constructive in nature, denying a strict definition or checklist approach. At the same time, the 1960s saw real changes to the way popular music was made, received and treated that allow us to trace the legitimation of popular music, and rock in particular, as art. The following section looks at the legitimation of rock and uses the case of the Beatles to consider some of these changes.

Tracing the legitimation of rock as art

It's tempting to look at the aesthetics of an object and their parallels in the fine art world to understand the legitimation of commercial popular culture. The more 'like art' an object is, the more we may expect it to be viewed as art. In reality, it is a complex interplay of internal and external factors that supports legitimation. Shyon Baumann draws on the work of popular music scholars to understand the legitimation of film as art and so it is not surprising that his analysis maps well onto the case of popular music. He identifies three main factors that sociologists of culture use to 'explain the public acceptance of a cultural product as art' (Baumann 2001: 405). These are legitimating ideology (as through critical discourse), changing opportunity space (external social change) and the institutionalization of resources and practices (such as the networks and organizations of art worlds mapped by Howard Becker (1984)). For rock in the 1960s, the legitimating ideology of popular music journalism, growing opportunity spaces of education, and changing institutional resources (e.g. the field of popular music studies) and practices (around recording and releasing music) each drew musicians and their output deeper into the realm of artistic legitimation.

The emergence and growth of serious music criticism can be seen as a major contextual factor aiding and reflecting the legitimation of popular music, and rock in particular, as art. Popular musicians had long been referred to as artists within the industry and by the trade press (record labels had 'Artists and Repertoire' divisions from the 1940s). Music journalism was also well established by the 1960s, with specialist music magazines like *Melody Maker* (est. 1926) and *Downbeat* (est. 1934) focusing on jazz and aimed primarily at musicians, and popular music (or, more accurately, the faces of popular music) featuring in teen magazines from the 1940s. But the type and scope of music criticism that developed in the 1960s achieved wider readership and more serious ambitions. Bernard Gendron notes the rise of the rock critic in this period as key to rock achieving cultural legitimacy, pointing to *Crawdaddy!* (founded in 1966) and the *Village Voice*'s 'Pop Eye' column as early examples of the rise of the rock critic (2002: 190).

What set such rock criticism apart from its predecessors? In *Writing the Record*, Devon Powers (2013b) looks at the rise of rock criticism through a focused study of the *Village Voice*'s early years and early pop critics. She demonstrates how critics like Robert Christgau and Richard Goldstein developed a new language for writing about popular music; intervened in mass culture debates (encouraging a reassessment of popular music and popular music journalism); and functioned as public intellectuals. Powers erodes the line often drawn between academic and journalistic work on popular music: parallels between the approaches were a result of both overlapping personnel and the concurrent development of popular music's role in formal education.

Popular music found multiple legitimating opportunity spaces in education in the 1960s. Traditional educational curricula were challenged by new subjects and new approaches, and education reforms sought to increase opportunity and equity for students regardless of background. In the UK, art education was broadened by the growth of art schools offering an alternative further or higher education route for often working-class and lower-middle class students. Indeed, many successful and influential musicians in this period counted art school as foundational training (John Lennon, Keith Richards, Jimmy Page, John Cale, to name a few) and many others emphasized art as an inspiration in their musical lives. Simon Frith and Howard Horne (1987) explore the connections between art school and pop music by examining how British musicians applied skills developed in art school to the attitude and style they brought to pop music. The art school experience for musicians laid the groundwork for negotiating the relationship between culture and commerce for 'in art schools', they argue, 'a particular tension between creativity and commerce is confronted' and 'pop music works as a solution' (Frith and Horne 1987: 3). That traditional artists themselves face commercial pressures opens the space for conceiving of commercial popular music as art.

At the same time, the study of popular music became institutionalized through academic research and inclusion in curricula. While academic journals and associations dedicated to popular music were not established until the early 1980s, the sociology of music was well under way by the 1940s and 1950s (though early contributors, like Theodor Adorno, hardly affirmed popular music as art). The foundation of Birmingham's Centre for Contemporary Cultural Studies in 1964, with its aim to take popular culture seriously, is perhaps a more direct predecessor of popular music studies and included popular music as an object of study.

Writing about self-taught artists, Gary Fine quotes Pierre Bourdieu's notion of the 'creator of the creator', which Fine describes as a 'consecrated discoverer who legitimates the work and the art' (2003: 156). In the 1960s, rock critics and scholars of popular music fulfilled this role. Through popular music criticism and education, key concepts from fine art become increasingly normalized as the basis for judgement of popular music: the depiction of musicians as artists and geniuses intermingled with notions of authorship; the significance of autonomy to creativity was informed by Romanticism; and, as highlighted above, authenticity was increasingly linked to the idea of pure expression.

While the development of criticism and education are reflective of changes to the cultural context in which rock was legitimated as art, technological and industrial contexts were also influential. Although technology has often been seen as a threat to authenticity, Frith (1986) argues that technological developments made the rock concept of authenticity possible (e.g. recordings allowed people to access aspects of a performance and experience emotions) and that technological change has been a source of resistance to corporate control (e.g. even punk relied on the availability and affordability of making records – a technological development). On the technology of magnetic tape, he writes 'The Beatles "Sergeant Pepper" LP symbolized the moment when rock musicians began to claim to be making complex artworks' (1986: 271). The active participation of musicians in recording activities further underlined their role as artists. Even the album format itself can be seen as a practice that supported a legitimating context: Keightley argues that 'the development of rock culture (c. 1965–7 onward) is crucially tied to a shift from singles to albums and an attendant shift in cultural legitimacy' (2001: 113). The album format offered the possibility of presenting longer, more complex aesthetic messages. I now turn to assessments of popular music content as art, using the Beatles as an example.

The Beatles: From teen idols to serious artists

The Beatles' journey from teen idols to artists might be seen as quite unusual by today's standards (with only rare cases like Justin Timberlake arguably making the leap from manufactured act to serious artist), but in the mid-1960s the group set the standard for their contemporaries and followers, fundamentally changing the attitudes and behaviours of record labels and the press. 'The narrative for the cultural accreditation of rock music begins', suggests Gendron, 'with the Beatles' "invasion" of North America in 1964 and reaches its apogee in 1967, contemporaneously with the release of the *Sergeant Pepper* album to a torrent of accolades' (Gendron 2002: 162–3). (Gendron focuses on the North American story while acknowledging that in Britain there was an openness to taking the Beatles and mass culture seriously earlier, hence Lennon and McCartney were named as 'the outstanding English composers' of 1963 by the London *Times* music critic William Mann (quoted in Gendron 2002: 164–5).)

The case of the Beatles also complicates assumptions about commercialization and popular music, a relationship that is central to understanding the parameters of selling out. That the Beatles went from successful teen pop group to 'serious and significant artists critiquing and contesting the dominant values of Anglo-American society' (Keightley 2001: 126) offers a counterpoint to the enduring rock mythology that positions organic culture as corrupted by commercialization.

Assumptions about the influence of commercial imperatives were challenged in the case of the Beatles by the increasing control they had over their output. For example, their insistence on releasing one of their own compositions as a single (1962's 'Love Me Do') rather than a song provided to them – and the success of this choice – gave them more subsequent creative control (Harvey 2016: 157). Their US label, Capitol, took longer to see the marketing value of ceding control to the group, continuing to choose different album covers, re-order tracks and re-package tracks until 1966's *Revolver*. In the language of Romanticism, the Beatles maintained levels of authorship and autonomy that were rare in the world of popular music. Put in the context of their extraordinary popularity, the exercising of such control opened up possibilities for similar displays by other musicians, including their California peers the Beach Boys and the Byrds and subsequent generations of musicians who valued independence as essential to supporting creativity. In *Our Band Could Be Your Life: Scenes from the American Indie Underground 1981–1991*, Michael Azerrad (2001) cites the Beatles, alongside Stevie Wonder and Bob Dylan, as predecessors to 1980s indie groups because of the control over their music they demanded and the link between control and credibility.

Of course, in order for the Beatles' control over their output to make an impression on fellow musicians and shape the practices of the music industries, they had to be identified as the decision-makers. The group's control over all aspects of their material (music, lyrics, presentation) was emphasized by the band members and their management, including through the description of the group as artists and their work as art.

Mark Harvey (2016) traces how the demands that the Beatles made in terms of the artistry of their output, from the use of eclectic sounds and instruments, to new forms of production and arrangement, shaped EMI's approach to negotiating control with artists, ultimately shaping the approach of other labels too. By the release of *Sgt Pepper's Lonely Hearts Club Band* in 1967, musicians, including the Beatles, were disrupting cultural boundaries between high and popular art through their use of avant-garde techniques like 'collage, *musique concrète*, and irony' (Gendron 2002: 1). As Gendron puts it, 'In three short years, rock 'n' roll had gone from being cast as vulgar entertainment not even suitable for adults to being hailed as the most important musical break-through of the decade' (2002: 1).

It is widely agreed that the success of *Sgt Pepper* 'drew a line between music as a commercial product and music as art, even if that "art" sold incredibly well' (Harvey 2016: 165). *Sgt Pepper* was actually the culmination of recurrent breaches of that line, from the group's earliest efforts onward: 'that the Beatles' recordings of fifties rock'n'roll, rhythm and blues and Motown songs were seen as homages, rather than commercially motivated covers, is evidence of the fact that the tastes of the musicians themselves begin to be taken seriously as signs of artistic ambition' (Keightley 2001: 118).

Lyrically, the Beatles were one of the early and most popular rock groups to elevate popular music to readings worthy of poetry, territory opened up by folk rock and the characterization of artists like Bob Dylan as poets (Gendron 2002). Academic and journalistic analyses of the Beatles' and other popular musicians' lyrics as poetry were published as early as the late 1960s (see, for example, Damian 1968 and Rorem 1968) and continue to make appearances (Ricks 2003 is an affectionate analysis of Dylan lyrics as poetry).

Aesthetic appreciation of the Beatles was not limited to their recordings: the way they presented themselves, both visually and verbally, indicated a group that was not manufactured or packaged in the way that pop groups were understood to be. Although John Lennon reflected critically on their matching suits as an indication that the group had 'started to sell out' (Williams 1969), it is also the case that the Beatles' extra-musical activities, including press conferences (though not the suits), were first to receive a positive aesthetic evaluation amongst mainstream commentators. Gendron explains of American Beatlemania-era press coverage that 'while in their formal musical performances they were judged to be talentless, they were heaped with praise for the inventiveness of their informal, unscripted performances' (2002: 167). Also contributing to the image of the Beatles as artists were John Lennon's book of poetry, published in 1964, and the release of *A Hard Day's Night* (with its art film techniques) in the US in the same year: both generated aesthetic approval.

White, male, middle-class rock and selling out

I am acutely aware that the story I am telling in this chapter, of popular music's legitimation as art and the introduction of selling out debates, is populated with musicians who are male, who are white, and who benefited from class background or class-linked privileges like art school education (even when working-class identity formed the basis of publicity campaigns). In the next section, I will explore why claims to authenticity, links with art, and accusations of selling out in popular music tend to be classed, raced and gendered in this way. Throughout the book, I broaden the focus to demonstrate the relevance of selling out beyond the (white, male, middle-class) rock-based perspective that often dominates, but famous early cases of selling out suggest that those demographic details established a pattern in terms of what it means to sell out and who can sell out under what circumstances.

The case of Dylan 'going electric' at the Newport Folk Festival in 1965 demonstrates the way that folk and rock draw on different understandings of authenticity, as noted above, and how the moment that Dylan was perceived as selling out the folk scene was, paradoxically, also the moment that rock asserted its own authenticity. The events leading up to, context surrounding, and fall-out from Dylan's electric performance at the 1965 Newport Folk Festival have been covered by many a written and documentary film account. The short version, for the purposes of understanding the role of authenticity and selling out, is this: Dylan had been one of the major draws for Folk Festival attendees, with large audiences gathered and expecting a set of acoustic favourites (original hits and folk classics). Instead, he and his makeshift band performed a short, ramshackle electric set, representing Dylan's emerging sound but surprising folk purists. So the myth goes, the set was met with boos and accusations of selling out. As Elijah Wald ably illustrates in his excellent account, there are in fact many competing stories about the response to Dylan's performance: 'What anyone experienced depended not only on what they thought about Dylan, folk music, rock 'n' roll, celebrity, selling out, tradition, or purity, but on where they happened to be sitting and who happened to be near them' (2015: 259). Perspectives on the response may vary but, as Wald concludes, 'it was the iconic moment of intersection, when rock emerged, separate from rock 'n' roll, and replaced folk as the serious, intelligent voice of a generation' (2015: 301). Rock may have replaced folk in this sense, but it also maintained certain elements of folk, including the sense that music could be an artistic statement, so that 'by the later 1960s it was considered insulting to call someone like Jim Morrison or Janis Joplin "commercial"' (Wald 2015: 301).

So, on the one hand, the negative response to Dylan going electric communicated anxieties about the desertion of folk aesthetics and values, and the impact of commercial appeal on folk music and on the folk community. On the other hand, the performance represented a new era of rock, which borrowed a sense of artistic worthiness from folk but defined authenticity differently, distanced from folk assumptions about tradition, politics and community. As Phil Ochs put it: 'I'm writing to make money. I write about Cuba and Mississippi out of an inner need for expression, not to change the world' (quoted in Frith 1981a). Artists like Phil Ochs and Bob Dylan, who rejected the folk position of representing the people, claiming instead only to represent themselves, reflected a new definition of authenticity (Frith 1981a). The aspect of authenticity retained by such artists was 'truth to experience rather than to class or organisation' (Frith 1981a: 164) and, consequently, 'For rock fans, Bob Dylan was a more "authentic" singer after he went electric than before' (Frith 1981a: 163).

While much of the focus on the Newport Folk Festival performance rests on the betrayed fans, who did not get the Bob Dylan they wanted, for supporters, the shift from protest songs to personal songs invoked the authenticity of honest expression: 'Dylan's "authenticity" was now lodged in his being true to himself as a poet, rather than in reflecting the needs and aspirations of a mythical folk community' (Gendron 2002: 182). The development of folk rock, of which Dylan's musical shift is one early and influential example, 'ushered in a complex array of modernist concepts and clichés—authenticity, genius, art for art's sake, shock, and avant-garde transgression—which would play a crucial though contested role in rock 'n' roll's aesthetic triumphs of 1967-8' (Gendron 2002: 183).

Authenticity had to be redefined for performers like Dylan (and other white, middle-class men). Recall the above discussion about folk musicians who were not from the communities of those traditions: because Dylan was, as a folk artist, performing a tradition and background that he did not come from, it makes sense that his development as an artist required complicating and ultimately reconfiguring what it means to be authentic. There was nothing he could do to more authentically represent the communities of folk traditions, so instead he asserted his authenticity through genuine expression of the self. The case of going electric may seem on the surface a strange example for locating rock authenticity, since it is usually told as a story of selling out, but it is uniquely useful in demonstrating popular music's relationship to folk art (which Dylan sold out) and popular music's relationship to modernist art concepts (which Dylan's recordings and performances helped define). Whatever Dylan's perceived folk transgressions, he is redeemed through his electric work and sets an example for rock authenticity, which is the basis of much selling out discourse. It also starts to explain the classed, raced and gendered nature of rock authenticity, serving as it does artists who cannot claim to represent oppressed communities. Paradoxically, this redefinition of authenticity that did not demand membership of such a community often excluded artists who were members. While there are exceptions, black musicians and women musicians have been routinely excluded from the criteria for rock authenticity.

For black artists, authenticity continued (and continues) to be linked to a sense of what is natural, and staying true to where you come from. Experimenting musically or leaving one's community (music or otherwise) is more likely to invoke accusations of selling out than assessments of genuine and artistically elevated expression. Consider the 1968 release of Muddy Waters' *Electric Mud*, for which the artist was accused of selling out the blues to rock. Despite the parallels between Muddy Waters' experiments with psychedelia and Bob Dylan going electric, it took considerably longer for accusations of selling out to give way to any positive aesthetic assessment of *Electric Mud*: today the album is a cult classic, inspiring appreciative musicians and making its way, via samples, onto new records.

Unlike their white counterparts, black musicians are expected to stay true to their race, however that is understood and interpreted by critics. In *Just around Midnight*, Jack Hamilton (2016) explores the relationship between popular music and race that led to the designation of serious, artistic rock music as the province of white musicians, despite the racially inclusive history of the rock'n'roll that came before and paved the way for rock. Rock ideology produced a 'sonic worldview in which black musical authenticity was defined in relation to a set of imagined aesthetic strictures imposed onto a group, while white musical authenticity was seen in terms of individuality' (Hamilton 2016: 16). Early rock critics reinforced the segregation of soul music from rock music, despite the obvious musical parallels and overlaps: 'The tendency was discursively to relegate soul music to the domain of dance and amusement (and thus "entertainment") while reserving the good white "rock" music (the Beatles, Dylan, the Who) for careful listening and "meaning" (and thus "art")' (Gendron 2002: 9).

Women musicians encounter a different but equally powerful barrier to achieving rock authenticity. They are often associated with pop – a genre considered commercial and trivial in comparison to rock – and with singing non-original material (Leonard 2007). Pop is the category into which 'rock dumps adult easy listening, bubblegum teenybop, and sell-outs, frauds and musical trifles more generally' (Keightley 2001: 128), and the rock/pop binary has been naturalized such that rock is automatically coded as masculine and pop as feminine (Coates 1997). 'She doesn't write her own songs' is the classic put-down that reduces women to essentially an instrument being played by male songwriters.

The Romantic concept of the 'artistic genius' may have valued feminine qualities like emotionality and sensitivity, but with such qualities being seen as 'natural' to women, female artists and their works have rarely been granted the tag of 'genius' (Battersby 1989). The gendered nature of the artistic genius likewise emerges in rock: women are often excluded from a definition of authenticity that relies on 'the image of the performer as a unique personality expressing their own individual truth' (Davies 2001: 305). or their acknowledged talents are undervalued as natural. The language of 'genius' – by critics, by fellow musicians, by fans – is overwhelmingly applied to male musicians. Women musicians are damned if they do and damned if they don't. If a female musician does not write her own music or is perceived as not in control of her own career, she is inauthentic; if she insists on control, then she is characterized as difficult (Davies 2001). As with black artists, the press again reflects and shapes a segregated system of aesthetic judgement: Helen Davies (2001) argues that notions of credibility and authenticity have been constructed in the music press to essentially exclude women from the world of serious music by, for example, describing them only in comparison to men, treating women musicians as a homogenous group and focusing interviews on femininity.

Because black musicians and women musicians are in these ways prevented from accessing rock authenticity, they are also less likely to be accused of selling out on the same basis as white, male rock musicians. That said, as I argue in Chapter 4, there are more parallels between different discourses of selling out in music than at first seem apparent. In short, commercialism remains at the heart of selling out debates, whether identified as explicit links with corporations or consumer brands, as is often the case for rock musicians, or through more implicit choices that are viewed as attempts to capture a mainstream audience (the reason why pop is limited in the artistic evaluations it can attain, and why 'going pop' and 'going commercial' are used interchangeably). I conclude this chapter with an exploration of the intertwined relationships between popular music, art and commercialism.

Popular music, art and commercialism

As I described in the introduction, the commercialization of culture has been explored and critiqued by scholars focused on the growth of advertising, particularly from the twentieth century, and the intensification of promotional culture, characterized by the embedding of marketing logic across a wide range of everyday experiences and activities. I also mapped out key examples and analyses of the relationship between art and capitalism that preceded the establishment of the popular music industries, but still apply to the case of popular music. I focus here on changes that set the stage for, and particular manifestations of, the relationship between popular music and art. Popular music's acceptance as art occurred, not coincidentally, alongside the playful embrace of commercialism and consumerism epitomized in Pop Art. Some of the strongest and most formal relationships between popular music and art developed out of the mutual embrace of commercialism. Commercialism operates to simultaneously affirm popular music (if art is commerce, then its commercial production and appeal does not exclude popular music as art) and cast it as forever suspect (commercialism as the heart of selling out debates).

The emergence of postmodern style and Pop Art together represent an important moment for the legitimation of popular music as art. While I note above, citing Keightley (2001), the role of Modernism in broadening aesthetic evaluation to include innovation and experimentation, an important shift for the definition of rock authenticity, it is also the case that the movement from modernism to postmodernism is associated with shifting values around and increasing accommodation of commercialism. Postmodernism was used to describe a range of forms and attributes, thus denying an easy and inclusive description, though a key defining feature is 'the erosion of the older distinction between high culture and so-called mass or popular culture' (Jameson 1998: 2). Pop Art is an early example of this erosion, having laid the groundwork for the possibility of mass art and the proposition that commercial culture can be art.

The emergence of Pop Art and popular music's legitimation of art occurred not only around the same time but through engagement with similar concepts and debates regarding commercialism, authenticity and creativity: 'Pop Art and post-Beatles rock music function interchangeably as cultural signatures of the 1960s yet are rarely if ever discussed in relation to one another' (Crow 2014: 3). Crow's *Long March to Pop* (2014) contextualizes the rise of Pop Art by considering its roots in folk art and through exploring various music and non-music examples.

The origins of British Pop Art can be traced to the early 1950s: the Independent Group within the Institute of Contemporary Art in London responded to 'the combined forces of American consumer culture and chic Italian design' (Crow 2014: 82). The group included proponents of the idea that 'Art was where you found it, and it need not be thought too great an honorific designation for the commercial and mass produced' (Crow 2014: 93). Alongside producing works drawing on consumer culture, artists associated with the group began to create commercial design that had much in common with the Pop Art to come, and their approach to the everyday and popular can be seen as a pre-cursor of cultural studies. Crow describes how many of the artists associated with Pop, including Andy Warhol, had worked in commercial design or applied arts; what was new was allowing overlap between those approaches (using the same means, producing a similar appearance) rather than keeping them separate. The unsettled debate about whether Pop had a political dimension hinged on whether it was seen to be placing a critical focus on commercial culture though, either way, use of the work could also produce such meaning (Crow 2014: 201).

Crow examines the interplay between Pop Art and popular music, focusing on 'how efforts in the domain of popular entertainment began to assimilate and turn to their own use what had been recondite and ultimately condescending in Pop aesthetics' (2014: 272). He identifies 1965 as the year that 'music proved more than able to take [Pop] up with renewed energy' (Crow 2014: 348). At this time, the Who identifies itself as pop art and the Beatles' output makes connections to the international Pop Art movement in cover art and film, the culmination and mainstreaming of which can be seen in *Sgt Pepper*: 'Much as the celebrity cut-outs on the Pepper cover congregate without regard to time or cultural provenance, the Beatles ushered the subject matter of Pop Art into a significantly larger imaginative universe than the one it had recently occupied' (Crow 2014: 354).

Also in 1965, in New York City, the Velvet Underground formed and before long the band began a collaboration with Andy Warhol, who suggested Nico's involvement with the group and who offered a base for them at the Factory: 'When Reed's Factory-inspired lyrics were then combined with the caustic music already being produced by his band, the result was a pop art group that was decidedly anticommercial' (Cagle 1995: 85). Their collaboration developed into the Exploding Plastic Inevitable, with the Velvets providing accompaniment to Warhol's film projections. When the band turned its attention to recording, Warhol's role decreased, though he was commissioned to design the cover of their first album, released in 1967. 'Warhol was one of the first to experiment with the notion of album cover as art piece. That same year, the Rolling Stones and the Beatles also presented album covers that violated the traditional standards of record jacket design' (Cagle 1995: 91).

Perhaps the best illustration of Pop Art in album form is *The Who Sell Out*, which John Dougan celebrates in the 33 1/3 series as 'nothing less than rock's greatest example of pop art' (2006: 25). From their earliest work, the Who identified with and drew on values associated with the Pop Art movement. A 1965 article in *Melody Maker* describes the group as 'linking their image with what they call Pop Art': 'They describe their current chart success, "Anyway, Anyhow, Anywhere", as "the first Pop Art single," and they have started designing their own Pop Art clothes' (*Melody Maker* 1965). Their third studio album, 1967's *The Who Sell Out*, plays with commercialism through concept, cover and commercial jingles: the album is presented as a pirate radio broadcast (pirate radio had been recently banned in the UK); the cover features the band's members in four panels of ads for real (Heinz beans) and fictitious (Medac acne cream) products; and album tracks intermingle with fake public service announcements and commercials. In fact, the promotional spots were going to be used alongside actual paid advertising spots but there was no interest, such that 'selling out' was 'more ironic aspiration than opportunism' (Crow 2014: 358) and Townshend instead composed them.

The album grapples with the centrality and contradictions of commercialism within popular music and culture more broadly. They were a band that 'had come to reckon with the powers of commercial machinery to outflank their best efforts at creative independence, yet had found a way to figure that state of ambivalence and contradiction within a vividly convincing musical and visual statement' (Crow 2014: 359). Designating the album as 'Pop Art pop masterpiece', Frith and Horne (1987: 107) suggest that Pete Townshend 'was using the vitality of commerce itself, the bombardment of sales patter, to both heighten the "realism" of the Who's music and draw attention to its spuriousness' (1987: 107).

Early and classic examples of the intermingling of popular music and Pop Art left a legacy on musicians for years and scenes to come, often expressed through a conscious and explicit relationship to commercialism, whether read as celebratory, critical or ambivalent. For example, Van Cagle considers the influence of Warhol and the Factory on musicians like David Bowie: 'In both the United States and abroad, Bowie and his glitter rock followers helped usher in a new post-1960s moment—a "revolt into style" as a social practice in which commercialization and consumerism were a means to a radical end' (Cagle 1995: 14). Post-Pop Art links between art and music continued after the movement itself declined – in the visual style of punk, for example, or the work of musicians like Sonic Youth's Kim Gordon who build on 'cross-fertilizations between art and music' (Crow 2014: 367). In more recent years, artists including Lady Gaga (Sullivan 2008) and the Black Eyed Peas (Mitchell 2009) have cited Warhol as an inspiration when describing their creative processes and goals. At worst, Warhol's name is used as a talisman against legitimate concerns regarding the commercialization of popular music culture.

As a consequence of the domination of Warhol's brand of Pop Art, market success became the indication of the best art: the 'commercialization of art has made it impossible to sustain a convincing Romantic or avant-garde role, and so the only means of artistic opposition left is to deny those roles' significance in the first place' (Frith and Horne 1987: 110). Of course, many musicians have continued to position themselves within Romantic and avant-garde frameworks, and the commercialization of art has not prevented fans and critics from accusing musicians of 'going commercial'. But certainly, by the 1960s, perceived boundaries between culture (whether painting or popular music) and commerce had become porous and productive.

If Pop Art offered the acknowledgment that all art is produced and operates within commercial culture, in the popular music world, fans and critics continued to distinguish between artists on the right side of commercialism and wrong side of commercialism. Authenticity did not cease to function as a valuable concept: 'Crucial to the convergence of creativity and commercial culture is, ironically, the maintenance of a *distinction* between authenticity and the commercial', which sustains 'the idea that there is a space outside of the market in which authenticity can take root and flourish' (Banet-Weiser 2012: 120). As Frith and Horne describe, the problem for art school graduates 'is not whether or not to "sell out" (to switch from artistic to commercial logic) but how to set up a relationship with an audience, a market, that is somehow different from a straight sales pitch, that confirms their status as "artists"' (1987: 171). Authenticity is cultivated through the crafting of a personal identity and relationship with an audience, and commercialism itself is not a hindrance to achieving artist status. That's the theory anyway.

In practice, there have always been and remain limits on commercial activities for musicians who aspire to authentic and artist labels. The use of music in advertising has been a relatively consistent hot button, though views have seemingly softened in recent years, a tendency I examine and critique in Chapter 5. Dylan may have dodged the charge of selling out in 1965 by appealing to a different form of authenticity, but his liaisons with advertising could hardly be defended on the basis of artistic experimentation: 'Many fans continue to think of him as embodying the rebel spirit of the 1960s, and when he made a commercial for Chrysler in 2014 the internet exploded with accusations and laments that he was selling out' (Wald 2015: 208). There are of course different rules for different musicians and genres with respect to commercialism, including the genres and musicians excluded from the rock rules along class, race and gender lines. Movements and scenes that have positioned themselves in explicit opposition to commercialism (e.g. DIY indie: see Chapter 3) or embrace of commercialism (e.g. poptimism: see Chapter 2) apply their own criteria or, purposefully, none at all. Pop Art may have added nuance to our understanding of commercialism, but commercialism continued to shape debates about authenticity and selling out for popular musicians and fans.

In this chapter, I have explored how popular music has appealed to the language of art and conceptualizations of authenticity in order to gain access to the status of art and the potential charge of selling out. I traced the transformation of the concept of authenticity from one based on folk traditions to a dominant mode with an origin in Romanticism – and the consequence of this shift on artists who do not fit a particular rock culture-based model. Popular music's legitimation as art crystallized in the mid-1960s, as demonstrated by the example of the Beatles, and formal links between popular musicians and the Pop Art movement.

The chapter has made clear two points with continuing relevance throughout the book. Firstly, selling out discourse attempts to protect communities at times (as per the folk tradition) but also delineates insiders and outsiders in ways that reveal construction (to sell out blues for rock is treated differently than selling out rock for disco). Despite its variation in use, I argue for the utility of the concept of selling out, and future chapters will consider the purpose served by such discourse at various times and across various popular music scenes, musicians and fans. Although different boundaries are policed for different ends, there are shared and consistent themes that run through charges of selling out, including authenticity and commercialism, both flexibly defined but nevertheless powerful.

Secondly, the relationship between culture and commerce, including popular music and commerce, is not straightforward. I suggest above that the Pop Art movement's incorporation of commercialism affirms that commercial production need not exclude popular music from artistic legitimation or evaluation. Indeed, the artists considered in this chapter – Dylan, the Beatles, the Who – were all commercially successful. But, paradoxically, commercialism remains at the heart of selling out charges. The next chapter considers challenges of maintaining boundaries between cultural and commercial imperatives from within a commercially successful sphere. It unpacks the notion of 'going commercial', and examines how the careful balance between art and commerce struck by musicians in the 1960s was challenged or dismissed as meaningless by musicians in the 1970s.

2

Popular music as big money

By the 1970s, certain genres of popular music were not only accepted as achieving artistic goals, but were also noted for the possibility of enormous commercial success. Members of the first generation of rock musicians were playing arenas, experimenting with their sounds and making millions of dollars – all activities that may be viewed dubiously by fans and commentators interested in symbols of authenticity and autonomy previously associated with less commercially successful art forms. It's no coincidence that the designations 'arena rock' and 'corporate rock' have been used interchangeably. Yet few musicians would admit to courting commercial success, whatever it takes. This chapter considers the challenges of maintaining boundaries between cultural and commercial imperatives from within a commercially successful sphere.

In the previous chapter, I traced rock's path to artistic legitimation and entry into long-standing selling out debates, highlighting the complex relationship of popular music to commercialism. The acceptance in the late 1960s of rock as an art that has something important to say occurred in tandem with unprecedented business growth in the music industries. The audience for rock music had expanded beyond the teenaged fans associated with the early days of rock'n'roll, whose spending power was limited and who were expected to age out in any case. Older and loyal audiences prompted developments in recorded and live music, and broadened the commercial opportunities available to musicians and the professionals who supported them.

In the US in the 1970s, music became the most successful sector of the entertainment industries, a shift which contextualized popular music analyses in that and the immediate period following. Steve Chapple and Reebee Garofalo's *Rock'n'Roll is Here to Pay* (1977) covers the first half of the decade, and opens with the success of rock music and its consequences: 'Rock music, which accounts for more than 80 percent of all records and tapes sold, is also the core of a $2 billion business that dwarfs other entertainment industries. It is bigger business than the $600 million made in 1974 in professional sports, or the $1.6 billion in movie revenues' (1977: xi). Their analysis situates rock 'as part of an ever-growing and highly profitable cultural industry' (1977: xii), and they argue that the 'major problem of the industry has been learning how to harness artistic creativity to corporate production and marketing structures without killing it' (1977: xiii). Simon Frith's classic *Sound Effects* (1981b) similarly opens with the music industry's extraordinary growth into big business: 'By the mid-1970s well over $4 billion was being spent annually in the world on musical products, and in America music had become the most popular form of entertainment' (1981b: 4). Frith writes that the rock story of increasing success and wealth is 'depressing for radicals like Chapple and Garofalo' (1981b: 151), whereas he himself downplays the power of commerce or corporate control on the basis that the meanings fans get out of music cannot be controlled. What both accounts share is the belief that understanding the power of music cannot be separated from understanding the music business.

The result of the music industry's financial success and newfound centrality within the entertainment industry could be seen in increasingly clashing values. Popular music may have become big money in the 1970s but, for many musicians, the perception that they are in it for the money went hand in hand with accusations of selling out. As profit-driven structures of the industry, including the establishment of professional roles and scaling up of operations, became commonplace, artists could expect to struggle to maintain distance (real or perceived) from money-making activities.

The professionalization of the rock music business offered a combination of advantages and disadvantages in this respect. As Fred Goodman (1997) documents, the 1970s saw the establishment and growth of new and enhanced roles in the music industries – agents, managers, publicists, critics – with role-holders wielding increasing power. On the one hand, such roles offered a clear separation between the creative and business aspects of making music, potentially allowing artists to get on with being artists, while leaving the business to the professionals. On the other, realizing the commercial opportunities for popular music could easily lead to treating popular music like any other commercial product expected to adapt to a mass market: 'Musicians and the creative personnel within the music industry were integrated into an entertainment business now firmly part of the American corporate structure' (Chapple and Garofalo 1977: 300).

With a range of dedicated (to making money, if not necessarily making art) professionals on the case, and reflecting the big, mainstream audiences at play, the sounds and experiences of live popular music in the 1970s became geared towards large scale. Again, such a shift can be interpreted both positively and negatively. Certainly, scaled-up spaces and strong financial backing supported, in some cases, the development and circulation of experimental sounds and visuals, of the sort associated with live music events. Likewise, while it's naïve to think that counterculture values could travel in a protective bubble into the mainstream, there is no doubt that ideas and values associated with the counterculture reached diverse and large audiences that were excluded from the smaller urban scenes of rock's roots. However, commercial success and commercial influence can pose a threat to the counterculture values that rock's originators might have hoped to spread. As I noted in the previous chapter, selling out debates distinguish acceptable commercialism (commodity form, financial success) from unacceptable commercialism (compromising values, deserting communities). While commercial success on its own may be compatible with artistic values, commercialism at the expense of artistic integrity and autonomy can quickly turn into cynical appeals to the lowest common denominator and merchandising blitzes that leave artists and fans alike shell-shocked.

This chapter explores discourses of 'success' and 'going commercial' that followed the mainstreaming of rock. It considers the characteristics, judgements and defences of arena rock to understand the relationship between popular music culture and commercial success, and questions how a multi-billion dollar industry can be a comfortable home to culture. Along the way, I explore artists and scenes that embraced commercialism and refused the terms of the selling out debate, including musicians that welcomed the challenge of writing commercially successful music, using the key example of Blondie; musicians that adopted artifice as an aesthetic; and pop enthusiasts (poptimists) who sought to redeem the value of pop music against detractors who treat rock values as innately superior (rockists). From its origin in early 80s Britain, the term 'rockism' has continued to be deployed by music critics, especially in the US, to critique the privileging of rock over pop (Morley 2006): for some, tensions remain unresolved. I also consider musicians who have managed a convincing anti-commercial stance alongside commercial success and in the face of rock's commercialism, with Bruce Springsteen serving as the 1970s paragon. As soon as the notions of 'selling out' and 'going commercial' were imported from other art worlds into popular music, they were challenged. The role of commercial success and commercialism in the 1970s highlights continuities in the debates, but also suggests that our understanding of and tolerance for commercialism has changed significantly since then.

Success, going commercial and selling out

The suspicion of mainstream success as an indication that an artist has actively pursued a more commercially friendly approach and has prioritized money over art is present across art worlds, historic and contemporary, high and popular. Concerns about artists going commercial or selling out are an inevitable outcome of the inherent tension between art and commerce, where commoditization threatens to shape cultural processes and objects. As Bill Ryan describes in Marxist terms, 'The undermining of its use value as a cultural object by its exchange value form is what underpins the contradictions of the cultural commodity and many characteristic dynamics of the culture industry' (1991: 5).

The challenge of balancing commercial and artistic success in popular music imitates struggles that fine artists have long faced and, like today's popular musicians, fine artists find themselves with fewer choices and more pressure to rely on corporate sponsorship. Popular music is also not the first of the popular arts to juggle different forms and perceptions of success: film went through a similar process of artistic legitimation and filmmakers often face similar choices and charges. A *Guardian* interview describes director Martin Scorsese's dilemma as 'how to combine commercial success with artistic integrity', with some of his artistically successful films leading to 'an uninterested public' and his popular films characterized as 'selling out to the studios' (Pilkington 2006). Replace 'director' with 'musician', 'films' with 'albums', and 'studios' with 'record companies' and you have the popular music version of the same narrative. For popular arts like film and popular music, the fact that the products originate within commercial systems does not eliminate the tension between art and commerce.

One way in which the tension is expressed is by hiding the commercial processes that underpin success. The presence of big business cannot be denied, but it needs to be seen to play a supporting rather than leading role. Indeed, the strategy of controlling exposure to an artist creates the impression of organic success. Goodman explains, 'By underselling the market, the demand for the act remained unsatisfied and appeared greater than it might be. Most important, whether it was true or not, the musician did not appear motivated by greed and could not be tagged a sellout by either the fans or the rock press' (1997: 313).

In many ways, the new music industry professionals of the 1970s participated in a continuation of the commercial exploitation of music that developed in the late nineteenth century with music publishing (Suisman 2009). Most of the music we hear in our everyday lives 'is connected in some way with the commercial economy of the music industry, in which value is gauged according to financial, not cultural or aesthetic, criteria. Music may still have cultural or aesthetic value, but neither governs its commercial production' (Suisman 2009:9). At the same time, the new professionals were, like the rock artists they represented, committed to (or held hostage to?) an ideology based on notions of art, authenticity and autonomy. Tin Pan Alley songwriters 'saw no irony, no contradiction, and probably no pejorative connotation, in the term *music industry*. They enjoyed the music, and they enjoyed the commerce' (Suisman 2009: 52). However, the relationship of early rock musicians to the music *business* and music *industry* was necessarily fraught.

The music industry has its roots in the early commercial exploitation of music in the United States, from the late nineteenth century developments of music publishing and the phonograph to the expansion of copyright and links with radio and film in the 1920s. Subsequent debates about mass culture brought new critiques of the processes and products of mass consumption. Theodor Adorno and Max Horkheimer's 1944 essay, 'The Culture Industry: Enlightenment as Mass Deception', documents their concerns about the culture industry's production of 'pseudo-individuality', its appeal to the lowest-common denominator, and the narcotizing effects of mass culture, which they view as laying the foundation for a similarly mechanized and controlled political system (1999). In his 1941 essay 'On Popular Music', Adorno singled out popular music as prime offender (1990). Frith's overview of the Frankfurt School's mass culture critique of popular music emphasizes Adorno's claim that 'it is the production of music as a commodity, to be consumed, that determines its cultural quality' (1981b: 43). From a critical theory perspective, 'Art has become entertainment, cultural response has become selection in the marketplace, popular creation has become the commercial attempt to attract the largest possible number of consumers' (Frith 1981b: 43).

Evaluations of the state of the music industry in the 1970s were explicitly informed or implicitly influenced by such thinking because the art values invested in rock were strained by the enormous scale of commercial operations that resulted from rock's success. The fit of the culture industry thesis for popular music is awkward, however. Frith (1981b) questions the classification of rock as mass culture, noting that some records will only have limited appeal while others will be directed at a large audience, and Stratton (1983) argues against the claims of standardization on the basis that capitalism also requires innovation and originality, and popular music artists and the Romantic values that often characterize them are thus important to the music industry. Chapple and Garofalo, however, are sympathetic to the idea that commercialization cannot but damage the values associated with rock's anti-establishment origins: 'The position of the music as an increasingly important cultural commodity within a consumer economy weakened any of the explicit antimaterialist content of the music' (1977: 300). A critique of materialism might be less inspiring when voiced by an artist in a materially rich position.

The tension between art and commercialism requires careful navigation, but in popular music it is also the case that artistic success and commercial success can occur together and not result in criticism. In the early days of rock's financial ascendency, artistic success and commercial success seemed to go hand in hand, nurtured largely by professionals who were themselves fans and who believed in the importance of artistic autonomy (Goodman 1997). Commercial success could be viewed as a validation of a musician's artistic ambitions: as Manfred Mann put it, 'the more people buy a record, the more successful it is—not only commercially but artistically' (quoted in Frith 1981b: 61). Record companies may have been led by commercialism, 'but many companies have found that music made as the artist would like to make it is itself commercial' (Chapple and Garofalo 1977: 178). In this formulation, musicians and producers focus on the art, and the business side of the music industry is left to the record company, which sounds like an ideal balance, though horror stories of record executives getting involved in production to its detriment suggest a less clean split. When such a division of labour works, artists can experience autonomy and benefit from the financial support and marketing of labels, while avoiding accusations of chasing commercial success. Goodman notes the example of David Geffen managing Laura Nyro's career: Geffen's 'success with Laura Nyro was proof that he could help an artist cash in without making it seem that he or she had sold out' (1997: 130).

When commercial success, or the perception of the pursuit of commercial success, does draw criticism, it may be for good reason. Positive examples of musicians finding commercial success without compromise may obscure the more typical experience for musicians who entered into contractual relationships with the big record companies at the height of the music industry's financial success. The music business of the 1970s made it 'possible for an established artist or act to write and record pretty much what it wants to, always operating within the bounds of commercial success' (Chapple and Garofalo 1977: 310). However, 'New artists with no proven ability to repeat their first successes are under more pressure to conform' (Chapple and Garofalo 1977: 310). While not censorship in the formal sense, the pressures of the business impose a sort of self-censorship by artists. Maintaining rock as counterculture within the context of the music industry presents a major challenge to musicians: 'As local live performers, musicians remain a part of their community, subject to its values and needs, but as recording artists they experience the pressures of the market' (Frith 1981b: 51). If rock's commercial success and centrality to the music business in the 1970s made it 'impossible to tell what is done for art and what is done for commerce' (Goodman 1997: xiii), some fans and critics were quick to point fingers at cases that suggested the latter.

'Going commercial'

Between the artistic legitimation of rock in the late 1960s and the opportunities afforded by the success of the music industry in the 1970s, the concept of 'going commercial' became especially relevant for popular musicians. Where jazz and folk musicians had in the past occasionally found themselves in demand, with commercial opportunities weighed against the accusation of 'going commercial', the entire structure of the music industry in the 1970s was based around the commercial success of rock, even if, then as now, the majority of artists signed were not profitable.

Sometimes used as a synonym for selling out, 'going commercial' is perhaps better understood as a more specific sub-category of selling out that usually focuses on music or music-related choices made to appeal to a broader audience. Other categories of selling out (e.g. corporate sponsorship) offer an immediate financial benefit, but do not necessarily require musicians to do anything different in terms of sound or performance. In the context of the 1970s and the increased commercial appeal of rock music, the concept of going commercial was typically used to describe musicians courting a mainstream that wasn't previously available.

The intermingling of artistic and commercial success following the legitimation of rock as art meant that some optimists believed the phrase and its negative connotations to be antiquated. Music critic Richard Goldstein's 1967 review of the Bee Gees' album *Bee Gees 1st* perfectly captures this position. Goldstein notes, 'The time when "going commercial" meant creating repetitive and simplified music is over, and this album is all the proof of that one needs' (1967: 84) before describing how the rock revolution has raised the expectation of artistic qualities in commercial music:

> You can approach the album assuming it will be complex; today's rock audience demands that. To be profound is to be professional. Good poetry sells. To blow the mind with radical departures is commercial. The pseudo-sound that passed for Pop music five years ago has become a vital, probing sound. Today, slick means skill.
>
> Goldstein 1967: 84

It's an alluring narrative and certainly reflects significant changes to popular music and the music business that ushered in the commercial success of the industry in the 1970s, but of course the phrase remained a part of the 1970s vocabulary, whether applied to bands who did not or would not go commercial; those who did go commercial but the results justified the decision; or those who did go commercial and attracted criticism. While 'going commercial' has in recent years been applied as a pun for music used in advertising, in the 1970s the phrase was mostly used to describe the sound of the music in question, from the proficiency of the musicians and slickness of the production, to explorations in new genres or the release of less challenging material.

The development of a more professional sound can be interpreted as going commercial particularly for groups that have previously exhibited a naïve or shambolic sound, due to lack of training, an ideological commitment to democratic music-making, or both. The classic quote 'This is a chord, this is another, this is a third. Now form a band' (from 1977 fanzine *Sideburns*) was a fantastic and punk call to arms, but most musicians become more proficient with time, even despite themselves! Post-punk band the Mekons, whose amateurish sound reflected opposition to notions of talent and stars, had to re-evaluate their music philosophies as the group's technical ability (and – limited – commercial appeal) increased. On the prospect of signing a big contract as a music industry 'intervention', a *Melody Maker* writer observed, '"Intervention" sounds so much nicer than "going commercial", doesn't it?' (Harron 1979).

The professionalization of the music business in the 1970s opened up the possibility of cleaner production, another change to sound that signals greater commercial appeal. The combination of experienced producers, more studio time and better equipment can smooth the rough edges associated with rock authenticity, though the result is not always decried. Consider a 1974 review of Southern rock group Wet Willie's *Keep On Smilin'*:

> The bad news is that Wet Willie, probably the hardest core Southern band, has finally gone commercial. The good news is that it sounds great.... More than anything else it's Tom Dowd's production that makes *Keep On Smilin'* stand out from everything else Wet Willie ever recorded before. He slickened it up and funneled the group's energy down distinct channels for a clear, concise, cohesive and well-layered sound.
>
> Esposito 1974

The review works against the usual expectation that 'going commercial' and 'slick production' are bad moves that result in less artistically successful material – in the process confirming that the negative connotations of such discourse are very much still in play in most cases.

Musicians who depart from their usual genre to explore a trendier one represent a classic case of going commercial, with the shape of the music charts seemingly shaping musical choices. San Francisco rock group the Flamin' Groovies recognized the temptation in a 1978 *Trouser Press* interview:

> But despite the constant lure of selling out, 'going commercial,' to make it, the Groovies have never swayed from their rock'n'roll purism. 'We could have copped out years ago,' said Cyril, 'and gone space fag rock in '72. In '69 we could have gone psychedelic. In fucking '75 we could have gone reggae. I mean we know how to play all that shit. But we never did that because we never wanted to turn our trip into a business to make money'.
>
> Goldberg 1978

Other musicians are accused of going commercial when they release less challenging material, in terms of instrumentation or song structure, than they did previously. While not technically straying from their genre, this version of 'going commercial' suggests a watering down of their output, going 'pop' to increase commercial opportunities. Having cut his teeth in bluesy rock group Humble Pie, and with his initial solo efforts offering little in the way of commercial success, Peter Frampton's enormously successful *Frampton Comes Alive!* resulted in an 'MOR musical stamp' (Valentine 1977), which suggested he had gone commercial by taking the middle of the road. His appearance in the terrible 1978 film adaptation of *Sgt Pepper's Lonely Hearts Club Band* strengthened the charge, and is a reminder that going commercial in sound is often accompanied by other commercial activities. Similarly, Frampton's 1976 shirtless *Rolling Stone* cover – which he came to regret for hurting his credibility – reflects Helen Davies' observation that the 'degree to which an artist's music is viewed as "serious" is often inversely proportional to the extent to which their image is foregrounded' (2001: 306).

As well as visual presentation and media image, other non-musical dimensions sometimes used as evidence of going commercial include the setting in which musicians perform or links to broader processes of commoditization. The contested position of the arena as music venue represents the former and the latter is often identified through sponsorships and merchandising. 'The process of selling records inherently coopted both music and musicians by commoditizing them' (Chapple and Garofalo 1977: 306), which is especially pernicious when products with no clear musical connection are involved: 'The biggest rock stars are commoditized to an even greater degree. Their image is transferred to everyday items of clothing, toiletries, and toys, and sold piecemeal to an adulating public' (1977: 306). (Chapple and Garofalo (1977) identify the use of rock in advertising as one result of rock music's success and co-optation, and highlight how it undercuts any revolutionary stance, a claim I pick up in Chapter 5.) When assessing whether musical choices are a case of artistic evolution or going commercial, critics may necessarily draw on such non-musical activities. Descriptors like arena rock and corporate rock, sometimes used interchangeably, bridge both musical and non-musical dimensions to describe commercially driven music and to suggest an elevation of profit above art. For many fans and critics in the 1970s, arena rock came to represent the worst manifestations of commercialism to infest the music business. In the following section, I consider what arena rock can tell us about the relationship between popular music culture and commercial success.

Arena rock

As described at the start of the chapter, by the 1970s the popular music industry was big business, having grown on the back of rock's success into the largest entertainment sector in the US (itself the largest producer of globally distributed entertainment). Live music was one area of the industry that met the increased mainstream appeal of rock by scaling up operations. The arena concert is the pinnacle of the audience- and profit-maximizing strategy.

The success of music festivals offered a precedent and template for arena tours in terms of scale. Cotten Seiler looks at late 1960s music festivals and the rise of the concert industry as examples of the claim that, in addition to its role in positive social change, 1960s 'rock culture must also be understood as a historical moment in the production of new coalitions of consumers and, consequently, of more supple, sophisticated, and activist strategies of capital' (2000: 207). Festivals offered a space and occasion for a countercultural meeting of hearts and minds, but their existence owed more to the business sense they made than to the social and cultural values derived by attendees. As Frith writes of the success of Woodstock, 'The Woodstock Festival of 1969 was, indeed, a symbol of the vast size not just of the "rock" community but also of the rock market' (1981b: 100) with high fees for artists becoming the norm for concerts.

The corporatization of rock through the concert industry was not uncontested: even some music business insiders were critical of the commercialized and profit-driven nature of festivals. Warner Bros executive Andy Wickham's view of the commercial underground was shaped by his friendship with protest singer Phil Ochs, who 'remained committed to folk music's political/activist tradition' and 'had little use for the increasingly commercial underground scene, which he viewed as hypocritical' (Goodman 1997: 77). When Wickham wrote (unused) programme notes for the 1967 Monterey Pop Festival, he declared, 'the artists and the festival's promoters were motivated solely by commerce and greed' (Goodman 1997: 77). Seiler notes that 1970s's Isle of Wight festival and later festivals attracted charges of commodification, evidence of the tension between claims of anticommercial values and profit-making goals, but suggests that such charges were less likely in later years: 'one factor in "the selling of rock and roll" to corporate America is the weakening—and in many cases, the severing—of the connection of rock music to utopian politics and to social progressivism more generally' (2000: 209–10). The more relaxed attitude towards the commercialization and corporatization of rock concerts laid the groundwork for the movement of concert tours from smaller, specialized venues to enormous multi-purpose arenas.

The transition to arenas was also eased by the fact that many of the earliest acts to go the arena route were the same groups that had helped to legitimate popular music as art in the 1960s: the Rolling Stones (whose 1969 arena tour is considered a game-changer for the concert industry) and the Who (who upgraded to arenas for their 1970 tour) brought with them into the arena existing credibility and respect. Read generously, such groups were simply meeting audience demand efficiently through arena tours – and there is no doubt they had paid their dues on the club circuit. Many more groups that followed, however, began their careers amidst the arena tour context and with the expectation of excess that came to define the setting and concert style. Steve Waksman (2009) quotes a young, pre-Aerosmith Steven Tyler taking in Madison Square Garden before a 1969 Led Zeppelin concert:

> When I got there, the road crew and the union people were all eating and the band hadn't arrived. The stage was empty and so were the 19,000 seats. The silence was deafening. I walked out to the stage and lay down, with my head hanging backward off the edge. I was overwhelmed by instant delusions of rock and roll grandeur, imagining that I was roaming the land, raping and pillaging, disguised as an ambassador of rock. And I said to myself, *Someday a band of mine is gonna fill this fuckin' place.*
> Quoted in Waksman 2009: 32, emphasis in original

As Waksman argues, Tyler's perspective demonstrates 'that the arena was an icon of success in its own right, and the possibility of drawing an arena-size crowd stood for an intensely coveted form of rock-and-roll grandeur' (2009: 32). That such grandeur involves musicians living out a gross, sexist and violent fantasy rather than a community of shared values reveals a truth of arenas, which served rock gods first and foremost, not rock communities, and essentially maintained the scale of festivals without the pretence of making the world a better place.

As more musicians and music fans experienced arena concerts, the arena as venue became crystallized into a style of music, with dominant characteristics, judgements and defences. 'Arena rock' ultimately came to stand not simply for the setting but for particular qualities of music that were befitting the space and spectacle, with an emphasis on big: big sounds, big choruses and, at times, big hair. The description is generally associated with hard rock and heavy metal, though arenas have housed more typically pop acts as well, and its use implies a relaxed orientation towards commercialization. At their most cartoonish, arena rock groups are greedy for money and success, are not afraid to say so, and are willing to do whatever they need to do to achieve it. 'Corporate rock' is sometimes used as a more explicit and direct synonym, and makes clear assumptions about the underlying motivations behind the development of the concert industry from smaller venues to festivals to arenas (i.e. as a business rather than artistic strategy).

The key judgement of arena rock, then, is that it is primarily profit-driven and any claimed artistic achievement of the environment or performance is either incidental or a distraction from the main purpose to pack as many paying customers into the space as possible. Criticisms of arena concerts preceded the establishment of arena rock in the 1970s: critical responses to the Beatles' Shea Stadium appearances in 1965 and 1966 – the second of which was closely followed by the group's withdrawal from live performance – focused on their inauthenticity (Waksman 2009). John Lennon himself remarked, 'I reckon we could send out four waxwork dummies of ourselves and that would satisfy the crowds. Beatles concerts are nothing to do with music any more. They're just bloody tribal rites' (The Beatles 2000: 229). Of course, rites and rituals can still be meaningful for fans building a community around shared music and values, and later large-scale concerts did not suffer from crowd noise overwhelming the sound of the performance as per the Beatles. Still, versions of those early critiques of the arena experience have persisted. Additionally, while earlier notions of a rock community included both performers and fans, another critique of arena rock focuses on the physical and psychological distance between artists and audiences created by the level of success defined by the arena setting.

Success can be isolating, in and outside the concert setting. Those who make a lot of money are distanced from their audience and lose touch with their roots: 'Top stars, the Rolling Stones being a particularly spectacular example, have become part of the standard bourgeois jet set' (Chapple and Garofalo 1977: 312). The impact of such a shift on musical output is not certain. Frith claims of the state of the popular music industry in the 1970s, 'There is, in fact, less conflict between art and commerce in rock than in any other mass medium' since 'the biggest acts have contracts that let them do much as they musically like' (Frith 1981b: 83). Though it's easy to imagine how musical vision may be shaped by the distanced superstar experience of 'moving leisurely, luxuriously, excessively between studio and stadium, cocooned (and cocained) by an entourage of servants and sycophants' (Frith 1981b: 64–5). The great sell out occurs when 'performers stop being artists and begin being Rock Stars, no longer concerned with their community or their vision, no longer even able to get in touch with them, capable now only of churning out more formulaic, inauthentic commercial product, marketing their own ghostly commodified star-image' (Tetzlaff 1994: 98–9).

Promoter Bill Graham cynically described the domination of arena and stadium tours in the 1970s as allowing bands to 'make more money in *less* time' so they could enjoy all the luxuries that commercial success had bought them (Waksman 2009: 31, emphasis in original). If arena rock has come to stand for

1970s rock star excess, it is also the case that it was a response to, not the cause of, popular music's commercial success. While there is no shortage of caricatures depicting rock stars as in it for the money, in reality we rarely encounter musicians who admit to being driven primarily by money. The more typical defence is that successful musicians can't help it – and shouldn't need to apologize – if their art happens to be enormously successful. As noted above, the most successful rock stars of the 1970s had leverage and musical freedom as a result of their success, relieving some of the art–commerce tension in rock.

The success of the popular music business in the 1970s, as reflected through arena rock, posed the question of whether a multi-billion dollar industry can be a comfortable home to culture. The simple answer is yes: there are plenty of examples across popular music genres and over the decades since rock first found mainstream popularity of artists enjoying success while maintaining their artistic vision. Yet the challenge of achieving the commercial success, scale and profit margins that proved possible in the 1970s necessarily led to pressures and compromises for some musicians. The next section turns to musicians who accepted and relished the challenge of redefining their art within a highly commercialized context and who cast doubt on some of the underlying rock mythologies that opposed artistic success to commercial success.

Commercial success, artifice and early poptimism

Arena rock was not the only style of music in the 1970s that challenged earlier rock notions of authenticity or that embraced commercial success as desirable. From the early 1970s, glam or glitter rock played with notions of artifice and sought to redeem pop genres like bubblegum that had been marginalized by rock. As noted in the previous chapter, Van Cagle describes how 'Bowie and his glitter rock followers helped usher in a new post-1960s moment—a "revolt into style" as a social practice in which commercialization and consumerism were a means to a radical end' (1995: 14). According to Cagle, Robert Duncan's suggestion that 'Warhol was inauthentically authentic' resonates in styles like glitter (1995: 202), and he concludes that glitter rock challenges 'the guiding maxim of rock criticism' (1995: 217) that pitted commercial success against authenticity, since authenticity was not a contested notion or problem for glitter musicians. Glitter was not alone in reconfiguring a relationship to authenticity against the rock mould: early electronic groups in the 1970s, such as Kraftwerk, likewise challenged the rock notion of authenticity and, in this case, the expected expressive performance of male rock artists. No sooner had the rise of rock constructed a version of authenticity that tied selling out to commercial ambition and appeal than other rock-based scenes emerged to question the shaky foundations of such values.

By the late 1970s, the torch for championing commercial pop had been passed to new wave, a phrase used to cover a broad range of sounds, primarily with roots in punk. Depending on the source, new wave was simply a more commercially friendly description of bands that would otherwise be classified as punk, or a term for the more pop-friendly groups to emerge from the punk scene, or a catch-all for music that had previously enjoyed only limited success in the music underground. On the one hand, punk and new wave emerged as a response to 'this new decadence, this new inauthenticity' decried by rock critics and embodied by such acts as Elton John, Led Zeppelin and Chicago (Gendron 2002: 231). On the other hand, new wave was characterized by critics as a more commercial, less authentic variation of punk. Emerging from the New York underground and going on to achieve worldwide success, Blondie was frequently at the centre of debates about punk and new wave, and the relationship between commercial success and selling out. The response of the group's members to charges of selling out complicate simplified dichotomies between art and commerce or authenticity and artifice.

Blondie's attempt to balance mainstream and underground activities and sounds provides the context for Kembrew McLeod's (2016) 33 1/3 series contribution on 1978's *Parallel Lines*: he suggests that the dynamic is key to understanding the group and their work. Although Blondie was regularly accused of selling out following the success of *Parallel Lines*, the group had not positioned themselves ideologically outside the commercial mainstream. Instead, members spoke enthusiastically about the possibility of commercial success: guitarist Chris Stein saw mass appeal as a challenge and drummer Clem Burke discussed his desire to be a successful pop star (McLeod 2016: 3). Given their perspectives on success, the selling out charge seemed inapplicable. In a 1999 interview, Burke reflected on the group being accused of selling out:

> Which was ridiculous. Our whole aesthetic was about being successful. It was more analogous with Andy Warhol in a way, mixing art and commerce together. We wanted to reach as many people as possible. That's why Warhol made paintings of Brillo boxes and Campbell's soup cans, because everyone could relate to that. It was about finding a common denominator, which is also what

> Blondie has always been about in a way. Some people at CBGBs had more artistic pretensions, which we had, too, of course. But we were also very focused on the commercial aspect of it.
>
> Burston 1999

There were other ways, too, in which Blondie's creative approaches did not fit with the basis of authenticity driving selling out debates. As McLeod explains, 'When Blondie went pop with *Parallel Lines*, it wasn't a typical mid-career sellout move, because sugary sweetness had always coursed through the band's collective veins' (2016: 21). Blondie's embrace of the 1960s girl group style that preceded the shift from rock'n'roll to rock both denied the distinction rock made between entertainment and art, and flattered through imitation the dismissed genre. As McLeod points out, the designation of rock as art, particularly through press appraisal of the Beatles, relied on criticism about the low quality of earlier rock'n'roll, denying the role and influence of girl groups on later bands, including the Beatles (2016: 57–8). Like glitter artists, Blondie also played with ideas of art and artifice, particularly through performance:

> Debbie Harry was pivotal in the shift from an emphasis on authentic self-expression—which defined the 1960s rock era—to an approach used by 1980s pop stars like Madonna.... Unlike earlier rock stars like Janis Joplin, whose appeal was grounded in 'honest' displays of emotional pain and ecstasy, Blondie's frontwoman was clearly acting, faking it. Irony and artifice would become the new authenticity.
>
> McLeod 2016: 125

While arena rock came to stand for music that didn't care about, or even think about, tensions between art and commerce, examples from glitter rock and new wave confronted the tension head on to insist that commercial pop can be valued aesthetically and that authenticity is a faulty rock tool that draws lines arbitrarily and disingenuously. Arena rockers had no use for a concept like selling out, whereas artists like Bowie and Blondie contributed to selling out debates by using their credibility to chip away at the foundations. These examples laid the groundwork for a backlash to rock and rockism that continued to develop in subsequent years into a position that became known as poptimism.

In fact, the seeds were planted just as soon as the rock myth was born: the legitimation of rock as art occurred alongside 'inauthenticist' and 'popist' moments of rock critics 'glorifying those mass-cultural features of the music that traditional critics found so repugnant, such as rapid obsolescence, market saturation, constant repetition, and the merger of economics and aesthetics' (Gendron 2002: 214). From the early 1970s, and especially in the 1980s, pop-positive perspectives developed into celebrations that 'rock is dead': 'The rotten core of this myth, or so the argument went, is the idea of musical authenticity. Pop musics conceived as anti-authentic became the predictably postmodern intellectual rage' (Tetzlaff 1994: 95).

More recent attempts to redeem artists and genres dismissed as manufactured and trivial have further disturbed the rock versus pop division (Keightley 2011). A 2004 *New York Times* piece by Kelefa Sanneh, 'The Rap Against Rockism', kicked off a debate among music writers that continued to attract new pieces over a decade later (see Austerlitz 2014, Loss 2015). Sanneh identifies (in what Jody Rosen (2006) calls 'the most-discussed piece of popular music criticism of the past several years—at least among pop music critics') the cracks in the rockism perspective, which he describes as beginning 'when British bands questioned whether the search for raw, guitar-driven authenticity wasn't part of rock 'n' roll's problem, instead of its solution; some new-wave bands emphasized synthesizers and drum machines and makeup and hairspray, instead' (2004: AR1). He portrays rockism as 'idolizing the authentic old legend (or underground hero) while mocking the latest pop star; lionizing punk while barely tolerating disco; loving the live show and hating the music video; extolling the growling performer while hating the lip-syncher' and asks, 'could it really be a coincidence that rockist complaints often pit straight white men against the rest of the world?' (Sanneh 2004: 32). (I considered this point in the previous chapter's discussion of rock authenticity and will pick it up again when I look at how selling out functions within hip-hop in Chapter 4.)

Saneh reminds readers of the utter joy that pop music can bring and encourages recognition and serious consideration of the great songs that come out of the pop marketplace. Rosen's (2006) response in *Slate* reveals the emergent label for the perspective: 'There is a name for this new critical paradigm, "popism"—or, more evocatively (and goofily), "poptimism"—and it sets the old assumptions on their ear: Pop (and, especially, hip-hop) producers are as important as rock auteurs, Beyoncé is as worthy of serious consideration as Bruce Springsteen, and ascribing shame to pop pleasure is itself a shameful act'. As critics have debated the faults and merits of poptimism for challenging the narrow rockist conception of authenticity, musicians too have continued to question authenticity as a useful criterion: David Grazian notes how some indie rock and hip-hop artists have acknowledged the constructed nature of authenticity and expressed 'their own critique of commonly held assumptions about the nature of producing music as simultaneously art, entertainment, and commerce' (2003: 239), questioning why credibility should be tied to professional or social marginality.

The fact that the rockism/poptimism debates are still going shows the endurance of the rock myth and the unresolved nature of commercialism in popular music. It's also worth pointing out that artists who are valued for taking a contrarian position regarding authenticity and selling out have often inherited or earned the credibility to be contrary, whether through the dimensions of race, class, gender and sexuality, or through the perception of having 'paid their dues'. Besides, active and vocal disavowal of concepts like authenticity and selling out still engages with the debate in a way that lots of purely commercial artists wouldn't. Finally, for many artists in the 1970s and beyond, anti-commercialism remained an essential mode for expressing authenticity.

Anti-commercialism, community and the punk response

As the above glitter and new wave examples illustrate, the 1970s was undoubtedly an interesting time in terms of challenging the newly established rock myth, its authenticity foundation and relationship to pop and commercial success. There were also examples in this era of artists – particularly those positioned more squarely in the rock mode – who achieved commercial success yet managed to maintain a persuasive anti-commercial stance, with Bruce Springsteen serving as an archetype.

Springsteen's ability to achieve enormous commercial success while maintaining an image of anti-commercial authenticity resulted from a combination of his genuine naïveté about the music business in the early years and a clear marketing and promotion strategy aimed at maintaining the image in later years. The story of Bruce Springsteen supports Goodman's (1997) argument that commercial and artistic success can go hand in hand if the professional roles are filled by the right people (i.e. music fans who have good instincts and give the artists their autonomy). In Springsteen's case, the role of his eventual manager Jon Landau, who had already established his credibility as a music critic with an acute understanding of the business, was critical to the artist's success.

Springsteen had initially agreed to unfair contractual terms with his first manager: a poor business move, but one which supports the myth of the artist who was driven by music alone, was uninterested in money and was 'willfully ignorant of the business' (Goodman 1997: 221). By 1977, when Landau negotiated much more favourable terms for Springsteen, and in the wake of the critical and commercial success of 1975's *Born to Run*, the singer was 'heralded as the keeper of the promise that rock—despite surrendering its ties to an anticorporate counterculture—was still about something more than acquiring the trappings of success' (Goodman 1997: 294). Springsteen was a convincing embodiment of 'the real thing' in part due to his positioning as an outsider to the music business: 'Despite being the beneficiary of one of the costliest, most sophisticated marketing campaigns the record industry could produce, he remained a naïf' (Goodman 1997: 294). The record industry and its marketing strategies had evolved significantly between the time of Dylan and this declared 'new Dylan', and Springsteen 'had trouble reconciling his own artistic aims with the record company's purely commercial decisions—or at least wanted to keep the company at arm's distance' (Goodman 1997: 302). In his role as manager, Landau became responsible for the commercial dirty work, while allowing Springsteen to avoid accusations of selling out and maintain an image counter to 'rock's creeping commercialism' (Goodman 1997: 304).

Stories of artists achieving or deserving commercial success without succumbing to the pressures of the music business or compromising their artistic integrity continue to circulate today. Radiohead, for example, are said to hold the 'secret to success without selling out' for their ability to gain popularity while 'making music increasingly divorced from anything that conventionally resembles commercial appeal' (*Toronto Star* 2006). 'Radiohead aren't sellouts', explains another journalist, because 'commercial success hasn't influenced the type of music they create' (Grewal 2003). In the 1970s and today, anti-commercial perspectives and activities have not proven a barrier to commercial success, offering evidence that rock's core values relating to authenticity, autonomy and community persist even as rock's commercialism grows.

Perhaps the charge of 'going commercial', while ostensibly concerned with the power of music business institutions and the lure of greater financial reward, obscures the real source of distress prompted by 1970s developments like arena rock. As discussed above, while critiques of the arena setting often focus on their profit-driven nature, another charge emphasizes the physical and psychological distance between arena artists and audiences. Drawing from its folk roots, early rock emphasized the personal connection between artists and audience, the lack of pedestal and the opportunity to identify kindred spirits. While Frith asserts this sense of community as a myth, he explains, 'the importance of the myth of rock community is that it *is* a myth. The sociological task is not to "expose" this myth or to search for its "real" foundations, but to explain why it is so important' (1981a: 168, emphasis in original). We can, for example, choose to understand accusations of going commercial or selling out as attempting to protect a community: if that community is just a romantic idea, it still promotes for fans the belief in values outside commodity culture.

The 1970s rock superstar was not simply distanced from fans, but distanced from the foundational values of the genre. Goodman characterizes the conundrum of 1970s commercial rock success in a nutshell:

> Monetarily, the marriage of the music and the business was an extraordinary success. But artistically and socially, it was a complete reversal of the values that had spawned the music. The underground scene started in earnest when rock assumed the mantle of meaning and intent from folk music, and it was founded on a search for authenticity and an explicit rejection of consumerism and mainstream values. But the resonance and appeal of that message had proven broad enough to supply the impetus for a new business—and that business had taken on a life of its own.
>
> 1997: 306

While an example like Bruce Springsteen proves that commercial success can go hand in hand with artistic success, and that core values of rock can persist within and despite the trappings of the music business, genres like glitter and new wave question whether rock concepts like authenticity need protecting at all. The most explicit critique of the commercialization of the music business came from punk, which Seiler describes as a response to the 'excesses of 1970s "arena rock"— giant concert venues and inflated ticket prices, impeccably and exorbitantly produced recordings, virtuoso performances, mythologized star personalities, and an expansion in merchandising' (2000: 217). Punk recast rock (in the form of 'aging superstar bands') as the site of commercial sellouts, the home of industry shills (Tetzlaff 1994: 97). 'According to punk thinking, rock had lost its power, partly because its stars had become rich and out-of-touch with the vernacular vitality that gave popular music its energy and legitimacy' (Hesmondhalgh and Meier 2014: 97). It is no surprise that punk became the centre of the most heated of selling out debates, as the next chapter demonstrates.

The dismissal of notions like selling out and going commercial as no longer relevant has been a part of popular music culture since the importation of the concepts from other art worlds. As this chapter shows, in the 1970s, values of anti-commercialism were challenged by the scale and success of the music business, encapsulated by arena rock, and values of authenticity were challenged by scenes like glitter and new wave that drew attention to the exclusionary nature of rockist ideology and celebrated pop and artifice. Moving away from extremes like arena rock and trying to pin down what counts as 'going commercial' and when it's a valid criticism proves more difficult.

For the purposes of this book, it's worth noting that commercialization in the popular music business has changed significantly since the 1970s. While artists like Blondie may have embraced commercial success as meeting the challenge of mass appeal, today artists have little choice but to consider commercial opportunities in order to make a living – whether that means adopting a more commercial sound or agreeing to a commercial sponsorship. In Chapter 6, I argue that recent challenges to the relevance of the selling out concept have taken on a different and more worrying character in terms of commercial pressures, gatekeepers and influences. But before those promotional developments came a period in which independent music scenes flourished.

In the next chapter, I explore small, independent networks and scenes that grew partly in response to the excesses of rock in the 1970s, and the increasing distance between performers and audiences. Influential discourses of DIY and independence in popular music offer a corrective to the rock star pedestal and a natural home for selling out debates.

3

Alternative goes mainstream

Maintaining cultural autonomy remains central to the decision-making processes of many musicians, and particularly those involved in genres that stress independence as a value. The choice to sign to a major label or not was a touchstone of selling out debates within punk and indie scenes of the 1980s and 1990s. This chapter explores cases for which the ideology around selling out was associated primarily with signing to major record labels, focusing on the examples of the mainstreaming of punk in the 1980s and the commercialization of independent music following the popularity of grunge in the 1990s. Indeed, the commercial success of Nirvana has been understood as marking the end of an indie era (Azerrad 2001: 8).

The charge of selling out suggests that external influences have led the accused to compromise their values in order to achieve money or power. For a politician, this could mean adjusting his or her position around an issue so as not to alienate a potential source of funding or endorsement. For a journalist, it could involve ignoring newsworthy transgressions of advertisers on which a publication is reliant. For an educator, selling out could reflect a curriculum shaped by political or religious pressure in the absence of strong, academically grounded evidence. Shared across these cases is the implicit assumption that a role-holder who should be trusted to act independently is no longer doing so.

In the context of popular music, as has been indicated by previous chapters, the perception of a loss of independence is often linked to straying from a sound, or engaging in commercial activity that was either disavowed previously or assumed to be at odds with generic values. For some artists, the assertion of independence is made explicit through engagement with alternative production, distribution and consumption networks that operate in opposition to the mainstream music industries. Independent record labels have provided a space through which values of independence are declared and the ability of the mainstream music industries to support independent artistic expression is questioned.

In this chapter, I consider the history and growth of independent labels in the UK and the US, from a practical and not especially political alternative subset of the recording industry through to their politicization in the context of punk and post-punk scenes, beginning in the late 1970s, maturing in the 1980s and confronting challenges to their foundations and continuing existence by the 1990s. For a brief period, the tension between independent and major labels became the central issue of selling out debates in popular music culture, before being made largely obsolete through the incorporation, at times welcome and at others aggressive, of independent bands and labels into the major record label system. I conclude the chapter by pointing to some of the ways in which the attendant values of independent labels persist within popular music culture.

Cultural autonomy and 'independence' in popular music culture

The notion of autonomy as critical to genuine artistic expression has its roots in the Romantic movement, and was imported alongside related ideas of authorship and authenticity into popular music culture and other areas of mass cultural production. As Mark Banks describes, 'at least since the late eighteenth century, autonomy in cultural production has been associated with freedom from the particular demands and constraints of the commercial world' and 'to speak of "creative" or "artistic autonomy" is to index a particular notion of freedom actively developed in the context of Romanticism' (2010: 252–3). The ideals of Romanticism, including originality and individual genius, encouraged a separation of artists from elements that might influence them and interfere with true artistic expression, such as the corrupting force of commercialism. In reality, then, as now, many artists had to negotiate the desire for creative independence with the need to make a living, often striking a compromise by supporting their artistic output with commercial work. No doubt the temptation to court a broader and more commercial audience was as present for some as the fear of being accused of sacrificing their valued cultural autonomy.

In the introduction, and drawing on earlier work with Leslie Meier and Devon Powers (Klein, Meier and Powers 2017), I use the term 'cultural autonomy', rather than 'artistic autonomy' or 'creative autonomy'. The choice of the word 'cultural' is intended to broaden the scope beyond creative or artistic activities to include practical choices that may reflect an ethos or ethical position (Klein, Meier and

Powers 2017). In popular music culture, autonomy has at times been linked to the decision to opt out of mainstream structures of distribution and affiliation: that choice may be reflected in artistic expression (e.g. commercially unfriendly music or lyrics), but not necessarily or obviously – especially as the mainstream has diversified to include a wider range of genres and regions (Toynbee 2002).

To understand autonomy in the context of large-scale cultural production like recorded music, we need a definition that is inclusive, encompassing even the non-creative decisions that can shape cultural production including and beyond creative expression. At the same time, because the notion of autonomy remains tied to traditional art discourses, we also need to understand the implications and limitations that accompany the term, especially as it is applied in the context of a wider range of cultural products.

For many scholars of popular music, Pierre Bourdieu has offered a route through which to unpack the importance and articulation of autonomy for musicians and for fans. The 'turn to Bourdieu' in the sociology of music embraced and applied Bourdieu's work on cultural taste and fields of cultural production to popular music genres, despite his relative lack of attention to the subject (Prior 2013). Bourdieu has been deployed in analyses of indie music and indie musicians (for example, Hibbett 2005, Maclean 2016, Moore 2007, Strachan 2007), often drawing on the concepts of habitus and cultural capital to explore indie taste, but also using his conceptualization of autonomy to understand the function of 'independent' in naming and defining independent music. While Bourdieu (1996) differentiated between small-scale and large-scale (or mass) production, linking the former to pure artistic cultural products and a high degree of autonomy, and the latter to commercial cultural products and a low degree of autonomy, the above-cited popular music scholars have identified in independent music scenes values that align more closely with the former, including a sense of autonomy defined against commercialism.

Excitement about the applicability of Bourdieu's concepts within the field of popular music production has been tempered by sober evaluations of the limits. While 'we can recognize the distinction between genres and styles that are positioned as experimental, innovative or "independent" versus more commercial styles of music', for Bourdieu, popular music was located in a field of cultural production where it lacked legitimacy because of its reliance on commercial logics (Prior 2013: 191). In fact, large-scale cultural production generally gets short shrift in Bourdieu's account, which hardly acknowledges or explores commercial cultural production or media, despite its popularity; as David

Hesmondhalgh points out, 'Large-scale production might be more differentiated than Bourdieu's work suggests, and the relations of heteronomy and autonomy might sometimes be more fluid and complex than he implies' (2006: 221). Noting examples from the Beatles to Radiohead, Hesmondhalgh explains that, in the field of popular music, 'prestige and popularity are not necessarily so much in contradiction as in Bourdieu's schema' (2006: 222). Links between major and independent record companies offer an example of how large-scale production establishes relationships with semi-autonomous subdivisions in pursuit of the production of quality cultural products.

Banks directly challenges Bourdieu's account of autonomy, alongside other dominant critiques of autonomy courtesy of Theodor Adorno and Michel Foucault, in light of the actual experiences of contemporary cultural producers. The critiques, which Banks characterizes as 'autonomy as pose' (Bourdieu), 'autonomy denied' (Adorno), and 'autonomy as false freedom' (Foucault), all 'tend to overemphasise the capacity of capital to determine the conditions of cultural production, and underestimate the extent to which autonomy is shaped by the somewhat more open dialectic of creativity and constraint that underpins what Bill Ryan (1992) has termed the "art—commerce relation"' (Banks 2010: 259).

Challenges to Bourdieu's conceptualization and mapping of autonomy demonstrate how research into creative work and cultural labour has complicated the meaning of autonomy beyond that with which a definition based on old divisions between high and popular culture can cope. For one thing, the reversed economy of 'loser wins', Bourdieu's description of a perfectly autonomous sector where the pursuit of profit is rejected, is simply unrealistic for the majority of cultural producers who, in the absence of birthright or patronage, need to make a living to survive and, often, to be able to create their own art. The increasing casualization of cultural labour also challenges idealistic notions of creativity: working in the cultural industries demands compromise, but autonomy can still be experienced through models of 'good work' (Hesmondhalgh and Baker 2011).

Banks considers how the continuous demand for new commodities gives cultural workers 'permission to rebel', which can result in radical autonomy (including challenges to capitalism) and, more typically, negotiated autonomy, understood as emerging through 'the more routine conditions of cultural production where workers find themselves engaged in a quotidian "struggle within" to try to mediate, manage or reconcile the varied opportunities and constraints of the art—commerce relation' (2010: 262). Banks (2010) identifies studies like Jason Toynbee's (2000) work on music-makers to highlight examples of autonomy being encouraged and exercised within highly commercialized environments. The permission to rebel, which offers an opening to autonomy, mirrors the positive consequence of the professionalization of the music business introduced in the previous chapter. Namely, a clear separation between the creative and business aspects of making music allows artists to get on with being artists, often with little intervention from the business side. For musicians, institutional autonomy is promoted by the 'tendency for the music industries to cede control of production (writing, performing, realizing) to musicians themselves' (Toynbee 2000: 1). (Hesmondhalgh (2006) notes a similar point made by Bourdieu (1996) in the context of publishing: the presence of professionals around creative personnel allows for a certain disinterestedness.)

While pockets of autonomy can persist in highly commercialized sectors of cultural production, it is also the case that narratives of the mainstream music industries are strewn with instances of compromise and control, of unsupported artists and artists who are pressured to move in one aesthetic direction over another. Similar stories are easily unearthed across the mainstream cultural industries, from television and film, to publishing and design. For this reason, some cultural producers choose to work outside the mainstream system and in independent alternatives. The idea of independence has particular resonance within popular music culture: 'Institutional musical independence has been very strongly linked to ideas of aesthetic, institutional and political *alternatives*: to the idea that independence might contribute to the formation of different and better ways of organizing cultural production and consumption, and society itself' (Hesmondhalgh and Meier 2014: 95, emphasis in original). As David Hesmondhalgh and Leslie Meier (2014) explain, the significance of independence, and independent record companies, for popular music culture highlights the importance of ideas such as artistic freedom and autonomy in this realm.

The development of alternative institutions in the form of independent record companies has offered the possibility of claiming and exercising independence in the seemingly constrained circumstances of mass production. While independence in popular music has often been linked with particular sounds and values, the term's most basic function is as a description of an alternative economic structure, as epitomized by independent record labels. Independent record labels operate separately to the major record companies that dominate the music business (the 'Big Six' of the 1990s has merged and consolidated its way to the 'Big Three' of today). While some independent labels strike distribution deals with a major, for purists, true independent labels will maintain the separation from the mainstream music business through reliance on independent networks of distribution. In either case, the structure of an independent label generally suggests a lower economic investment in the artist, a lower risk for artist and label, and a lower limit on possible returns. All this might imply an excessively modest scale, but consider the typical experience of releasing a record on a major label: the label's initial investment is a debt that most artists will never or barely pay off, and high risks are taken by major labels on the basis that a minority of commercially successful artists will subsidize the label for the majority of sunk costs.

Motivations for aligning with an independent record label are multifarious, ranging from the practical to the political. For some artists, the choice to record for an independent label is purely practical. It may be that an independent takes an interest where majors have not. And if nobody else will do it for you, you can Do It Yourself by starting your own label. For others, recording for an independent label is an ideological choice. Some musicians feel that for music to make a political or emotional difference, it cannot be tied to the yoke of a corporation, a stance which is grounded in rock discourses around art, commerce and creativity (Strachan 2007). In his 1985 book *One Chord Wonders*, music journalist Dave Laing describes the connection of early punk to independence, explaining, 'To be "independent" did not automatically signify a different type of music from mainstream rock. But if the independent sector was less than an artistic revolution, it was also more than simply an economic one.... Instead of the associations of leisure/relaxation/passivity characteristic of mainstream music, there were counter-associations of alternatives/seriousness/experimentation' (2015: 175). Independent label proponents who positioned their activities in ideological opposition to the corporate and controlling approach of major labels made signing to a major label a focus of selling out debates in the late 1980s and early 1990s (Kruse 2003, O'Connor 2008). Punk is central to the development of independent labels from practical to ideological alternative.

Independent labels: Early history, punk and after punk

The early history of independent record labels was largely unconnected to the politics of art and commerce that underline selling out debates. Within the rock domain, independent record companies, like Joe Meek's Triumph or Andrew Loog Oldham's Immediate, had been in operation since the 1960s 'but they were, in the main, small companies trying to be big, like Island or Virgin' (Savage 1991: 297) and typically held the same values as the majors (Laing 2015). The range of semi-independent or seemingly independent labels expanded in the late 1960s and 1970s to include vanity projects for rock stars, where a label is a wholly or partially owned subsidiary of a major but with much control ceded to the star. This is a tradition that continues today.

While some early independent labels were formed to accommodate artists who may be considered too controversial, risky or unprofitable for the majors, a successful independent label could expect to be purchased or otherwise supported by a major without objection. A notable exception comes in the form of an even earlier independent precedent: black-owned label Black Swan was critical in bringing attention and respect to black artists in the 1920s, and was condemned for agreeing to a deal with Paramount. Owner Harry Pace 'countered that he would have sold out to a black-owned company if another one had existed in the business' (Suisman 2009: 236). For the most part, however, a clear distinction can be seen between earlier independents – run by entrepreneurs, not typically politicized – with those that emerged in the punk era which, unlike their predecessors, openly opposed working with the major corporations or courting mainstream success (Hesmondhalgh 1997). As Simon Frith describes, the 'ideology of "independence"' (1981b: 155) developed by punk musicians in the late 1970s with a basis in DIY production 'moved attention back from markets to musicians, to the ways music works to symbolize and focus communities' (1981b: 156).

The history of punk is well rehearsed, but also a necessary context to understand the relationship between independent labels and selling out. I direct readers to Jon Savage (1991) and Dave Laing (2015) for fantastically vivid and thorough accounts of the roots and development of punk. Here, I focus specifically on the role of record labels in that development.

While many punk groups used their musical platform to question authority, the major record labels to which most early punk acts were signed hardly registered as part of a corporate enemy. Instead, punks directed their disdain at hippies and members of the counterculture, viewed as sellouts whose movement was a failure. The association of anti-corporate and anti-mainstream values with hippies led many early punk artists to cynically embrace the opportunity to work with major record corporations. The relationship between early punk bands and the major labels that supported them was not always easy, however.

Early US punk seemed to have a generally positive attitude towards major labels. Those bands that released records independently typically did so with the hopes of gaining major label interest (particularly for distribution deals) (O'Connor 2008). The Ramones, for example, 'signed with Sire in late 1975 because no big record label would even listen to them. Although it was an independent label, [founder Seymour] Stein operated no differently from the majors' (O'Connor 2008: 1). Sire's independent status may have allowed it to take on riskier punk and new wave artists in the mid-1970s, but the label had major label distribution deals both before and after this period, finally being acquired by Warner Bros in 1978.

The most successful early punk acts in the UK had a more complicated relationship to the major labels that supported them. The case of the Sex Pistols reveals the tensions that can exist between band and label, where both sides want to take advantage of what the other offers but in the absence of trust or shared vision. Signing to a major was always a part of manager Malcolm McLaren's plan for the group: 'It was central to McLaren's ethos that the Sex Pistols would sign with a major record company' (Savage 1991: 213). Signing to EMI 'vindicated their self-image as the Punk elite ... with EMI's production and promotional back-up, there was every chance that the Sex Pistols would become Rock stars, able, if they still so desired, to act out their theatre of nemesis not only in the UK but also worldwide' (Savage 1991: 225). EMI ultimately dropped the group in the wake of the moral panic catalysed by a string of publicity stunts and protests, including the 'Grundy incident' in December 1976. The Pistols' language and behaviour during an interview with Bill Grundy on the evening news programme led to hysterical pearl-clutching among viewers and within media. The group's March 1977 signing with A&M was staged for the press in front of Buckingham Palace, but didn't last long: the contract was broken by the label within a week following a number of violent confrontations. 'God Save the Queen' was instead released by Virgin, the third label to sign the group in less than a year.

Clearly the big labels did not want to miss out on the potential profit attached to the group, despite a mismatch between how they do business and how the band did music. The band, on the other hand, could frame their relationship to the major labels as a scam, attracting support rather than censure from those critical of the mainstream music industries. As Rough Trade Records' Geoff Travis commented, 'I thought the scam aspect of the Sex Pistols signing to EMI was brilliant, but my romantic notion of building my utopia was to avoid the record industry completely' (quoted in Savage 1991: 297).

The relationship that the Clash had with CBS may not have been as volatile as the Pistols' experiences with major labels, but there were again signs of mismatch. Sellout critiques emerged amongst punks who felt an alternative system of production was necessary for the maintenance of integrity, and the group and label wrestled over artistic control. Among their detractors were anarcho-punk group Crass, whose 1978 song 'Punk is Dead' includes the lyrics 'CBS promote the Clash/ But it ain't for revolution, it's just for cash'. Mark P, founder of seminal UK punk fanzine *Sniffin' Glue*, recalls his disappointment with the band's CBS deal: 'It was a blow that they got signed; the music business hasn't really changed, but if a band as big as them had done that [released their music themselves with the support of small record shops] then it might have been a lot different' (quoted in Savage 1991: 304).

Worries and criticisms of fans were borne out by the group's struggle to control their creative output in the face of the label's professional marketing operations. The story of Clash songs 'Remote Control' and 'Complete Control' encapsulates the struggle. As Savage describes, in 1977 CBS 'had released a weak track, "Remote Control", as a single, against the Clash's wishes. Not only did it flop, but it raised the question of "artistic freedom" promised by the contract' (1991: 398). The group responded to the situation with the song 'Complete Control', released on the US version of their debut album. The lyrics 'They said we'd be artistically free/ When we signed that bit of paper/ They meant let's make a lotsa mon-ee/ An' worry about it later' confirm the track as 'a hymn to Punk autonomy at its moment of eclipse' (Savage 1991: 399). Although cynics marvelled at the group's apparent naïveté in signing with the major label (what do you expect when you sell out?), resulting debates proved an energizing force: 'In the UK and in the USA (where the Clash's debut album sold 100,000 copies on import alone) the debate about such "selling out" helped to fuel the growth of a new generation of labels, inspired by the Do It Yourself ethos of punk' (Hesmondhalgh and Meier 2014: 98).

Models for independent punk labels existed in both the UK and US in the form of early independents that released punk bands without being formed specifically for that purpose. In the UK, two key labels emerged out of the pub rock scene. Lack of interest in pub rock from the majors led to the establishment of independent labels Chiswick and Stiff (and the system of independent label economics central to punk). By eliminating the overheads associated with the major labels and keeping record costs downs, these independent labels could break even with a much smaller number of sales (Laing 2015). While not established for punk groups, Stiff and Chiswick proved a good fit: both released records by the Damned, for example.

In the US, too, some immediate predecessors to independent punk labels were established prior to the development of a coherent punk ethos or genre. Noted antecedents include self- or independently released records by Television, Patti Smith and the Flamin' Groovies in the mid-1970s (Dale 2008). US proto-punk label Bomp! was formed in 1974 and early punk label Dangerhouse was formed in 1977. Like many early examples, Dangerhouse was a relatively short-lived venture, but its foundation illustrates the association of independent motivations with punk from the start. The failure of such labels to thrive in the same way as UK counterparts (whose records charted) may be due to lack of opportunity, rather than lack of appetite among potential listeners. Although these early independent labels were based in LA, among the big players, their small scale and the absence of popular national radio likely limited their impact.

If there is one defining moment credited with fuelling the growth of the independent label sector, it's the release in 1977 of the Buzzcocks' *Spiral Scratch* EP, considered the first self-released punk record. As Savage explains, 'Chiswick and Stiff were releasing Punk-related material, but not as if from within: what was perfect about the Buzzcocks' EP was that its aesthetics were perfectly combined with the means of production' (1991: 297). Following the example of the Buzzcocks, 'independent labels and shops promised some degree of autonomy from the music industry' (Savage 1991: 417) and ushered in the transition of independent labels from a pragmatic alternative to the major label system into a reflection of a value system: 'The independents began as a classic example of supply-side economics, but they quickly developed an ideology' (Savage 1991: 417) which became more fully articulated with post-punk. Here, the model of selling out laid down in the late 1960s – 'of something to "sell out" (a cause, a vision, a pact with the fans) and somewhere to sell-out to (the record industry, occupying a separate space from that of the original pure creation)' (Laing 2015: 150) – was reclaimed by punk ideologues. As it turns out, it is possible to be both anti-hippie and anti-corporate.

The *Spiral Scratch* EP was soon joined by other releases that similarly acted as 'signal, catalyst, call to action' (Reynolds 2005: 94) for those looking for an alternative to the majors. Accounts frequently point to the Desperate Bicycles, whose 1977 debut single contained the clarion call, 'It was easy, it was cheap, go and do it!', reinforced by a brief explanation of how they did it and total production costs (£153) printed on the sleeve of their second single. In the wake of punk, many musicians and fans took up the bid to release records independently and, by the 1980s, independent labels were a central component of multiple scenes stemming from early punk.

In the UK's post-punk movement, independence grew from a practical alternative into a powerful tool and a crucial component of the political message delivered by bands like Gang of Four and Scritti Politti. Counter to approaches that treat punk as a moment/movement that died with the election of Thatcher, Hesmondhalgh (1997) considers the role of post-punk in terms of the democratization of media production. Using the Rough Trade label as a case study, he argues that the operation of such labels challenged the Romantic notion of artistic autonomy: musicians were often in close contact with staff involved in commercial activity, and sometimes did work for the label themselves. He demonstrates the significance of the indie versus major division for musicians and music production, characterizing the chief impact of punk as 'continuing suspicion of corporate cultural practice' (Hesmondhalgh 1997: 272). Hesmondhalgh's argument about the wider cultural influence of post-punk's independent approach encourages us to think of other iterations of musical independence as serving a more significant purpose of challenge, rather than as mere blips in the dominant corporate timeline. The values underpinning independence in popular music culture justify the activation of selling out in this context.

Likewise, independent music production in the US began to develop a coherent set of values opposed to those communicated by the mainstream music industries. The hardcore punk scenes that developed in Southern California (e.g. SST Records, Black Flag), San Francisco (e.g. Alternative Tentacles Records, Dead Kennedys), New York City (e.g. Bad Brains, Agnostic Front) and Washington DC (e.g. Dischord Records, Minor Threat) espoused anti-corporate values and located independence (of music-making as of thought) as central to identity. If early US punk did not have a strong antagonism towards major labels (or, indeed, much of a relationship to the nascent term and genre 'punk'), then, as Steve Waksman notes, the 'independent turn' of the 1980s prompted new perspectives within hardcore on its punk forebears: 'earlier bands such as the Ramones, the Sex Pistols, and the Clash may have outlined a valid musical path, but they did too little to assume control over the means of musical production. Indeed, it became common to refer to such bands, especially the Pistols, as sellouts for their apparent pursuit of something like mainstream success' (2009: 216). The same moniker was applied to contemporaries, 'bands which supposedly craved commercial success' (Moore 2004: 321).

Where the newly developed independent sector in the UK found itself successfully competing with the majors in music culture and charts, US hardcore was seemingly 'Devoid of a strategy which could make the do-it-yourself ethic into a basis for inclusion or the foundation of a mass movement' and instead 'ridiculed outsiders and condemned all gestures toward accessibility or popularity as "selling out"' (Moore 2004: 324). The harsher sound produced by groups within the hardcore scene may have ensured a reliable distance from mainstream appropriation, but many other sub-genres of punk and indie soon found themselves on a different trajectory with respect to major labels. The next section explores the incorporation of independent music into the mainstream music industries.

Indie incorporated

In its incorporation, as in its development, independent music was treated and received differently in the UK and the US. While there were exceptions on both sides, independent music was more genuinely supported by mainstream music industries in the UK and aggressively co-opted by mainstream music industries in the US, which explains why the focus on signing to major labels as central to selling out debates was more salient and enthusiastic in the US.

The UK variant can be appreciated through the presence of independent music in the 1980s music charts. While the newly established independent sector was enjoying occasional hits in the standard UK singles chart by 1980, the approach to compiling the charts, which counted record sales at national chains but not small regional shops, put independent artists at a serious disadvantage. The first independent chart came from participants in the independent music scene and was published in trade paper *Record Business* in 1980. The independent chart was clearly defined (records not distributed by the major record companies), compiled by the Media Research Information Bureau (MRIB) from 1981, joined by complementary independent charts and published in weekly music newspapers. By giving independent music its own chart, the profile of the sector was raised, resulting in greater exposure and sales and, paradoxically, closing the gap in scale and values that had distinguished independent music from its mainstream counterparts.

Crossover success from the late 1980s/early 1990s blurred the line between independents and majors, with independents entering into a range of relationships with major labels; while signing with major labels in the period of post-punk and early indie may have been met with disapproval (Fonarow 2006), as relationships with major labels became more common, objections were muted. Other boundaries between independent and major label artists similarly receded in this period. For example, the appearance of indie and punk bands on *Top of the Pops* prompted debate in the 1980s, but by the mid-to-late 1990s bands described as indie were the programme's majority (Dale 2008).

Crossover success was possible in the UK because mainstream charts were already more receptive to the sort of music and musicians coming out of the independent sector. Contrary to the shiny, manufactured imagery associated with the US mainstream music industries, the UK charts were marked by a diversity of sounds and artists, including some decidedly non-commercial, and less corporate paths to entering the industry. In the 1980s, claiming unemployment benefit (the 'dole') was viewed as driving creativity in popular music since it provided artists with the time and financial support to develop their music (a practice that was revived formally in the late 1990s by New Labour with the 'rock'n'dole' scheme).

The example of independent label Creation Records, half of which was sold to Sony in 1992, demonstrates the pros and cons of the close relationships forged between independent and major labels in the late 1980s/early 1990s. For independent record companies trying to strike a balance between financial solvency and resistance to selling out to major record companies, 'selling out' doesn't capture what might be gained through partnership: 'The term "sell-out" masks not only a potential range of motivations behind collaboration with other sources of capital, but also the achievements which such collaboration sometimes allows' (Hesmondhalgh 1999: 44). Creation's deal with Sony could be understood not as a sellout but 'as a logical culmination of the company's desire to develop a new generation of classic pop stars in an era of increasing internationalization in the recording industry' (Hesmondhalgh 1999: 46), though not without compromise: their reliance on corporate capital and the pressure to succeed underpinned 'a return to rock ideologies of authenticity and masculinity which many other independents had previously sought to challenge' (1999: 50). The Creation story is thus not a straightforward narrative of the triumph of independence, but the label's centrality to the success of Britpop (Oasis was signed soon after the Sony deal) ensures its place in ushering independent music from the margins to the mainstream.

As a result of independent music's success in and assimilation into the UK's mainstream, the terms independent and indie were transmogrified, such that 'in the twenty-first century the descriptor "independent" no longer denotes the strong separateness from "the majors" which it did when the indie chart was first instigated in the UK' (Dale 2008: 172). The abbreviation of independent to 'indie' in the 1980s and its application as a genre name in the UK is often noted as proof of independence being drained of meaning, but the genre naming itself holds huge significance. As Hesmondhalgh explains:

> no music genre had ever before taken its name from the form of industrial organization behind it. For indie proclaimed itself to be superior to other genres not only because it was more relevant or authentic to the youth who produced and consumed it (which was what rock had claimed) but also because it was based on new relationships between creativity and commerce.
>
> 1999: 35

Variously applied definitions of indie can appear disjointed:

> (1) a type of musical production affiliated with small independent labels with a distinctive mode of independent distribution; (2) a genre of music that has a particular sound and stylistic conventions; (3) music that communicates a particular ethos; (4) a category of critical assessment; and (5) music that can be contrasted with other genres, such as mainstream pop, dance, blues, country, or classical.
>
> Fonarow 2006: 28

But, despite some definitional messiness, these categories are historically and ideologically linked. The independent structures predated the value system, and were reclaimed and used to communicate an ethos in response to the commercialization of popular music and to promote music-making for everyone. The music associated with such scenes was absorbed by and replicated in the mainstream, hence the use of 'indie' as a description of a sound rather than necessarily a position vis-à-vis major labels. Evolution of the terms 'independent' and 'indie' does suggest a decline of the ideology of independence, as demonstrated by increasing links with majors: it is important that the major versus indie division is not reduced to consumer choice, given its significance for musicians and media production within the music business (Hesmondhalgh 1997). The more aggressive strategy of co-optation in the US, and the defensive response among some musicians and fans, embodies the struggle over ideology.

Where UK indie benefited from mainstream support (e.g. the promotion by DJs like John Peel, independent charts), a closely-knit community of music-related organizations within the London-centred music industry and well-developed national media networks (e.g. public service radio, independent music distribution), in the US the indie underground essentially stayed underground through the 1980s. Another notable difference is the relationship to 1960s rock authenticity. UK punk and post-punk cast suspicion on counterculture values, but such views were more muted in the US scenes that articulated an authenticity not unlike their 60s antecedents.

In *Our Band Could Be Your Life: Scenes from the American Indie Underground, 1981–1991*, Michael Azerrad cites the Beatles, Stevie Wonder and Bob Dylan as indie predecessors because of the control over their music they demanded and the link between such control and credibility. Azerrad explains that the 1960s provided inspiration although the indie community did not 'want to replicate the baby boomers' egregious sellout' (2001: 8). He characterizes 'interesting parallels between indie rock and the folk movement of the early sixties' in terms of adherence to values of 'purism and authenticity' (Azerrad 2001: 8). In both cases, he argues, 'the music's own eventual popularity derailed its crucial authenticity: the folk movement came to a symbolic end with Bob Dylan's heretical electric performance at the 1965 Newport Folk Festival; the indie movement was changed forever when [Nirvana's] *Nevermind* hit number one on the Billboard charts' (Azerrad 2001: 8). In this account, from the time immediately after early punk, the context of independent music in the US necessarily positioned the scenes that followed as opposed to popularity and mainstream success. US indie would not be incorporated into the major label system without a fight.

As with the UK context, genre naming in the US carried connotations of values rather than simply conveying information about musical sounds. The term 'college rock' indicated the significant role of college radio stations in promoting independent music and suggested a grassroots, non-corporate movement from below, whereas use of the term 'alternative' had a stronger association with the attempt of major labels to establish college rock into a marketing category. The number of independent labels grew substantially from 1980 and, while college radio existed prior to the punk era, 'those stations became an invaluable American network, linking the nascent punk rockers of each city to one another, and providing all the bands within a community with a way in which to prosper' (Arnold 1993: 23). Like their UK counterparts, many of the more successful bands did sign with major labels, which sometimes led to rejection by college radio and members of the underground, without whose support a band could end up selling fewer records than when they were independent (Arnold 1993).

The antagonism between college radio's bottom-up approach and the mainstream music industries' top-down approach can be overstated. In reality, college radio stations acted as a well-known breeding ground for future major label employees and had a strong presence in the wider music industries. The chart compiled for college radio's trade publication (*CMJ New Music Report*), for example, was used in music magazines like *Rolling Stone*, and by the late 1980s a 'modern rock' chart, drawing on college rock airplay, featured in trade magazine *Billboard*'s standard chart rankings. Dalliances with the mainstream music industries aside, college radio was seen by its advocates to promote independent music for love of the music, whereas major labels mined independent music for potential gaps in the market: 'By the early 1990s major labels perceived the value of "alternative" as a term that could be used to sell the idea of individuality and distinction to a broad range of young music consumers' (Waksman 2009: 255). The marketing of independent music as 'alternative' by major labels produced an uncomfortable paradox.

Many indie labels viewed themselves as 'defenders of musical art against its old enemy, commerce (or at the very least, untrammelled commerce)' and, unlike their mainstream counterparts, independent artists 'risked considerable diminution of their appeal by partaking in such industrial devices as corporate sponsorship and product promotion. Indeed, to be marketable, alternative rock artists must shun, or, at the very least, appear to shun corporate affiliation' (Seiler 2000: 220). Indie scenes wrestled with a particular set of terms and conditions:

> Whenever a band with alternative credibility signed with a major label, whenever an independent label entered into a financial relationship with a major label, whenever a college radio station adhered to playlists and rotations, the inherent tensions within a social, economic, and cultural formation that professed to eschew the mainstream success it was experiencing were exacerbated and a new version of the battle over what counted as alternative/indie/college music was joined.
>
> Kruse 2003: 14

Groups that signed with a major label under the banner of 'alternative' were presented as holding anticommercial views while being packaged and sold as commercially viable commodities in the music market, an incongruity that reflected the more general trend in this period for alternative or oppositional styles to be co-opted and flogged by mainstream companies (Seiler 2000).

The bind of being on a major label's alternative roster shaped the perceptions of bands and fans who rightly recognized the 'transition from underground to "alternative"' (Azerrad 2001: 59) as involving some compromise towards making commercially friendly records. Music critic Gina Arnold's account captures the feeling of distrust for the mainstream music industries among underground participants: she describes the music industries as 'busy playing games with their tainted cash, purchasing the services of former college radio program directors, stocking major label staffs with underground experts who've decided to go corporate, ruining real rock bands by promising them the moon, and, of course, concocting MTV formats by which to sell our once-lovely youth movement back to unsuspecting squares' (1993: 53).

The feeling of distrust for the mainstream music industries was manifest through anxieties about signing to a major and ambivalence about commercial success. Navigating such territory while retaining creative independence and the loyalty of existing fans is no easy feat, as many independent bands discovered. The case of Minnesotan rock group Hüsker Dü offers an early example that represents common motivations for signing as well as difficulties faced having done so.

Azerrad identifies Hüsker Dü as the first group 'from *the community*' (2001: 159, emphasis in original) to make the leap to a major label, demonstrating the commercial potential of college rock, en route to its branding as alternative. Having expanded their audience beyond their original punk fans, Hüsker Dü began to feel that the scale of SST, the influential indie label that released their earlier records, limited their sales and distribution potential. If they were able to retain creative control, a larger label would offer the group a more appropriate level of support without compromising their values. When a fanzine interviewer asked about the possibility of breaking into the mainstream by signing to a major label, bassist Greg Norton's reply that 'becoming popular was not necessarily the same thing as selling out' was unlikely to hold up: 'in the absolutist logic of the underground, anything that was popular was bad, ipso facto' (Azerrad 2001: 186). Indeed, the group's move to Warner Bros in 1985 'sent shock waves through the community' and, according to Azerrad, 'the glare of the major label spotlight' (2001: 159) contributed to the group's demise.

Despite the group's insistence on retaining control, Hüsker Dü's autonomy was under pressure from both the mainstream music business and the indie community even before the group signed with Warner Bros. Increasing attention from the mainstream, especially with 1984's critically acclaimed *Zen Arcade* album, couldn't help but exert influence. As guitarist and vocalist Bob Mould described, 'I don't think it's about selling out, it's just that all of a sudden, your world becomes invaded by other people, by the mainstream ... To me, you think, "Finally, we're changing things." But you're being changed *by* things as much as you're changing things' (Azerrad 2001: 183, emphasis in original). On the other side is the influence from the indie community, policing change and compromise. The group was held hostage to the style of *Zen Arcade* since, as Mould explained, 'when we went to Warner Brothers we couldn't change because we would have sold out' (Azerrad 2001: 195).

Signing to a major didn't necessarily sound the death knell for indie bands, but many that followed in Hüsker Dü's footsteps found that their achievements could exceed the capacity of independent labels while failing to meet the expectations of major labels. Some returned to an independent label after releasing a record or two on a major. Amidst the hand-wringing over selling out and going commercial, there were also major label success stories. Sonic Youth was one band that managed the transition effectively. The group's contract with Geffen, which gave them creative control and let them sign other bands, 'preserved their underground credibility through the transition' (Azerrad 2001: 271). While some still viewed the move as a sellout, Sonic Youth's musical experimentation and association with avant-garde art scenes made them less vulnerable to charges of commercialism. Rather than sell records, Sonic Youth were expected to attract other bands to the label, which they did most famously in the case of Nirvana, who bassist Kim Gordon encouraged to sign to Geffen. The *New York Times* described Sonic Youth as 'hipster guidance counselors for younger artists like Nirvana and Beck, who sold more records than Sonic Youth but were similarly distrustful of commercial success' (Foege 1998: 46). Nirvana's subsequent success led to a 'grunge gold rush' (Knopper 2018), drove the growth of an 'alternative industry' (Coyle and Dolan 1999: 21) and raised the volume of selling out debates centred on the independent versus major divide.

Corporate rock whores

Formed in Aberdeen, Washington in 1987, Nirvana released its first album, *Bleach*, on Seattle independent label Sub Pop in 1989, before signing to Geffen subsidiary DGC records and releasing 1991's *Nevermind*. When the album's first single, 'Smells Like Teen Spirit', found itself in heavy rotation on MTV and radio, the group was propelled into the mainstream as torchbearers of alternative rock and poster boys for grunge. 1991 became known as 'The Year Punk Broke': the resurgence of classic punk was credited to the success of grunge bands (see, for example, Morris 1992: 1), and *1991: The Year Punk Broke* was the title of a

Sonic Youth tour documentary, which also featured alternative rock groups Dinosaur Jr, Babes in Toyland and, of course, Nirvana. As Holly Kruse identifies, 1991 is a particularly significant year in indie rock's history due to '(1) the commercial success of Nirvana's *Nevermind* album, and (2) the first Lollapalooza concert tour, a popular and profitable touring "festival" of alternative bands. Both events generated a substantial amount of debate over whether indie or alternative acts were "selling out" when they reached a wide audience' (2003: 22). In Nirvana's case, there was disagreement over whether the band had sold out or not, with some pointing out that the group had not strayed from its original sound or values, and others indicating that signing to a major label and selling millions of records was incompatible with alternative credibility (Kruse 2003).

Ambivalence about Nirvana's signing and success can be attributed in part to the Seattle scene with which they were associated. With historical ties to hard rock and metal, Seattle was arguably less rooted in punk DIY ethics than other regional indie scenes, including nearby Olympia. Azerrad writes that 'Sub Pop's jokey big-business posture simultaneously mocked and embraced that culture, self-promotion disguised as self-deprecation' (2001: 443) and Ryan Moore describes Sub Pop's use of 'ironic capitalism' to maintain a necessary distance for the avoidance of criticism (2009: 122). In contrast, Olympia's K Records is viewed as reflecting an explicit DIY approach and focus on anti-commercial culture that laid the foundation for a successful model of independent music (Moore 2009, Azerrad 2001, Arnold 1993). Against this context, the move from Sub Pop to Geffen was less severe than signing to a major from within a more staunchly DIY scene. Yet concerns and debates about selling out left an obvious impact on Nirvana's Kurt Cobain: following the singer's suicide, Cobain's widow Courtney Love claimed he 'had been "tortured" by accusations of "selling out"' (Branigan 2001: 4).

Unsurprisingly, Nirvana's success captured the interest of the mainstream music industries, which increased attention to alternative scenes. Moore explains, 'After mostly ignoring them for more than a decade, the music industries took an interest in localized music scenes in the early 1990s with the success of Nirvana and Seattle's "grunge" scene, as "alternative" became a new advertising buzzword in marketing to young people' (2009: 10). Moore documents major label interest in local scenes through the case of San Diego, one of many cities treated briefly as a potential next Seattle by the major labels. Many bands discovered downsides to signing with a major label beyond possible rejection from the indie community: 'Bands who were accused of "selling out" were in fact more likely to end up in debt and without any musical product to sell' (Moore 2009: 152). Alongside the music industries' seemingly indiscriminate signing of any band that looked or sounded 'alternative', the post-Nirvana period also saw an increase in distribution deals between independent and major labels and the short-lived tactic of majors releasing music on 'fake indies' (Azerrad 2001: 495).

If Nirvana's signing and success signalled the end of an indie underground for some, for others it galvanized a commitment to DIY values. In the years immediately following 1991, major label signing remained at the heart of debates in scenes that were associated with punk. As Pete Dale argues, 'Since the early 1990s, the punk-related DIY ethos has been more vehemently adhered to in the US than in the UK' (2008: 187), driven in part by the success of Nirvana and the response of some independent labels to maintain DIY values.

Pop-punk group Green Day, who made the leap from small independent Lookout Records to Warner subsidiary Reprise with their commercially successful 1994 album *Dookie*, were among those accused of selling out by early fans and the Berkeley, California punk community in which they had formed and grown. The group's success – with *Dookie* and most pointedly in 2004 with Grammy award-winning *American Idiot*, which was adapted into a critically lauded and hugely successful stage production – can be taken as proof that they had exceeded Lookout's capacity to support them. But for some early fans, the personal loss of a band from their DIY community combined with the ideological transgression of receiving corporate support proved difficult to accept. The transition was difficult for the band, too, whose alienation from their new, mainstream fanbase echoed the experience of Nirvana. Within the punk community, debate about major label signings reached a fever pitch: punk magazine *Maximum Rock'n'Roll*'s 1994 special issue *Major Labels: Some of Your Friends Are Already This Fucked* can be regarded as the zenith of label-related sellout debates, and many of the comments contained within were directed at Green Day. A 2015 *Vice* article revisits some of the punk albums released by major labels from 1994 into the 2000s, including *Dookie*, observing, 'Though it seems petty and dumb in retrospect, "selling out" was a thing people cared about once' (Ozzi 2015).

Unlike Nirvana, Green Day managed to weather the storm of sellout accusations (Coyle and Dolan 1999). As their career evolved beyond the initial post-signing period, many other cases of major label signings worked to normalize the decision, and most vocal detractors resigned themselves to the new music industry order. (This period also saw some bands reflecting on sellout debates in their material: see, for example, 'Boxcar' from punk band Jawbreaker, a premonition of the group's subsequent major label signing.) Plus, the positive consequences for labels like Sub Pop or Lookout in terms of back catalogue sales and financial security suggested that independents and majors could thrive in symbiosis. Yet the fate of many of the bands that signed to major labels is a reminder that the discourse of selling out rested on legitimate concerns about the mainstream music industries. Artists were unsupported or dropped when they did not achieve the commercial success demanded by majors and when the trendiness of alternative had passed. Jawbox, Royal Trux and Mudhoney were among the groups that returned to independent labels following a mixed experience with a major label.

Enduring indie values

Selling out debates that focused on the indie versus major divide drew attention to the forms of cultural autonomy that independence enabled and the pressure to compromise that signing a contract with a major music company might entail. Since that period in the 1990s, the boundaries and differences that once marked the divide have become less meaningful. Complex distribution and publishing deals are standard for many independent labels and bands, and both independent and major labels have been forced to respond to challenges presented by digitalization (see Klein, Meier and Powers 2017, Hesmondhalgh and Meier 2014). The rise in the twenty-first century of digital platforms as music gatekeepers was initially cheered for its potential to democratize music production and distribution, but companies like YouTube and Spotify can be understood as reducing music to content (Hesmondhalgh and Meier 2014, Negus 2019), revealing a commercially driven, aesthetically neutral mode that amplifies the worst tendencies of major labels. Major labels responded to digitalization's threat to recording revenue by tightening their grip across artist revenues in so-called 360 deal contracts (which give the label a percentage of all income streams) (Stahl and Meier 2012, Marshall 2013) and by negotiating deals with digital platforms using the market share leverage that independent labels lack (Hesmondhalgh and Meier 2014). I pick up on these recent developments in Chapter 6.

The persistence of DIY/independent labels and scenes suggests a continued desire on the part of some musicians for cultural autonomy associated with opting out of the mainstream music industries, even as the new digital music industry has tempered the anti-corporate stance that once fuelled selling out debates (Hesmondhalgh and Meier 2014). Rather than operating as small-scale versions of majors, the practices of micro-labels are shaped by negative perceptions of the mainstream music industries and powerful discourses relating to art and commerce (Strachan 2007: 247). Punk's history of anti-commercial ideology continues to be expressed by some modern punk and metal bands. Like early US hardcore groups, the authenticity of extreme metal, for instance, is often judged on the commitment of groups to sounds and themes that will not appeal to radio programmers or corporate sponsors. The value of independence has also travelled outside the generic and geographic boundaries of the 1990s selling out debates, with UK grime artists celebrating their independence from major labels (Khalili-Tari 2017), and DIY indie bands in East Asia championing autonomy in music-making (Jian 2018). Recalling the mainstreaming of indie and alternative in the West, the popularization of indie in East Asia is leading to co-optation, with bands signing to 'sub-labels of mainstream record companies' (Jian 2018: 12).

Hesmondhalgh and Meier propose 'a revisiting and perhaps redefinition of what independence means and could mean for popular music' (2014: 111) against the context of the new cultural industries, which finds the power of the major record companies both contested and abetted by tech giants. The selling out debates of the 1990s are an example of the enthusiasm once conjured for challenging corporate power and for preserving values of musical independence. While the dominance of digital gatekeepers complicates the practice of musical independence, the continuing assertion of independence by artists indicates an opening for revived deliberation of media power and cultural autonomy.

The independent record shop is one space where enthusiasm for independence in popular music culture persists. The annual celebration of Record Store Day is recognized in countries around the world and the current vinyl revival has provided independent shops with a boost. The value of independence is also retained and championed in other cultural and retail sectors. In February 2017, news reports that large book retailer Waterstones had opened small, unbranded shops in three towns in the South of England led to accusations of deceiving customers and local independent competitors. While the Waterstones boss defended the decision as enhancing local high streets and maintained that its booksellers do have the autonomy associated with independent shops (BBC

2017), critical responses revealed key issues bubbling beneath the surface. What is lost when 'independence' is reduced to an aesthetic? What does a large retailer gain from appearing to be independent? What do communities gain from genuinely independent businesses? In Chapter 7, I revisit autonomy as a key value in popular music and beyond, which selling out discourse seeks to protect.

4

A different kind of selling out

Tensions between cultural and commercial objectives and the presence of selling out debates have varied over time and across a range of factors, including genre, class, race and gender. Narratives of selling out have been particularly prevalent in relation to rock music, a genre whose performance and study has long been dominated by straight, white men. Questions of what it means to sell out have understandably been inflected by a rockist bias that constructed an 'authentic' benchmark by which other cases were judged. This chapter steps back to consider the variation in the way selling out discourse has been used, and what the differences and similarities tell us about the values which underpin it. It offers a focussed study of the case of rap's relationship to commerce, racial authenticity and selling out through examples including the mid-1980s partnership between Run-DMC and Adidas (a brand that was no stranger to the benefits of sponsorship) and the twenty-first century rise of rappers at the helm of business empires, epitomized by the successes of Jay-Z and Dr Dre.

As previous chapters have demonstrated, from the legitimation of rock music as art in the 1960s to the colonization of independent rock by major labels in the 1990s, the concept of selling out in popular music culture has had the most traction with and endurance for the rock genre, particularly when it comes to questions of corporate partnership. Many of the key selling out debates have centred on rock music, whether the exploitative company hails from within the music industries (as in the cases of major recording companies squeezing the cool out of potentially marketable scenes) or outside the music industries (as in the cases of consumer brands seeking sponsorship or licensing deals).

Jack Hamilton (2016) focuses on the 1960s in his consideration of how rock'n'roll, rooted in interactions between black and white musicians, evolved to exclude black musicians into separate genres and to celebrate white musicians as exhibiting rock authenticity. The discourse of 'soul' proves particularly revealing: 'The far-flung musicality embedded in the word's implications made it an ideal vehicle for a host of complicated discussions about cultural ownership versus cultural availability, racial essence versus racial transcendence, music as a utopian sphere of unraced democracy versus music as a delineation point of racial authenticity' (Hamilton 2016: 172). Genres associated with black artists have since continued to be evaluated – by artists, by critics – on the basis of racial essence and staying true to culture and community, in contradistinction to the construction of rock authenticity in opposition to corporate partnerships and commercialism. This is perhaps especially the case with rap, where a fixation on authenticity is not incompatible with explicit commercial partnerships such as sponsorship, endorsement, product placement and licensing.

Rap is no stranger to the discourse of selling out, though in this case the version that emerged from the 1960s within popular music culture intermingles with a race-based understanding of the term, resulting in an application that is both broadly applied and flexible. A 2017 roundtable discussion on Genius (which began as Rap Genius, a forum dedicated to hip-hop) brought together veteran and current rappers to discuss what it means to sell out in rap. Kurtis Blow, Erick Sermon, A$AP Ferg, Vic Mensa, Denzel Curry and Soulja Boy considered the journey that selling out has taken in rap, where it originally was applied to artists achieving mainstream success, then to those perceived to have changed for success, then to commercial endorsements and to signing to major labels. Selling out, the rappers agreed, is generally seen as irrelevant now. As Erick Sermon explains, 'It sounds crazy now, but if you was doing McDonald's or any type of commercial, it was a sellout to the culture. Now, it makes no sense hearing that' (Genius 2017).

Asked to name a rapper who didn't sell out, it's telling that Vic Mensa turns instead to a rock example: 'I think Kurt Cobain definitely stood by his ideals and morals. I feel there are a lot more examples in punk and rock music, of people just unwilling to sell out, like the artists that won't put their music in a car commercial because they don't believe in turning their art into capitalistic solicitation like that' (Genius 2017). Association with brands (through the appearance in a commercial, for example) may not have the same stakes for rappers as rock artists, but there are other dimensions for which the phrase resonates. As A$AP Ferg describes, 'You could define a sell out in different ways. Some dudes might define a sell out by changing the sound of your music or jumping on commercial records or some dudes may define sellout by like, you not hanging out or associating yourself with old friends or not hanging out in your neighborhood anymore' (Genius 2017).

Authenticity is a core value across hip-hop culture, and the way in which authenticity is communicated and evaluated has been central to the accounts of many of its scholars (see, for example, McLeod 1999, Forman 2002, Harrison 2009, Jeffries 2011). Unlike rock, rap presents a case where authenticity remains of central importance but is not defined consistently against the type of commercialism represented by partnerships with consumer brands. A rapper's relationship to money and to the mainstream can attract scrutiny, but sponsorships, endorsements, product placements and licensing deals are not necessarily barriers to authenticity.

In this chapter, I explore rap's relationship to commercialism and selling out by examining how black artists have been historically mistreated by the music industries and how interest from consumer brands has been viewed as comparatively supportive and, in many cases, organically linked to rap, the wider hip-hop culture, and the communities in which both developed. Rap's particular relationship to commercialism, whereby commercial success and commercial partnerships with consumer brands can be celebrated within a framework of authenticity, is inextricably linked to the genre's roots in African-American culture. (While hip-hop has always been multi-ethnic (Harrison 2009), most commercially successful rappers have been African-American, and usually men (Jeffries 2011).) I consider how commercialism offers an unexpected home for displays of authenticity, how selling out debates about racial identity relate to the popular music version of the concept and how rap's growing popularity and eventual mainstream dominance demonstrated for other popular music genres that authenticity and commercialism need not be opponents.

Race and the music industries

Practices in the music industries are shaped by external forces. If the wider society is racist, you can expect the music industries to include racist practices. If the wider society is beholden to the logic of the free market, despite deleterious effects on disadvantaged communities, we should expect no more from the music industries. The intersection of racism and market logic within the practices of the music industries has led to and continues to result in pernicious consequences for black musicians. As Anamik Saha (2018) argues, commodification acts as a technology of racialized governmentalities through processes of bureaucratization, formatting and marketing/packaging. In other words, standard practices within the music industries produce and reproduce differences based on race (even when black cultural producers are working as intermediaries).

Keith Negus looks at how '"the street" operates as a metonym for a particular type of knowledge which is deployed by executives throughout the music industry, a type of knowledge which legitimates the belief that rap *is* and *should be* outside the corporate suite' (1999: 86, emphasis in original). He argues, 'One consequence is that this maintains a separation of experiences and contributes to the ongoing reproduction of the broader economic, cultural and racialized divisions across which r 'n' b and rap have been and continue to be made' (1999: 86). While Negus doesn't develop this point about race, Saha suggests that his study does demonstrate how 'what appears as common business sense belies its racialist effects in terms of the containment of rap' and 'disguising racist logic as common business sense is not merely disingenuous or a discursive trick, but something that is structured into, or embedded within the very industry logics of cultural production' (Saha 2018: 125).

The tendency of the music industries to at once exclude and exploit black music has a long history. David Brackett (1999) describes the initial exclusion of black music and white hillbilly music from music-making institutions. In the 1940s and 50s, whereas hillbilly music was adapted as country and western by the mainstream music industry, rhythm and blues relied on support from independent companies. 'Country and western' still had a major entree lacked by 'rhythm and blues' (a more polite name used for 'race' music after 1949): its practitioners were almost all white, whereas rhythm and blues musicians were almost all African-American. While the former had been met initially with derision, the latter was met by outrage, a response replicated by the growing popularity of rap in the late 1980s and early 1990s. Such comparisons help us to understand music genres as working through social issues. Genre is not just about similar internal qualities of music, but connects to the social context of music production and consumption: '"Similar" elements include more than musical-style features, and groupings often hinge on elements of nation, class, race, gender, sexuality, and so on' (Brackett 2016: 4). Using case studies from the 1920s to 1980s, and looking at changing trade magazine treatments and radio formats, Brackett (2016) traces how the categorization of sound by genre links to social practice. He reminds us that the power of genres to impose ideas cannot be seen simply as a top-down process: 'genre labels arise through broad processes that create projections of our shared and not-entirely-conscious social preoccupations, somewhat in the sense of modern-day mythical fables in which a society works out its collective concerns' (Brackett 2016: 32).

The division of music by raced genre labels has reflected and reinforced real material differences in terms of music production and distribution for black musicians, from the rhythm and blues artists of the 1950s through to rappers in the 1990s (during the genre's mainstream ascent). Unfair treatment in previous eras provides the context through which today's rap artists established their own business practices and orientation to commercialism. I first look at some of the key historical differences that distinguish the experiences of black musicians before considering how consumer brands offered themselves to rappers as an alternative source of support.

Production, distribution and segregation

In terms of music production, the history of underpayment of black musicians stretches back to the early days of popular music recordings and contracts. Whether as session musicians or in terms of record label contracts, black musicians have since the 1920s been routinely underpaid. Hamilton describes 'the historical backdrop of an American music industry that had long seen white artists disproportionately compensated in comparison to their black counterparts, even—indeed, especially—when the forms being performed were African-American in origin' (2016: 182), which emphasizes the disparity as not about the sound, the music, but about the race of the performer.

In many cases, black musicians simply were not hired or offered contracts by recording companies at all. When recording companies deemed black musicians profitable, they reduced the risk of investment by locating artists in a separate division for black music, a practice that developed in the late 1960s and early 1970s, though with roots in earlier practices such as the development of race music labels from the 1920s (Negus 1999). Conveniently, divisions can be made smaller or shut if deemed poor performers, which helps to manage risk for recording companies. Negus (1999) suggests black divisions suffer disproportionately and not purely for economic reasons. His analysis draws on a case study of the music industry at the time of rap's rise to the mainstream (he conducted interviews in 1996), and the trends he identifies can be seen as setting a standard for the treatment of the genre by major recording companies even as such divisions have been rebranded 'urban'.

The strategy of major recording companies to exclude black music until proven profitable, then to exploit black music until it has been drained of its value, has been demonstrated repeatedly by tales of black labels that have succeeded against the odds, from Black Swan in the 1920s to Motown in the 1960s/70s. In both cases, the innovation and success of a black-owned label with a roster of black musicians resulted in acquisition by one of the big music companies to the detriment of the label's original mission.

1920s jazz and blues label Black Swan Records was the most successful black-owned label of its time and demonstrated that there was a market for black music (Suisman 2009). As a result, it faced increasing competition from the big (white-owned) labels, which had previously shunned black music (at least made by black musicians) as unmarketable. As competitors engaged in price-cutting and developed their rosters of black musicians, and unable to withstand the challenge to sales presented by radio broadcasting, Black Swan went bankrupt and was acquired by Paramount Records in 1924, who soon after discontinued the label. It's hard not to feel like the cards were stacked against the label.

While acquisition didn't spell the end of Motown, it was a part of a mainstream marketing strategy that did entail significant compromise for the label. As Mark Anthony Neal (1997) argues, Motown's growth in the 1960s/70s and entry into the mainstream – reflected in the move from Detroit to Los Angeles in 1972 on the back of the success of the Jackson 5 – placed constraints on black expressive culture. The shift in orientation towards a mainstream audience limited the company's ability to serve the black community from which it originated and to address important post-civil rights issues of the time, and its sale to MCA records in the mid-80s further eroded any differentiation between the label and the major recording companies.

Motown can be understood as a template for marketing black music to mostly white audiences (and was itself a result of civil rights progress), and for gaining the interest of corporate America (Neal 1997, Neal 1999). While the integration of the black popular music industries into the mainstream music industries can be seen as a success for black musicians, it also 'significantly eroded African American financial control over a segment of the industry that segregation had empowered them to control' (Neal 1999: 117). Incorporation into the major recording companies did not result in better contracts or increased freedom for artists, nor did it result in significant power for black executives, and certainly not of the likes enjoyed by Berry Gordy with Motown. The sacrifice of black departments during times of financial challenge and the lack of black executives in top roles are trends that have continued into an era when R&B and hip-hop dominate the charts (Mitchell 2018).

The distribution of royalties was one dimension of contracts that remained starkly unfair for black artists as the major recording companies opened their rosters. Bad deals agreed in the 1950s and 1960s continued to haunt artists as the copyright revenue that they might have relied on to support them in old age was not forthcoming. Matt Stahl (2015) considers the royalty reform movement that emerged in the mid-1980s to secure royalties for ageing R&B artists that they were denied by record companies through a racialized intellectual property regime. Copyright law and implementation as applied to the music industries privileges the rights of corporation owners over creative workers (Klein, Moss and Edwards 2015), and the situation is often even worse for black creators, whose creative processes and musical traditions may not fit with the narrow definitions of ownership and composition in copyright law (Hines 2005).

Justifications for paying black musicians less than their white counterparts have been explicitly grounded in market logic that links profits to potentially larger, white audiences, though implicitly draw on assumptions about race and about authenticity. The assumption that white audiences would not buy black music was woven into the practice of early rock and roll covers by white artists of black artists. Moving into the rock era, black musicians were associated with blues-based authenticity, but respect was not paid in dollars: artists who achieved the greatest financial and commercial success using a blues style have been white (including Elvis, Dylan, Jimmy Page, Janis Joplin) (Grazian 2003: 152). The myth that 'the most "authentic" black music was that which was farthest from the market, the white market in particular' (Hamilton 2016: 42) structured mainstream or commercial possibilities and evaluations of black music. Motown demonstrated there was a substantial market for black music beyond black audiences in the 1960s (Neal 1997, Neal 1999), yet old assumptions were revived in the context of rap in the 1990s, where low investment was defended on the basis that labels expected a short catalogue life and limited international appeal (Negus 1999).

Disparities in treatment by race in the popular music industries extended into distribution from the earliest era of music radio to the age of the music video. Divisions by race in record catalogues in the 1920s and 1930s were re-affirmed with the introduction of the music popularity charts; radio formats like 'urban contemporary', 'quiet storm' and 'soul' are among separate genre names assigned to stations for black music from the 1960s onward, distinguished from mainstream top 40 and rock formats (Brackett 2016). Race-based differences between genres were perpetuated by music critics and music industry workers even when similar aesthetics were revealed by crossover success. MTV's initial programming included few non-white artists: Jane Brown and Kenneth Campbell (1986) note in their early comparison of MTV with video programmes on BET (Black Entertainment Television) that the small number of black artists on MTV tend to be more rock-oriented. The introduction of *Yo! MTV Raps* in 1988 was a significant moment in the evolution of MTV, but it took longer still for black artists to be more fully integrated into the channel's programming.

Of course, interested white audiences have always found a way to access and celebrate black music, even when the mainstream channels of distribution offered little in the way of exposure. In the segregated US south of the 1950s and 1960s, for example, young white audiences were drawn to the 'beach music' – often R&B or soul – played by the bars along the beaches of North and South Carolina. The northern soul scene in the UK provides a striking example of interested audiences collecting and celebrating black American soul that was often not promoted nationally in the US, much less internationally. And, as the example of Motown demonstrated, popularity with white consumers – which can be sparked by grassroots communities of fans – is a key factor in drawing the attention of the mainstream music industries to black genres. Tricia Rose explains that 'rap has followed the patterns of other black popular musics' in terms of its initial rejection by (both black and white) middle-class listeners, and by major recording and radio companies that became interested only after independent labels and companies produced success (1994: 6). However, the success of black music among white audiences has not spelled the end of race-based strategies for maximizing profits. For example, 'black artists and executives sponsor white artists and market their music to a white audience' (Hess 2005a: 373). From Dr Dre's support of Eminem to Usher's support of Justin Bieber, successful black artists are acutely aware of the potential audience and sales of white artists performing in styles still largely regarded as black music. I offer this short history of the role of race in production and distribution processes within the popular music industries to set the scene against which to consider why rap artists might be wary of mainstream music institutions and why rappers have been particularly receptive to overtures from consumer brands looking to build relationships. I turn to some of those relationships now.

Rap and commercial opportunities

As Negus suggests, in the 1980s 'major companies had neither the inclination, the understanding nor the skills to deal with rap. It was partly anxiety, partly lack of expertise and incomprehension on the part of the majors that allowed many small companies to carve out a considerable niche during the 1980s' (1999: 90). For this reason, early rap was largely released and promoted by small, independent labels. However, though the mainstream popular music industries were relatively slow to take rap seriously through substantial investment and promotion, early cases of partnerships between rappers and consumer brands offer a prescient example of an alternative route to revenue and exposure that now seems ordinary. As well as generating alternative resources for artists denied fair treatment by the music industries, the appearance of artists in commercials or endorsing products demonstrated shrewd business awareness (Negus 1999). The partnerships between Run-DMC and sportswear brand Adidas, and between rappers and malt liquor brand St. Ide's, offer two examples that embedded commercial opportunities in the business of rap early on.

The relationship between Run-DMC and Adidas is perhaps the best known and most celebrated case of endorsement in rap, because it was an early and novel example, and because it was perceived as an 'organic' partnership, a moment of branding serendipity. While it's true that the group wore Adidas and wrote the 1986 single 'My Adidas' before they had been in contact with the brand, the strategy of using endorsement deals was not new to Adidas.

Where earlier hip-hop crews sported flamboyant, and often futuristic, stage attire, Run-DMC represented a new era of rappers who chose to wear the street style typical of young people in the neighbourhoods from which they hailed – Queens, New York City, in this case. The 1986 single 'My Adidas' confirmed the group's street style as a meaningful choice: not merely a celebration of the sneaker brand, it was a challenge to judgements of hip-hop culture. As DMC explained, 'It was a song that was about our sneakers, but it was bigger than just talking about how many pairs of sneakers we had' (Blanco 2011). He continued:

> It came from the place of people would look at the b-boys, the b-girls and go, 'Oh, those are the people that cause all the problems in here.' And, 'Those young people are nothing but troublemakers and those young people don't know nothing.' So they was judging the book by its cover, without seeing what was inside of it.
>
> Blanco 2011

The impact of the song on sneaker culture and endorsement deals was enormous. 'My Adidas' connected with fans donning the same style, and often the same sneakers, as the group, creating a three-striped spectacle at live performances. As the story goes:

> Angelo Anastasio, a senior Adidas employee, was attending a 1986 Madison Square Gardens performance of the Raising Hell tour when he was struck by the sight of tens of thousands of fans lifting their Adidas sneakers into the air, answering the call of those on stage. Inspired, Anastasio reportedly ran back to the Adidas New York headquarters and within days, Run-D.M.C. became the first hip hop group to receive a million-dollar endorsement deal. Success was immediate; a limited edition shell toe 'Superstar' sneaker was released, soon followed by the now immediately recallable cross-branded clothing range, which is still in production under the Adidas Originals label. Big budget advertisements depicting the band in the brand were soon everywhere, and sales skyrocketed.
>
> Mellery-Pratt 2014

Through their deal with Adidas, Run-DMC helped to cement the centrality of clothing to rap marketing (Negus 1999: 100), and extended the tradition of partnerships between musicians and consumer brands to new genres, markets and product types. The deal's 'rampant success paved the way for the kind of endorsement deals that saturate the music industry today and forged Adidas' long-running association with hip-hop, which has seen the sportswear giant sign deals with Kanye West, Missy Elliott, Snoop Dogg, Ciara and Pharrell, amongst many, many more' (Mellery-Pratt 2014).

The story is incomplete without the significant detail that future president of Def Jam Lyor Cohen, then road manager for Run-DMC, had invited the Adidas executive to the show, in the hope of brokering a formal partnership. Furthermore, Adidas's history of sponsorship complicates the possible interpretation of the brand as a brave champion of a musical form that was considered risky by the music industries and that had yet to be identified by other brands as a source of lucrative partnerships. While the sponsorship of sports by sportswear companies now seems an obvious marketing strategy, it was not born with sport. As it happens, Adidas was an early leader in sports sponsorship, which offered a template for other forms of commercial sponsorship (Philips and Whannel 2013). The brand's early role with rap extends long-standing marketing strategies that moved beyond conventional advertising into sponsorship and endorsement. While Run-DMC's endorsement deal with Adidas cannot be classified as entirely serendipitous or organic, given the strategic motivations on both sides, the band did have a genuine affection for the brand, which it wore and wrote an ode to before the deal. There is no question that the partnership was a good fit, and the reception to it positive: Run-DMC was not accused of selling out. But not all early rap endorsement deals were equally uncontroversial.

In 1988, beverage firm McKenzie River Corporation ended their deal with Motown soul legends the Four Tops to promote their St. Ides malt liquor, and turned instead to members of the underground West Coast rap scene. The company gave an unprecedented amount of control to producer DJ Pooh, who tapped rappers King Tee and Ice Cube to appear in St. Ides commercials. Over the next few years, some of the biggest names from both coasts – Snoop Dogg, Wu-Tang Clan, Notorious B.I.G. – appeared in the radio and television spots, rapping the praises of the malt liquor brand and solidifying the link between the cheap but strong alcohol and rap.

Like sportswear, malt liquor already had a place in rap culture and 'McKenzie River decided to cash in on this subcultural trend' (Quinn 2005: 3). What became known as gangsta rap in this period was particularly well suited to such a commercial opportunity. As Eithne Quinn explains, 'Economic self-determination and creative autonomy – the touchstones of rap "representing" – fueled the publicity images of these St. Ides endorsers' (2005: 2). With the desire to make money and entrepreneurial flexibility omnipresent in the lyrics of the gangsta rap subgenre, endorsing a brand and appearing in a commercial was just another hustle: 'Instead of incurring the common accusation of "selling out" from its core audience, the promoting of St. Ides actually worked to enhance rappers' "keepin' it real" image' (Quinn 2005: 5). Reflecting on broader changes in the culture, Quinn (2005) notes that at a time of declining public funding under a government supportive of corporate growth, rap artists saw an opportunity to get money from companies that some tracks were endorsing anyway for free. The interest in rap from consumer brands also served to validate the artists: 'To rappers in the early 90s, hawking malt liquor on TV wasn't selling out—it was a sign of cultural legitimacy and upward mobility' (Coward 2015).

The endorsement of malt liquor by rappers was not without critics, including from within the rap community. Chuck D, one of the highest profile detractors, wrote the 1991 Public Enemy song '1 Million Bottlebags' about the white corporate exploitation driving such partnerships (Quinn 2005: 5): 'They drink it thinkin' it's good/ But they don't sell that shit in the white neighbourhood/ Exposin' the plan, they get mad at me / I understand, they're slaves to the liquor man'. As the lyrics suggest, the link between malt liquor and rap culture reflected the strategy of malt liquor producers to target their marketing at poor, inner-city, mostly black populations – relying on a combination of poverty and alcohol abuse to popularize the product. The promotion of malt liquor as drink of choice by rappers only raised the volume of critique for those concerned about related marketing ethics, or lack thereof. Furthermore, unlike Adidas, St. Ides was a 'brand with no inherent ties to hip-hop completely building its identity around the genre' (Coward 2015).

We would be surprised to see major rap artists today endorsing downmarket brands of liquor or anything else: from the mid-90s, rappers turned their consumerist gaze towards luxury brands, and advertisers were increasingly eager to sign rappers to deals. As Kyle Coward writes, 'Today—when Dr. Dre is an Apple executive, Jay-Z has partnered with Samsung on an album release, and Snoop Dogg has appeared in Chrysler commercials—the St. Ides campaign appears strange, a relic from a time when hip-hop culture hadn't yet earned wider Madison Avenue respect' (2015). These early cases are responsible for laying the groundwork – and testing possible limits – for the bonanza that was to follow as rap moved up the charts and into the suburbs.

Chart success and corporate interest

Rap became increasingly popular from the late 1980s and through the 1990s, and a rush of corporate interest – from music companies and beyond – followed. Paradoxically, the qualities encouraged by the major recording companies were often the same qualities that made rap and rappers risky partners for consumer brands.

From the perspective of the major recording companies, rap was potentially high risk but also a comparatively cheap investment because sampling replaced live musicians and 'young urban Hip-Hop artists could be paid a fraction of the rate of more established adult acts because of ineffective representation, unsophisticated negotiating strategies, ignorance of the recording industry, and racism' (Neal 1997: 128). The 'boutique model', whereby deals with independent labels allowed majors to control the market while leaving the responsibility of production and promotion to the independent labels (Jeffries 2011), further minimized risk. Under this model, independents did most of the work, but got less of the payoff and power: Neal (1997, 1999) describes managers of boutique labels as (at least initially) distanced from the real power represented by ownership of recordings, and control over decisions. One way that majors wielded power during rap's ascent in the 1990s was through privileging lyrics about sex, violence and consumption, typical of the gangsta rap style that was viewed as particularly marketable to the young fans driving rap's sales (Rose

2008, Jeffries 2011). The most critiqued aspects of rap were encouraged by mainstream marketing by major labels: 'gangstas, pimps, and hoes are products that promotional firms, working through record companies for corporate conglomerates, placed in high rotation' (Rose 2008: 23).

The economic structure of the mainstream music industries is reliant on big hits and will milk dry the qualities linked to chart success. Rose points to 'artists (especially those who have become moguls and entrepreneurs) who gleefully rap about guns and bitches' (2008: 25) as among those who allowed the shift in commercial rap in the mid-90s towards gangsta to occur, a reminder that, as Saha (2018) argues, it's the logic of cultural markets that shapes racialized production, not simply or straightforwardly the race of producers. The shift that occurred with the interest and investment of major labels created an ongoing tension for consumer brands, who were both keen to exploit the popularity of the genre and nervous to be associated with some of the common themes promoted.

With the approaches of Adidas and St. Ides leading the way, sportswear and beverages were two of the product areas that saw consumer brands eager to build associations with rap artists through sponsorship, endorsement, licensing and product placement strategies. Like Adidas, other sportswear brands, including Reebok and Nike, took advantage of the popularity of their products with b-boys and b-girls, drawing on hip-hop style in advertising campaigns and agreeing formal deals with rappers. MC Hammer appeared in a British Knights commercial in 1990, and the Digital Underground's Shock G appeared in a Nike commercial in 1994. In 1999, Nike collaborated with the Wu-Tang Clan on the Dunk High sneaker, and Converse partnered with Master P for the Converse All-Star MPs. These examples foreshadowed the current era in which sneaker collaborations are standard for successful rappers. Examples of formal relationships say nothing of the free publicity that these and many other sportswear (and later preppy and designer clothing) companies enjoyed as a result of rappers wearing their products and mentioning brand names in lyrics. Fans would be forgiven for assuming that artists have deals when, in many cases, they promoted the brand in exchange for free products or for nothing at all.

Unlike sportswear companies, beverage companies could not rely on free publicity: soft drinks are not a required accessory and don't often earn lyrical mentions. The relationship between rappers and soft drinks was instead cemented through sponsorship deals and, most visibly, the appearance of rap artists in television commercials. Coke, Pepsi and Sprite were among the brands that viewed rap and hip-hop culture as a route to reach target audiences and encourage brand loyalty. Coke advertisements featured Run-DMC (1988) and LL Cool J (1998), while Pepsi ads featured Young MC (1990) and MC Hammer (1991). But it was Sprite that forged the strongest bond, positing its commercial campaigns as genuine support of hip-hop culture. Sprite's roster included Kurtis Blow (Sprite, 1986), Heavy D (1990), A Tribe Called Quest (1994), KRS-One and MC Shan (1995), Nas and AZ (1997), among many others. The connection between soft drinks and hip-hop culture has continued for decades now with partnerships between the big brands and top artists, including Drake for Sprite (2010) and Cardi B for Pepsi (2019). Soft drink commercials featuring rappers have spanned eras and rap subgenres, demonstrating the success of the partnership for consumer brands, and the more relaxed orientation of rap towards commercial opportunities compared to rock: whether to license a song for an advertising campaign became a significant source of hand-wringing and selling out debates for rock artists around the turn of the twenty-first century, as Chapter 5 documents.

In 1994, Rose described commercial marketing of rap as 'a complex and contradictory aspect of the nature of popular expression in a corporation-dominated information society. Rap music and hip-hop style have become common ad campaign hooks for McDonald's, Burger King, Coke, Pepsi, several athletic shoe companies, clothing chain stores, MTV, anti-drug campaigns, and other global corporate efforts ad nauseum' (1994: 17). By the end of the 1990s, commercial partnerships between rappers and consumer brands were standard business. Rappers endorsed products across a broad range of consumer goods, brands sponsored individual artists as well as tours, products were placed in music videos and songs were licensed for use in visual media, including commercials. The relatively tension-free relationship between rap and consumerism created the possibility of featuring rappers in all-encompassing, synergistic campaigns. As *Billboard* reported in 2001:

> Not only are urban artists selling music by the truckload, they're also helping major corporations market and sell their products as well. Everyone, from Sprite and Foot Action to Radio Shack and American Express is tapping the shoulders of black artists, wooing them with endorsement and licensing deals, tour sponsorships and various opportunities that will align their brands with the industry's biggest and brightest stars.
>
> Baraka 2001

Marketing firms like Maven Strategies arranged deals for rappers that 'would have an artist write a brand name into a song, feature the brand in a music video and partner with the brand in other promotions, getting paid by the brand's owner along the way' (Williams 2005). While some rappers and consumer brands had previously favoured a more 'organic' approach – agreeing a deal because the artist was already a loyal consumer, or limiting the relationship to free products that the artist could decide whether or not to use – as time wore on, limits all but disappeared. Reported discussions of a possible product placement deal between Def Jam and Hewlett-Packard, for example, were declared 'groundbreaking' for challenging 'the established ethos in the hip-hop community of not "selling out"' (Kim 2002).

The Pillsbury Doughboy (1988), Fruity Pebbles' Barney Rubble (1992) and Barbie (1992) featured among a growing list of fictional character MCs spitting original rhymes as 'rap emerged as a staple facet of advertising jingles' (Forman 2002: 214). Fast forward to the present and even conservative brands employ (classic) rap and rappers to sell products and services: Macy's featured De La Soul's 'Me, Myself and I' in a 2016 commercial, and Ice-T starred in a Geico insurance ad in the same year. As the focus of brand mentions in rap has shifted towards luxury goods, not all companies want to formalize a relationship to rap, though a New York-based brand consulting executive describes clients 'happily sending product to rap artists with hopes that they will love it enough to put it in a song' (Billboard 2006).

The desire of some brands to have it both ways – to benefit from rap publicity without formally agreeing a paid deal – is perhaps unsurprising. Even those consumer goods and brands that have enjoyed the longest and deepest relationships with rappers have proven tempestuous partners, willing to rescind an opportunity when controversy is detected. In 2013 Reebok dropped Rick Ross over lyrics alluding to the use of date rape drugs, and PepsiCo's Mountain Dew ended a multi-million dollar endorsement deal with Lil Wayne over a controversial reference to civil rights icon Emmett Till. Perhaps most tellingly, in 2002 Pepsi stopped an ad campaign featuring Ludacris following a call to boycott the artist by conservative Fox News commentator Bill O'Reilly, on the basis that Ludacris degrades women. The irony was not lost on the rapper when O'Reilly was fired by Fox in 2017 after it emerged that he had settled half a dozen sexual harassment lawsuits.

As happy as brands are to enjoy an association with rap and hip-hop culture when it suits them, the reputation of the brand will always come first. The on-again, off-again relationship of clothing company Tommy Hilfiger to rap is a more mundane example of the capriciousness of brands (Indvik 2017). There are examples of ties being severed in the other direction too: Jay-Z called for a boycott of Cristal when the owner's comments about the popularity of the brand with rappers was interpreted as racist ('What can we do? We can't forbid people from buying it') (Century 2006). However, such examples are unlikely to affect the brand to the extent that a terminated endorsement deal does an artist, and occasional critiques of individual companies has not led to an anti-commercial awakening to challenge the comfortable fit between rap and commerce.

Rap, commerce and entrepreneurialism

I suggested above that the unfair treatment of black musicians by traditional music institutions pointed to commercial partnerships as a potentially preferable arrangement for rappers. It is also the case that the socio-economic circumstances of many aspiring rappers and the consumerism-focused lyrics of some subgenres of rap made such opportunities an obvious fit.

The development and growth of rap has often been linked to a sense of entrepreneurialism shared by its early proponents, who had to exercise creativity in locating performance spaces and channels of distribution. Kevin Powell (1996) describes succinctly 'the conditions that created the rap game in the first place: few legal economic paths in America's inner cities, stunted educational opportunities, a pervasive sense of alienation among young black males, black folks' age-old need to create music, and a typically American hunger for money and power'. In the absence of educational and career opportunities, the neighbourhoods that nurtured hip-hop culture were also home to a bustling street trade that ran the gamut in terms of legality.

The same entrepreneurial attitude drove rap practices: 'Many rappers have come to use the narrative of the street hustler, always working and surviving by any means necessary, as a story easily transferable to their lives in the music industry' (Jeffries 2011: 96). Quinn highlights the broader economic context for entrepreneurialism in gangsta rap: 'The resonance of gangsta's ruthless brand of entrepreneurialism amongst young people who had lost faith in the legitimacy of the wider society extends beyond the survivalist ghetto and into the hustling dynamics of the rampant free-market 1980s and 1990s' (2005: 65). In other words, limited employment opportunities (especially for young black men) combined with free market rhetoric to create a context in which capitalism is celebrated rather than critiqued. Eazy-E's attendance at a Republican fundraiser, and explanation that it was a publicity-stunt to garner press (Quinn 2005: 31), is a useful political parallel in how the financial ends can justify the means.

Entrepreneurial spirit defines the ideal pathway in rap, where many artists aspire to progress to executive roles as producer or label-owner. Artist-owned labels, responsible for the development of identifiable regional rap styles, were a response to 'years of bogus contracts, management conflicts, and poor representation' (Forman 2000: 69), but also an opportunity for substantial reward: 'For many recording artists, to gain wealth and material remuneration for their work suddenly meant learning the production and management side of the industry and exercising entrepreneurial skills as well' (Forman 2000: 69). The growth of artist-owned, dedicated rap labels began to challenge the dominance of white executives in the music business and represented the idea of 'making it'. In a 1992 article on capitalism's incorporation of hip-hop culture, Ice-T explained, 'When it comes to the economics of culture, hip-hop musicians, in general, are not fools' and Def Jam co-founder Russell Simmons offered drily, 'Being a starving artist is not that cool in the ghetto' (Marriott 1992).

As artists who embrace the value of 'individual and financial success' and exude 'entrepreneurial energy' (Rose 2008: 108), career progression for rappers has extended beyond the music industries into business empire building, with portfolios including their own brands and brand partnerships. Fashion labels and clothing lines became a popular investment in the 1990s (King 1999). Wu-Tang Clan established Wu Wear in 1995, and Diddy launched Sean John while Jay-Z launched Rocawear in 1999. In the twenty-first century, rap moguls diversified further. As John Jackson Jr writes:

> Hip-hop recording artists, learning their lessons from the exploited musical labor of mid-century black soul singers, have upped the ante on artistic business acumen with an almost fetishistic impulse to own, and own everything—from publishing rights to subsidiary record labels, from production companies to clothing lines, from soul food restaurants to bookstores, perfume brands to hair-care products.
>
> 2005: 182

Jay-Z and Dr Dre represent paragons of the business empire model of success. New York City rapper Jay-Z began his career by starting independent label Roc-A-Fella records in 1995 to release his debut album. Following his increasing chart success (especially the 1998 album *Vol. 2 ... Hard Knock Life*) and the success of the label, the rapper expanded his music interests and began investing in other product lines. Clothing line Roc-A-Wear (1999) has since been joined by sports bar chain 40/40 (2003), entertainment company Roc Nation (2008), wine and spirits company Sovereign Brands (2014) and streaming platform Tidal (2015). He also has financial stakes and decision-making power in a range of other ventures as, for example, co-brand director for the Budweiser Select beer, and co-owner of the Brooklyn Nets NBA team. Jay-Z's development from rapper to businessman is documented in the book *Empire State of Mind: How Jay-Z Went From Street Corner To Corner Office* by *Forbes* editor Zach O'Malley Greenburg (2015).

West Coast rapper Dr Dre followed his success in N.W.A. by co-founding Death Row Records in 1991 and releasing solo debut *The Chronic* in 1992. The album was hugely popular and came to define the gangsta rap subgenre G-Funk. After leaving Death Row Records, in 1996 Dr Dre established Aftermath Entertainment, a boutique subsidiary of Interscope Records, and consolidated his achievements as an artist with his work as a producer (of Snoop Dogg, Eminem and 50 Cent, for example). Dr Dre's music achievements opened up other business opportunities and, with the exception of some endorsements along the way, he has largely stayed close to his music roots: his first Beats by Dr Dre headphones were released in 2008, with additional styles released and deals agreed over the following years. The 2014 sale of Dr Dre's Beats Electronics company to Apple for $3 billion provides the entry point for 2017's four-part documentary series *The Defiant Ones*, which traces the partnership between Dr Dre and Interscope Records founder Jimmy Iovine. Both Dr Dre and Jay-Z were among *Forbes*' top 100 highest-paid celebrities in 2018, and Greenburg published *3 KINGS: Diddy, Dr. Dre, Jay-Z and Hip-Hop's Multibillion-Dollar Rise*, which documents the artists' success as businessmen, in 2018.

Critics have drawn attention to the ways in which investments outside music may be shaping rap itself. Rose argues that the 'dumbing down' of rap can be attributed in part to the tendency of rap's biggest artists to 'expand their product lines and dedicate lyrics to promoting them' (2008: 219). She quotes comedian Chris Rock on the effect of the corporate mentality on the quality of rap: 'You know how shitty Stevie Wonder's songs would have been if he had to run a fuckin' clothing company and a cologne line?' (Rose 2008: 219). Against occasional criticism, celebrations of rap mogul success inhabit music and business press coverage.

As well as the entrepreneurial spirit driving the success of rap moguls, rap's relationship to commercial opportunities has been influenced by internal qualities of the form, as suggested by the cases of Adidas and Run-DMC. Generic conventions, from the focus on consumerism, to the explicit mention of products and brands in lyrics, create an opening for partnerships with companies. Although rap's 'explicit focus on consumption has frequently been mischaracterized as a movement *into* the commodity market (e.g., hip-hop is no longer "authentically" black, if it is for sale)' (Rose 1994: 40, emphasis in original), Rose explains that hip-hop already had a relationship to the commodity system, even if early participants didn't think profit was possible, before it was incorporated by multinationals. Paul Gilroy has noted the irony of hip-hop's commodity obsession against a context where 'forms of conspicuous consumption contributed to the strategies that the minority pursued in order to win and to compel recognition as human beings, as fellow citizens and as Americans with a profile that belied the lowly, racial specifications of foolish, childlike negrohood' (2010: 9). Brands take advantage of the free publicity afforded by the conspicuous consumption displayed by some rappers as status symbol, as is the case with luxury goods, the celebration of which demonstrates how rappers and the communities they often come from are denied a more traditional path to self-worth (Jeffries 2011: 71).

Brand mentions in lyrics are also usually unpaid, but absolutely pervasive in the genre. Rap contains the most mentions by far of brand names across popular music genres, with clothing and shoes the most prevalent category (Craig et al. 2017: 258). (Brand consultancy project American Brandstand has been tracing brand name mentions in lyrics since 2003: most are in hip-hop songs.) Where deals for lyrical mentions have been struck, both parties can be strategically coy. An executive involved in sponsorships stresses the need for deals to be secret: 'corporations want consumers to assume that rappers name-dropping hamburgers, cell phones, or cars wrote the brands into their lyrics because they love them, not because they were paid' (Craig et al. 2017: 261). An open relationship between artist and brand can be celebrated, but paid brand mentions in lyrics crosses a line into control over creative decisions, and threatens the perceived authenticity of the relationship (Kim 2002).

And there are other lines too, which reveal a careful balance of values and the relevance of selling out discourse beneath a celebratory surface. Ice Cube's intro to 1990 single 'Turn Off the Radio' was an early gesture towards the intersection of race and commerciality as potentially thorny for rap artists. His 'message to the Oreo cookie' implies that artists who compromise for radio play or crossover success are still regarded by the white music industries in racist terms. 'Think about it, fucking sellout'. The notion of 'going commercial' explored in Chapter 2 resonates, but what is interesting and distinctive about this discourse in the rap context is that business success can forgive such transgressions. Jay-Z's 1997 single '(Always Be My) Sunshine', a collaboration with Foxy Brown and Babyface that features a cheery pop chorus, drew accusations of selling out and going commercial, but some fans forgave the rapper given his subsequent business success (see Hagan 2014 for this and other examples).

Going commercial can still attract censure but, for rap, there is no inherent tension between commercial partnerships and authenticity, which explains why even socially conscious artists like A Tribe Called Quest, De La Soul and KRS-One have licensed to or appeared in advertisements. Mainstream music companies have not been good allies, and consumer brands are not necessarily any worse. Indeed, it is the *lack* of payment from consumer brands that attracts censure: as Jay-Z put it, 'You're talking about something you like and it catches on in culture. You're an unpaid spokesman for this brand. You're generating millions and millions of dollars for that brand. And for that brand not to say at least thank you it's a huge slap in the face' (Phillips 2016). The complex role of authenticity and selling out for rap across and between commercial and racial dimensions offers multiple layers to unpack.

Authenticity within commercialism

Authenticity, often expressed in hip-hop culture through the concept of 'keeping it real', is communicated and maintained through a variety of associations. As Kembrew McLeod (1999) argues, staying true to yourself, black, the underground, hard, the street and the old school are associated with being real, while following mass trends, white, commercial, soft, the suburbs and the mainstream are associated with being fake. The movement of authenticity across measures of success, signs of compromise and assumptions about race indicate the complexity of 'keeping it real' for rappers. While rap's ultimate dominance of mainstream music charts – overtaking rock as the most popular genre in the United States in 2017 – has arguably eased the tension between the underground and the mainstream, *how* rappers achieve mainstream success continues to be evaluated through the lens of authenticity.

Rappers can achieve authentic commercial success as long as they are not seen to put money first: the acquisition and display of wealth is typical in hip-hop settings, including by rappers who are viewed as authentic, like Jay-Z (Jeffries 2011). Jackson Jr acknowledges that financial gain, especially for an artist with humble beginnings, figures into assessments of the real self, though only if financial success is not perceived as gained through compromise of the real self. He refers to 'the juggling act: privileging money as ur-category for evaluating the *real* while also avoiding criticism that one has crossed some shifting line and, therefore, compromised an internal and interior *real* self in slave-like service to others in the music business' (2005: 192–3, emphasis in original).

The potential contradiction between 'keeping it real' and mainstream success can be resolved by rappers through enduring relationships to the communities that nurtured them:

> Successful acts are expected to maintain connections to the 'hood and to 'keep it real' thematically, rapping about situations, scenes and sites that comprise the lived experience of the 'hood. At issue is the complex question of authenticity as rap posses continually strive to reaffirm their connections to the 'hood in an attempt to mitigate the negative accusations that they have sold out in the event of commercial or crossover success.
>
> Forman 2000: 72

Moreover, the potential contradiction between authenticity and marketability is resolved in part by the market's demand for authenticity in rap, an example of the 'doubleness' of authenticity in rap music, where credibility and marketability are collapsed (Hess 2005b: 298). Recording companies and consumer brands invest in artists perceived as authentic. Authenticity is what sells rap. As Neal writes, 'One of the challenges faced by corporations in their efforts to annex the black popular music industry was to deliver a commercial product that would be deemed "authentic," particularly to black audiences' (Neal 1999: 116). The strength of black record labels in locating authenticity before commercial viability may be one of the reasons why subsidiary or boutique rap labels have remained prominent despite deals with the majors and rap's chart dominance.

The significance of community ties and credibility among black audiences highlights how the authenticity of commercial success is evaluated through race: by 'disassociating oneself from "blackness," a hip-hop artist opens himself or herself to charges of selling out' (McLeod 1999: 141). The rap sell out thus lies at the intersection of commerce and race, as when a rapper is seen to put 'exploitative economic gain before race/class affiliation' (Quinn 2005: 85), or to aspire to commercial success by abandoning the 'connection to black urban populations and resistance to assimilation by commercial capitalism' (Jeffries 2011: 134) on which rap's authenticity is built.

Blatant attempts by rappers to gain mainstream appeal have attracted accusations of selling out: in the early 1990s, MC Hammer, with his commercial sound, poaching of old hits, merchandising and endorsement deals, 'personified who young artists *didn't* want to be' (Rabin 2012, emphasis in original). But rap also stands out for its consistent challenges to the notion of selling out as linked to mainstream success. In 1991, when Tone Loc was labelled a pop rapper and sellout, he responded: 'I never understood what people mean by sellout. Sell out of record stores? Sell out a motherfuckin' concert? That's the only type of selling out I do!' (Nelson 1991). Russell Simmons echoed these remarks when he noted that 'Black kids want to be sold out, as in there ain't no more records left, no more tickets for your concert. Black people like to see people large. The more cars and houses and places rappers go, the badder they are' (Marriott 1992).

At the same time, 'Rap's mainstream marketability during 1990–1991 prompted a widespread lyrical shift from claims of performer skill to concerns of crossing over, selling out, and keeping it real' (Hess 2005b: 302). If the rock version of authenticity, with its strongly anti-commercial stance, held little sway for rap in its ascendance, success prompted intense reflection on racial authenticity: 'For African Americans, arguably the most depersonalized American group, issues of authenticity—delineations between who is "real" and who is a "sellout"—have a long history' (Harrison 2009: 116). Rap is hugely popular, commercially successful and culturally influential, yet at the same time an incredibly important and visible space for reflection on issues affecting black people (Rose 1994). Selling out emerges through tensions between expression and commercialism, and between mainstream and minority audiences.

Selling out and race

In Chapter 1, I argued that, for black artists, authenticity continues to be linked to a sense of what is natural, and staying true to where you come from, an inheritance from folk ideology that has been imposed on artists by (often) white critics and audiences, and that places strict limits on black musical expression.

Comparing the treatment of 1960s rock artists with Motown Records artists, Hamilton notes, 'cosmopolitan versatility among African American artists was not heard as identity transcendence but rather as racial betrayal, in accusations that were frequently lobbed by white critics' (2016: 15). He cites the example of Jimi Hendrix 'who during his career was judged by many as a fraud or a sellout, his blackness rendering his music as inauthentically "rock" at the same time that his music rendered his person as inauthentically black' (Hamilton 2016: 16). For rap, ideological investments into racial authenticity are made by those who seek to exploit artists – such as major recording companies and consumer brands – and by those who seek to hold artists to account for their connection to the communities they came from. The latter evaluation of authenticity helps illuminate how selling out debates and discourse can defend important values for popular music culture (e.g. community) while at the same time creating an opening for potentially damaging ones (e.g. commercialism and materialism).

Before the concept of selling out was imported into popular music, it was used against African-Americans who were viewed as deserting or aiding in the oppression of their community by choosing to pass as white or otherwise be accepted by whites. While acknowledging that a straightforward definition does not capture the messiness of the term, Randall Kennedy writes, 'A "sellout" is a person who betrays something to which she is said to owe allegiance. When used in a racial context among African Americans, "sellout" is a disparaging term that refers to blacks who knowingly or with gross negligence act against the interest of blacks as a whole' (2008: 5). Kennedy considers how the term has been applied widely and with significant negative consequences, but disagrees with those who would renounce the concept entirely, identifying 'policing the group's boundaries' as a 'requirement for maintaining any community' (2008:9), though suggesting that 'indictments for racial betrayal be drawn more cautiously and taken more seriously' (2008: 10).

Kennedy highlights the presence of the selling out concept in contemporary African-American media and culture, noting its reflection in novels, films and lyrics. Accusations of selling out have perhaps been flung a bit too freely between rappers at times, but such invocations point to the role that rappers can play in supporting their communities. While local community experiences vary, 'by recognizing blackness as the marker for mistreatment and hood connectedness as a source of pride, rappers build a discourse of collective identity and social awareness', which is strengthened through 'the rhetoric of authenticity' (Jeffries

2011: 68). The sellout instead uses their newfound wealth to abandon the black community: Ice Cube's 1992 single 'True To The Game' criticizes artists for 'moving out your neighborhood' and exhorts sellouts to 'Give something back to the place where you made it from'. (Driving the point home, the video features sellout rappers being kidnapped and schooled in black nationalism (Rabin 2012).)

Long before the mainstream music industries showed interest, 'black popular music was historically integral to black communal formations and the production and distribution of communally derived narratives. In this regard, the mass commodification of black expression undermined many of the processes associated with the development of narratives of resistance from within the black community' (Neal 1997: 120). Selling out discourse in rap can be seen as an attempt to salvage the role of black popular music to maintain community, a goal made explicit through rappers' investments in local communities and philanthropic efforts. Highlighting the contributions of some prominent hip-hop philanthropists, Rose notes, 'At the same time that these artists are shrewdly "giving back"—a well-known and successful public relations and marketing strategy—they have heartfelt ties to the young people in the poor and fragile communities to which they contribute' (2008: 205). As philanthropic efforts have become more corporate and less political, hip-hop activism has provided a more direct critique of capitalism and state power, including specific cases of injustice (Kumanyika 2015).

For rap, the role of racial authenticity in brokering the relationship between art and commerce makes it possible for artists to enjoy tremendous chart success, partner with consumer brands, and develop (into) global brands, all without being accused of selling out. However, given the historical contexts through which it grew, the relaxed relationship of rap to commercialism is as much a result of racist exclusion, as a triumph over it.

The popularity of rap among US music listeners of all backgrounds may feed narratives of inclusion and social integration, but rap's success, especially in the United States, has not ushered in a post-racial utopia or signalled racism's demise. Tracks like Boogie Down Productions' 1989 'Who Protects Us From You' and Public Enemy's 1990 '911 is a Joke' made visible important issues routinely neglected by mainstream media (in these cases, police profiling and violence, and the unequal distribution of public services, respectively). Thirty years on, and music serves as soundtrack and megaphone for the Black Lives Matter movement (Orejuela and Shonekan 2018). Consumer brands have positioned themselves as supporters of rap and hip-hop culture, but with disclaimers, get-out clauses and a safe distance from serious issues. Pepsi's tone-deaf ad capitalizing on imagery from the Black Lives Matter movement, featuring Kendall Jenner offering the beverage to a police officer at a protest march (Victor 2017), is a particularly painful example of the willingness of brands to wade into political waters only far enough to serve their own goals.

Although there have been examples of rap artists criticizing hypermaterialism, alongside the more common rap targets of violence and sexism (Ogbar 1999), critiques have rarely been directed at the pro-commercialism stance represented by partnerships with consumer brands through sponsorship, endorsement, product placement and licensing. In a 2018 episode of documentary *Hip-Hop Evolution*, journalist and historian Davey D said of MC Hammer:

> He was the epitome in terms of success. People was looking at him like, that's not hip-hop, that's not real. They were critical of him, only to find 20 years later, everybody's trying to do the same thing. 'How can I get a soda deal? How can I get a cartoon?' Before Jay-Z said, 'I'm a businessman, I'm a businessman', Hammer was executing that in a very methodic and systematic way.
>
> *Hip-Hop Evolution* 2018

While Jay-Z pursued his entrepreneurial vision in a way that contrasts with MC Hammer's opportunistic business deals, it is also the case that Jay-Z built his empire at a time when commercial opportunities of all kinds were looked upon more positively.

In this chapter, I have explored rap's relationship to commerce, racial authenticity and selling out as a revealing contrast to the rock version of authenticity based on anti-commercialism that drives many of the debates throughout the book. Rock's anti-commercialism can be understood in this light as resulting from its position of privilege within the mainstream music industries. Early support of rock by the major recording, radio and television companies meant that rock artists did not need to look for alternative sources of revenue and exposure. Rock could afford its anti-commercial stance.

Rap is not alone in its complicated relationship to mainstream music industries that exclude and exploit in turn. Other genres offer analogous cases where partnerships with consumer brands through sponsorship, endorsement, product placement and licensing have filled the gap left by unsupportive music institutions. For example, the early roots of country music – associated in the United States with the white, rural working class – include its use to draw crowds to advertising, particularly the selling of patent medicine (Peterson 1997: 15–16). Commercial advertisements and stars promoting products formed part of the barn dance radio programmes of the 1920s and 30s (Peterson 1997). These early associations, along with the genre's initial dismissal by the music industries as hillbilly music (Brackett 1999), start to explain the more congenial relationship between country music and consumer brands. Artists in the current UK grime scene have taken rap's lessons to heart: an emphasis on independence, and DIY methods of music production and distribution, sits comfortably alongside lucrative brand partnerships (Elan 2016, Khalili-Tari 2017). Digging beneath a genre's apparent comfort with commercialism reveals that differences in orientation towards consumer brands and corporate power are not innate, but result from particular histories and power dynamics.

The case of rap brings attention to some of the concerning consequences of commercialism for popular music. Endorsement deals and recording contracts offer their own ethical faults and merits, but the treatment of consumer brands as partners in music making obscures the power differential at work. Consumer brands take what they want from music and leave the rest. Brands drain music of its value by demanding non-specific and inoffensive meanings, including a detachment from politics. Brands also use music to target vulnerable populations: while the days of malt liquor endorsements are history, the shift in brand mentions to premium and luxury brands brings its own concerns. Quoted in an *Atlantic* article on hip-hop's corporate relationships, Quinn avers, 'Mainstream hip-hop's relentless promotion of high-end brands is deeply problematic. It fuels consumerism and materialism, which is often felt most keenly by those who can least afford to buy the brands' (Coward 2015). More broadly, commercial partnerships promote the false promise that we might gain from consumer goods the sense of genuine fulfilment and enrichment that we can, ideally, get from music.

The mainstreaming of rap helped normalize commercial affiliations for other genres and artists and, if rap's rise in the 1990s provided a template for how authenticity and commercialism can co-exist, it couldn't have come at a better time. By the late 1990s, the consequences of corporate consolidation and digitalization forced indie and rock artists previously opposed to commercial partnerships to re-evaluate their stance. In the next chapter, I consider how licensing music to advertising went from heated debate to standard practice.

5

Popular music in advertising

The use of popular music in advertising has provided a key battleground for debates over whether popular musicians have sold out, or compromised their values for financial gain. However, as the practice of licensing to advertising has become an important source of revenue for musicians and a more common practice, the stigma once attached to it has lifted. This chapter focuses on how and why selling out has emerged and receded as a valuable concept for understanding the use of popular music in advertising. It looks across both historical and contemporary cases to understand the practice of licensing popular music to advertising as an increasingly standard yet at times contentious activity within popular music culture.

Music has played an important role in advertising since the beginning of broadcasting: sponsorship of music radio programming and the rise of jingles were among the precursors that married music to advertising and paved the way for music licensing (Taylor 2012). Like other forms of popular entertainment, early popular music, including early rock'n'roll, caught the attention of consumer brands and services interested in the potential benefits of an association with music artists and audiences. Early rock'n'roll stars promoted and were sponsored by consumer brands, from companies obviously related to music (e.g. radio or phonograph companies) to those less obviously linked to music (e.g. cigarette companies, food producers, and services and charities). Stars could be seen standing by logos in promotional photographs and mentioning corporate sponsors during public and media appearances. *The Ed Sullivan Show* (1948–1971), the biggest showcase for new and top musical acts, was one of the most attractive (and expensive) spots for sponsors during its run and especially at the height of its ratings success, with Elvis and the Beatles attracting the largest viewing audiences. While Elvis trivia aficionados point out that the King only performed in one television commercial (for Southern Maid Donuts in 1954), he displayed no strong anti-commercial or anti-corporate beliefs: Elvis's affiliation with brands through various appearances was not at odds with his own brand of rebellion. Merchandising and commercial sponsorship played a central role in Beatlemania until the group's transition from entertainers into artists. While early rock'n'roll's position as pure entertainment minimized any culture versus commerce conflict for advertisers, it must not be forgotten that advertisers are led by profit, not culture, and their interest in culture is ultimately in the service of profit. There was always potential for strain, particularly as popular music became legitimated and established as art.

The intermingling of popular music and consumer brands from the early days of rock'n'roll to the present has been marked by both moments of tension and cosiness. In Chapter 1, I explored the influence of the folk revival on folk rock and, later, rock ideology: the avoidance of corruption through commerce was one value that rock artists adopted from their folk predecessors. Pete Seeger himself quit folk group the Weavers in 1958 after the group recorded an advertisement for Lucky Strike cigarettes, an affiliation that Seeger, a non-smoker and critic of commercialism, referred to as 'pure prostitution' (quoted in Wald 2015: 29).

Some brands were more successful than others at creating a seemingly natural association between their products and popular music. Coke and Pepsi have been particularly effective at using popular music to differentiate themselves from other consumer products and, subtly, from each other (Klein 2009). Coke's 'Things Go Better With Coke' campaign involved some of the best-selling artists of the 1960s (for example, Roy Orbison, the Moody Blues, the Supremes) singing the brand's jingle in their respective music styles. Full-length versions of Coke's 1971 jingle 'I'd Like to Teach the World to Sing (in Perfect Harmony)' went on to achieve chart success for the Hillside Singers and the New Seekers, solidifying Coke's reputation as supporting and driving popular music culture, rather than simply exploiting it. In the 1980s, Pepsi's advertisements featuring Michael Jackson and Madonna were themselves media events, on par with music video world premieres (Klein 2008b, Love 2019).

For 'serious' rock groups, the commercial success of the music business in the 1970s, as explored in Chapter 2, came with the expansion of corporate sponsorship: the big money stakes of the music business attracted big money campaigns and deals with consumer brands. Fragrance company Jovan's 1981 sponsorship of a Rolling Stones tour – with the brand and the band appearing on each other's products – was an important moment in corporate sponsorship (Seiler 2000) which utilized cross-marketing beyond standard practice. As music journalist Michael Goldberg put it in 1983:

This is rock & roll? Welcome to the Eighties. 'The mood of the country has changed. Rock music has become depoliticized,' explains Jay Coleman, president of Rockbill, a company that specializes in pairing rock bands with corporations and was responsible for the Stones-Jovan tie-in. 'Ten years ago, people were blowing up Dow Chemical. The same kids today are lining up for jobs. They don't go to concerts to protest something. It's more of, "Hey, let's go out and party."'

...

It was the 1981 tie-in between the Rolling Stones and Jovan, followed shortly thereafter by Rod Stewart's association with Sony blank tape, that legitimized rock bands in the eyes of advertisers, while at the same time making corporate sponsorships seem okay to many bands. 'After those two made the front page of Billboard, a lot of groups started calling us,' says Coleman. 'And once a few companies did it, it made it more kosher.'

Goldberg 1983

Overt, expensive and complex sponsorship deals naturalized the relationship between bands and brands, and pointed to television advertising as a suitable space to develop such partnerships.

While the legitimation of rock as art – and related anti-corporate and anti-commercial values – in the late 1960s might suggest an uneasy relationship between bands and brands, the use of music in advertising did not receive consistent objections until the 1980s and, even then, it was typically extreme examples (like Nike's use of the Beatles' 'Revolution' in 1987) that led musicians and fans to erupt in outrage. As the use of popular music in advertising became pervasive in the mid- to late-1990s, and with more frequent use of genres and artists invested in or associated with anti-commercial values (e.g. counterculture rock, indie), the practice became a key focus of selling out debates. But then something changed: new challenges faced by the music industries prompted musicians and fans to reassess the role of commercial opportunities, including the use of music in advertising.

Industry struggles, advertising heroes

In recent decades, the use of popular music in advertising has been promoted by music and advertising industry insiders as a salve for problems faced by the music industries, including barriers to radio play and decreasing music sales. In the mid- to late-1990s, media deregulation, enacted through legislation like the Telecommunications Act of 1996 in the US, allowed large corporations to dominate the radio industry and led to low-risk and standardized playlists (Taylor 2007, Klein 2008a). Television advertising, considered previously by many musicians to be an unsavoury setting for their work, began to look like a legitimate avenue for wide exposure: supporters celebrated advertising as the 'new radio' (Klein 2008a, Barnhard and Rutledge 2009, *Music Week* 2013). Advertising also offered a potential revenue stream, with advertisers paying the copyright holder for a music synchronization, or sync, license, which allows copyrighted music to be used in visual media. Tentative musicians were further persuaded to license to advertisers when digital music met the internet and spawned numerous platforms for acquiring music immediately and free of charge. While legitimate streaming sites and services have replaced the peer-to-peer platforms that first raised the alarm, earnings (and, importantly, the cut that makes it to an artist) will quite possibly never return to pre-digital levels. As a result, copyright exploitation, including sync licensing to advertisers, has become a central revenue stream for the music industries.

In the past, popular music in advertising attracted the scorn of critics and fans concerned with artists selling out; now it is a standard practice and rarely registers as controversial. The shift in perspective is likewise reflected in the evolution of scholarship on the use of music in advertising. Much of the earlier defining contributions to the study of music in advertising focused on composed and/or classical music used in television commercials (see, for example, Huron 1989, Cook 1994, Tota 2001), but the growth of popular music placement around the turn of the twenty-first century encouraged a focus on popular genres that had previously made only rare appearances in advertising, from pop and rock (Allan 2008, Klein 2008b) to world music (Taylor 2000) and electronica (Taylor 2007, Klein 2008a). Books have explored the economic and cultural context of the practice (Klein 2009), the history of popular music's relationship with advertising (Taylor 2012), the textual structure of ads themselves (Graakjær 2015) and the role of particular companies in setting standards for collaboration (Love 2019). Contributions to the literature on popular music in advertising reflect the interests of different fields (marketing and advertising; popular music studies and musicology; media, communication and cultural studies), and different approaches in both method (textual; production studies; historical) and orientation (instrumental; interpretive; critical).

While earlier scholarship on the use of popular music in advertising typically acknowledged debates about selling out, recent publications suggest that the use of popular music in advertising is no longer infused with tension. Music is still an important dimension of advertising from a marketing point of view (Cartwright, McCormick and Warnaby 2016), but its movement from 'ultimate sellout' to 'one of the best opportunities for many musicians to gain access to mainstream markets' (Eckhardt and Bradshaw 2014: 167) means that concerns about artistic integrity or commercialism may not even figure into current research.

Could we be witnessing a happy marriage between popular music and advertising? A confident bridging of the historically uneasy gap between culture and commerce? Echoing Timothy Taylor's assessments that 'there is no longer a meaningful distinction to be made between "popular music" and "advertising music"' and 'selling out is no longer an issue' (2012: 229), Nicolai Graakjær writes that 'accusations of "selling out" have lost significance and have become increasingly rare' (2014: 519) and Giana Eckhardt and Alan Bradshaw assert that 'although music and commerce have always been in bed together, they now truly seem to be in love' (2014: 181).

Rather than conclude with the observation that selling out is no longer a relevant concept for understanding the use of music in advertising, I choose to take this shift in attitude as a starting point. What does the use of popular music in advertising, and its changing relationship to selling out, tell us about promotional culture more generally and the role of branding in society? Practices that seem to blend culture and commerce, or art and business, can help us better understand the centrality of promotion to cultural production: what Devon Powers (2013b) describes as a '"state" of promotion' for popular music, why Leslie Meier (2017) explores popular music *as* promotion, and how Nicholas Carah (2010) considers musicians as co-creators in experiential branding. Sarah Banet-Weiser's work on branded creativity reminds us that even blurred boundaries are meaningful. While artists have always collaborated with commercial industries and organizations, the notion that commerce corrupts authentic art still circulates and structures decisions (Banet-Weiser 2012).

Investigating the use of popular music in advertising can reveal new practices in the advertising and music industries, but it can also provide rich examples to explore and debate tensions between culture and commerce. The use of popular music in advertising is perhaps the most blatant and public example of acquiescence to commercialism and consumerism that fans encounter. The aim is necessarily commercial for artist and advertiser, the advertiser has the final say, and the song is there to serve the advertisement, not the other way around. In the following section, I revisit how artists have assessed placement opportunities (Klein 2009) and consider the influence of recent developments on the trajectory of the practice.

To license or not to license

Some of the most controversial cases of popular music in advertising have incited an additional layer of outrage because the artist in question did not control the rights or approve of the usage. In order to use a song in an advertisement, a sync licence, including both master rights (the original recording) and publishing rights (the composition), must be purchased. While master rights are typically owned by the record label that financed the recording, publishing rights are automatically owned by the composer. Publishing rights can, however, be sold to another party, in which case the composer has no say over a song's use.

The use of the Beatles' 'Revolution' in a 1987 Nike ad is the classic example: the three Beatles alive at the time objected to the use of the song to hawk sneakers, but did not own or control the rights (see Klein 2009). For many music fans, this example proved a lesson in copyright and an opportunity to reflect on the moral dimensions of music licensing. Why does the use of music in advertising sometimes feel like a degradation of the song? Shouldn't the artist have a say over its use, whatever the technical status of copyright? For advertisers, the debate that followed Nike's use of the Beatles song suggested a cautious and considerate approach to music licensing, though subsequent cases with similar circumstances have sometimes revived the discussion. In 2001, Wrangler used Creedence Clearwater Revival's 'Fortunate Son' as a patriotic anthem to promote their jeans, despite the topical mismatch (it's a powerful anti-war song) and the songwriter's opposition to the use (John Fogerty did not control the rights). For musicians, these scandals delivered a warning, and few artists today would concede their publishing rights completely. The strength of feeling expressed by music fans gave musicians an additional warning: artists should wield their rights prudently.

All of the potential rights holders have reason to tread carefully when it comes to licensing to advertising. Publishers (who are often assigned copyright in order to license the work and collect royalties on behalf of the artist) and record companies (who typically own the rights to the master recording) need to consider a composition's future value since overuse or a use that prompts a negative response may limit future licensing opportunities. Musicians can add to this concern the worry that their artistic integrity will be questioned: they may be accused of selling out. Artists must balance such concerns with the reality that there is more pressure than ever to agree to licensing offers. To do so, artists consider the fit of the song with the product, service or company; the artistry of the commercial; and the various benefits and risks of licensing.

Brand alignment

When musicians discuss licensing a song for use in a commercial, the alignment of the music or artist with the product or service is often at the heart of the decision-making process. Musicians are more likely to be open to a licensing opportunity when the product advertised is felt to be a 'match' with the image or values of the artist (Klein 2009, Meier 2017).

Belief that the image of the advertised product shares characteristics with the image of the artist is often considered as a justification for licensing. In 2006, rock group the Donnas, who have licensed to commercials for brands including Target, Budweiser and Nissan, identified the then holy grail of spots: 'Why can't we get that iPod spot? Those spots are like having a video on MTV' (quoted in Paoletta 2006: 22). The combination of a music-related product with a 'cool' brand is about as safe a choice as an artist might hope to make. And the Donnas know about selling out:

> 'It's funny,' Robertson says. 'Some of our fans thought we were selling out when we were on an indie label. So, when we signed with Atlantic, they thought we were complete sellouts.'
>
> Toss several music licenses into the mix and the band is, for many, a poster child for selling out. 'But if you're not in a band, you don't know what it's like,' Robertson adds. 'We shop at Target. We like the Olympics. We love Budweiser.'
>
> Paoletta 2006: 22

Like the Donnas, many artists cite their own use of a product or company to explain why they agreed to license a song when they have declined other opportunities. Artists also evaluate the ethical fit of the advertiser against their own values. For example, Welsh rock band the Super Furry Animals rejected a seven-figure offer from Coca-Cola, citing the company's treatment of its workers.

Few artists rule out future opportunities entirely, however. Even John Densmore, who has been vocal in his disapproval of the practice and who has prevented the use of the music of the Doors in advertising, has commented, 'There's a possibility if something came along that's very "green" that agreed with where we're at, then maybe' (quoted in Newman 2006: 24). By evaluating each opportunity against personal connections or ethical perspectives, artists can be open to licensing without compromising their values or taking an anti-commercialism stance that rules out all consumer brands.

Being a user of a product or service, or sharing the values of a company, offers a more genuine connection than the arbitrary link typically forged by music placement. If an artist already supports an advertiser through custom or shared values, music placement can be viewed as simply extending that support. Bob Seger, for example, agreed to license 'Like a Rock' to Chevrolet, despite turning down offers from many other advertisers, because he was from the Detroit area, had worked for GM and wanted to support the company (Diamond 2016). The inverse is also true: when a company is already seen to care about popular music culture, a placement can be viewed as another vehicle through which the company can offer support to artists. DJ Steve Aoki saves his endorsements for brands that 'care about the culture' of Electronic Dance Music: to gain approval, companies 'really do have to support [EDM] from the ground up. You have to help build the culture. You can't go in and buy the culture' (Hall 2015).

Ultimately, both artist and advertiser seek a music placement that scans as authentic. As one branded entertainment executive puts it, the content of the advertisement must be perceived by the target audience as 'authentic to the brand' (Elliott 2009: B6). Of course, contributing to popular music culture is neither altruistic nor anonymous. Brands may sponsor tours, provide free products to musicians, or host competitions for musicians, but their contributions are invariably a part of a company's marketing strategy. The concept of authenticity may be too slippery to ever successfully pin down, as discussed in Chapter 1, but the perception of authenticity can make all the difference to the success of an advertising campaign and to the likelihood of selling out accusations.

Creativity in advertising

At the extreme ends, what advertising often represents is at odds with what music can represent: music can be an important source of human expression and connection, experiences completely detached from the commercial and consumerist trappings of advertising. In reality, popular music can be unapologetically commercial and advertising can embody genuine creativity. A spot with artistic aspirations can offer a more comfortable home for licensed music.

Artists who evaluate the creativity of a commercial as part of the decision-making process are still seeking an alignment between song and spot, though focused on the fit between sound and visual rather than artist and company values. Advertising spots described as 'creative' and 'artistic' may feel like a more natural fit for popular music, and can allay concerns about affiliation with the advertiser. Jim James from indie rock group My Morning Jacket, whose song 'Mahgeetah' was used in a Coors Aspen Edge beer commercial in 2004, recognizes the creative possibilities of advertising as part of a broader rationale for licensing music:

> It's a difficult thing, because I grew up coming from a school of music being used in commercials is an evil thing. It's a really confusing time to be a musician, because it's so hard to make your living and so hard to get your music out there. Sometimes you see music used in creative ways in advertising, and at least some kid out there watching TV is hearing a great song.
>
> Quoted in Cohen 2008

With award-winning ad campaigns offering 'proof that the final ad can be every bit as creative as the music which soundtracks it, acts are finding it harder than ever to say no to the right offer' (*Music Week* 1999: 24). Advertising's validation as a creative medium is promoted through industry awards, like the American Advertising Awards and the Clio Awards, and affirmed by the involvement of film, television, and music video directors. Directors including Wes Anderson, Sofia Coppola, Michel Gondry and David Fincher have all lent their talents to TV commercials, giving credence to advertising as a creative form. Musicians are understandably persuaded by the artistic treatment that is likely to result with a film director at the helm. Indie rock band Lilys were persuaded by Roman Coppola's involvement in the 1997 Levi's advertisement that featured their song and indie pop group Ladybug Transistor entrusted Errol Morris to use their song creatively in a Citibank advertisement in 2001. More significantly, the acceptance of advertising as an art form has been both affirmed and deepened by the involvement of artists of all kinds. Many advertising creatives, including music supervisors, bring art and music backgrounds to the practice via formal study or practical experience (Klein 2009: 48–52).

As the head of a sync agency explains,

Most artists these days are OK with sync as long as their music is used in a creative way and with an ethical company. I do admire artists such as David Byrne and Tom Waits who have a blanket 'No' on all advertisements as that is what they truly believe in, but it would be interesting to see if they would have the same view now if they were just starting out.

Quoted in Goldie 2008: 8

For musicians fortunate enough to be offered a placement for a commercial whose product and creativity assuage concerns of selling out, the decision can be easy. For most, the presumed exposure and income that comes with music licensing is enough to take the risk of raising the ire of critics.

Benefits and risks

The exploitation of copyright, including licensing music for use in commercials, has become central to the business of making music and making money from music. The use of popular music in advertising is ubiquitous and normal. For musicians, the key benefits claimed include exposure, which may lead to radio play and record sales, and income. In this section, I explore how the assumed benefits to artists have been celebrated and challenged by both variable practices and changing perceptions.

Lou Reed's defence of licensing 'Walk on the Wild Side' for a 1984 Honda scooter commercial in which he also appears – 'for money and to try to sell my records' (quoted in Fong-Torres 1986) – has been echoed by many artists since. As noted earlier, in the late 1990s and in the wake of deregulatory measures in the US, which tightened the control of a small number of large corporations over radio markets, the licensing of music for use in commercials was heralded as the 'new radio'. Unlike the increasingly conservative approach of commercial radio, advertisers were willing to take a chance on unknown bands, independent labels and sounds that stand out from chart music.

Perhaps the best known and most often cited case relates to Moby's 1999 album *Play*. The mainstream success of the album is credited to the licensing of every track across a range of media, including many television commercials, effectively opening a space for the promotion of Electronic Dance Music at a time when radio was unlikely to add EDM artists to their playlists (Klein 2009, Taylor 2007). Placement in an ad, it seemed, could lead to an enormous spike in record sales and radio play. In the years that followed, the story of bands breaking through as a result of music placement was a regular item in the music and advertising press: Feist, the Walkmen, Jet, and the late Nick Drake are among the artists who feature in this narrative. Singer-songwriter Aimee Mann described why some musicians are attracted to licensing opportunities in light of the state of radio:

> It might be the only airplay they get. I've become totally disillusioned with mainstream radio. I hate the music they play.
> What's amazing is that the music you hear on the radio sounds like jingles, but the music you hear in commercials is cool. I'd rather hear a Moby song in a commercial than a Britney Spears song on the radio.
> Quoted in *Toronto Star* 2002: J06

However, the positive outcomes of placement in an advertisement risk overstatement. The so-called 'Apple bump' – used to describe the sales increase that results from placement in an Apple advertisement – has always been variable (Bruno 2009: 14) and the benefit of exposure through advertising has arguably become less reliable over time. While commercials continue to feature popular music, including artists that could benefit from the exposure, the excitement surrounding the 'new radio' has diminished and the sort of success stories that were commonplace fifteen years ago are now rare. (Name the last band you recall as achieving success via a television commercial.)

Once popular music was used to break through the clutter of advertising that confronted would-be consumers across a growing number of media spaces. But advertising needs new and different techniques to stand out and, while an especially imaginative use of music might highlight a particular spot, the use of popular music in advertising has become ordinary. For every spot that allows an advertising creative with great taste to tip us off to a new or independent artist, there are many more that simply use popular music as another obligatory apparatus in a promotional machine. Furthermore, even if a song does break through the clutter, attracting audience and radio attention, record sales are unlikely to follow. Revenues from physical formats fell from over $25 billion in 1999 to $4.7 billion in 2018 (IFPI 2018, IFPI 2019) and the yearly increase in digital revenues (up to $11.2 billion in 2018) is not making up the difference, particularly for the majority of artists, whose streaming royalties remain scant.

Income through exposure, radio play and record sales is, at best, an erratic outcome. Musicians are, however, guaranteed income in the fee earned through the licensing agreement, typically split between a record label (for the master rights), the composer (for the publishing rights), and a publisher (if the composer has a publishing deal). A single sync agreement can make an enormous difference to an artist. Many artists describe how a sync fee has supported their music-making either directly, by paying for recording or touring, or indirectly, by providing an income that obviates the need for a more traditional 'day job'. As Meric Long of indie rock duo the Dodos puts it, 'I've been able to experience, for the first time in my life, getting paid to play music and nothing but' (Pequeno 2009).

For artists who don't need the money, the opportunity to donate the fee can be motivation to agree a sync license, even with a distasteful advertiser. In 2017, Grace Slick allowed fast food chain Chick-fil-A to use Starship's 'Nothing's Gonna Stop Us Now' 'specifically so she could use her payment to fund causes to which the chain's management is opposed' (*Guardian* 2017). The chain's owners have drawn criticism for their open support of anti-LGBTQ organizations and legislation: Slick donated the fee to Lambda Legal, which provides legal support to LGBTQ people. It's an approach used previously by artists including Moby (James 2001) and Chumbawamba (*Toronto Star* 2002) who donated fees earned for licensing to car commercials to 'environmental, alternative energy, and animal rights organizations' (MTV 1996) and 'anti-corporate activist groups' (McAvoy 2002) respectively. Whether the value of redirecting the fee to relevant charities offsets the cultural value an advertiser gains through the implied endorsement of music placement is surely a question that weighs heavily on artists. Still, the possibility of donating the fee to charity (or, in some cases, the advertiser promising a donation to charity) represents an additional justification for licensing.

Sync fees have always varied considerably and it has typically been the case that those musicians who could benefit the most (small, independent artists) often receive the least, while megastar, millionaire artists can be offered seven-figure fees. Today, the disparity persists and the average fees have decreased from the time when music licensing was first hailed as a panacea for the ailing music industries. As music supervisor PJ Bloom described in 2013,

> If you expect nothing, then you'll probably be very pleased. If you expect to get one of those $50,000 sync fees then you're probably going to be quite disappointed. There was a good moment 7–10 years ago when the retail record business was starting to fail and sync was starting to take over in a lot of ways. We were spending a lot of money: our budgets were higher, the notion of licensing music

had much more value so the fees were much higher. Fees have systematically gone down and down over the years and that's going to continue to happen.

Quoted in Pakinkis 2013

As the practice of licensing music to commercials has become more ordinary, the stigma once attached to it and the fees once expected for it have decreased in tandem. It is a result that could have been predicted when the same effect was witnessed for particular brands: a decade ago, Apple used its 'leverage in breaking artists' and the fact that artists 'want to be associated with a hip, cool brand like Apple' to justify a much smaller than average fee for master and sync rights combined (Moran 2008). The suggestion that labels should be paying for music placement, rather than advertisers paying copyright holders, is shared half-jokingly by music supervisors. With an abundance of artists looking for a break through placement in a commercial, it's no surprise that sync companies operating a 'pay-to-play'-style system have emerged (Klein and Meier 2017).

For artists signed to a major label, successful negotiation of a high sync fee may be overshadowed by the unfavourable terms of so-called 360 deals, contracts that allocate a greater proportion of an increasing number of revenue streams, including copyright, to record companies (Marshall 2013, Stahl and Meier 2012). Regardless of contract (or lack thereof), while one placement can be a significant boon for an artist, 'most musicians earn a relatively small portion of their revenue from sources directly related to copyright' (Dicola 2013: 339). Ultimately, there is a lot of competition for what translates into a comparatively modest amount: while sync income has risen steadily, it still accounts for only 2% of global music industry revenues (IFPI 2019).

The presumed benefits of licensing popular music to advertising have been tested by the ubiquity of the practice and the decreasing stigma attached to it, reason enough to be cautious of overly celebratory attitudes towards music licensing. A linked consequence of the pervasive and celebrated use of popular music in advertising is the obsolescence of selling out and the values that underpin in.

No such thing as selling out?

Throughout this book, I have highlighted activities and practices that were once a focus of key selling out debates, but which appear to no longer offer a space for such discussion. And so it goes with popular music in advertising: a growing chorus of voices within the advertising and music industries has proclaimed in recent years that there is 'no such thing as selling out' or that selling out 'no longer exists'. The view that selling out no longer has a role in debates about the use of music in advertising has attracted the attention of scholars and music journalists alike.

As highlighted earlier, Taylor's claim that 'selling out is no longer an issue' (2012: 229) has resonated with other scholars of popular music in advertising. Music journalists have similarly explored changing perspectives among musicians and how and whether selling out continues to hold relevance for the use of popular music in advertising (see, for example, Berkmann 2010, Hopper 2013, Molotkow 2012). Changes to the shape and structure of the music industries resulting from digitalization have occurred alongside an unprecedented growth in promotional culture (Klein, Meier and Powers 2017) and the evolution of advertising into the dominant cultural industry (Lewis 2013). If decreasing record sales have provided a practical rationale for the use of popular music in advertising, then the omnipresence of marketing and branding for all communicative practices has provided the cultural rationale. Together the forces of digitalization and promotion normalize practices that join culture and commerce through activities that purport to overcome barriers of clutter and inattention, and that benefit both parties.

The truth is more complicated. The reliance of artists on corporate patrons opens the door to greater corporate influence, giving corporations the power to censor artists or control the distribution of music (a DJ fears, for example, a festival sponsor dictating the line-up (Hall 2015)). Advertising does not offer a space for all sounds and messages, and can be a tempestuous champion. Advertiser tastes and demands change over time and vary by target audience. As one music publisher described in 2008, 'Folky music had become the new advert music, but now commercial briefs are saying that they specifically don't want that sound' (quoted in Goldie 2008: 8). The portrayal of advertising as a radio replacement may lead to the neglect of other, less commercial, spaces and opportunities. Operating in a challenging environment for public media, independent music venues and state funding of music (where it exists at all), musicians are encouraged to position themselves as brands and entrepreneurs, prepared to adapt to commercial offers.

The sheer abundance of promotional messages surrounding us, combined with the ability of media consumers to mute, skip or block advertisements, presents a challenge to advertisers. In order to reach consumers and retain their attention, advertisers rely on all techniques that offer a potential advantage.

Popular music has proven itself as an important tool in the advertising arsenal. When done well, the use of popular music in advertising can be creative, funny and beautiful.

Artists may consider the product being advertised, the creativity of the spot and the benefits and risks involved, but many musicians cannot afford the luxury to discriminate, as licensing opportunities are sought to make up for the loss of record sales. Paradoxically, the ubiquity of music licensing has made the benefits (exposure and income) less reliable, and the protective values attached to the concept of selling out less relevant.

We are at a crossroads, where selling out can be viewed as the preserve of unrealistic purists who don't understand how the music business works, or it can be viewed as a tool for upholding values that seek to protect cultural autonomy and that demand popular music be treated respectfully, through careful use and fair payment. Debates about the use of popular music in advertising have been peppered with reductive claims that favour the former view.

One claim is that capitalism is capitalism, and making, selling or buying music is equivalent to making, selling or buying any other consumer product. But our experience of cultural products like popular music tells us this is not the case and the argument for 'why music matters' (Hesmondhalgh 2013) points to popular music's potential to aid human flourishing. Another claim is that the relationship between popular music and advertising is mutually beneficial. In an ideal scenario, music placement benefits the artist, though I make the case above for why this outcome cannot be relied upon. Moreover, advertisers are looking out for the interests of advertisers, not music-makers: the relationship to music is 'more parasitic than philanthropic' (Klein 2009: 20). Both claims drive the belief that the loss of the concept of selling out is a sign of progress, that capitalism has united the goals of advertising and popular music, with music licensing an exemplar of the successful alliance. On the contrary, the loss of selling out in popular music culture is a sign of submission and the consequences may be severe. The standardization of advertising's role in popular music culture increases the power of marketers as gatekeepers, directly and indirectly privileging advertising-friendly sounds and messages. It is crucial that we reframe the conversation about selling out to capture the cultural value of autonomy that the concept has sought to protect and to ensure meaningful support for popular music culture outside the world of marketing.

That is, if it isn't too late. The economics of the music industries in the digital age has resulted in increasing mergers between creative and promotional strategies, such that the use of popular music in advertising seems almost a quaint courtship between culture and commerce. The ubiquity and normalization of promotional activities in popular music culture recasts musicians as 'artist-brands' (Meier 2017): the next chapter explores the consequences for music-making activities and musicians.

6

Promotion in popular music

The concurrent growth of digitalization and spread of promotional culture have together produced a framework for music-makers that challenges the boundaries around which selling out has been historically policed and within which artistic integrity has been traditionally understood and maintained. A central factor driving the re-evaluation of conventional boundaries is the economics of the global music industries in the digital age, shaped by changes to industry practice and government policies. Threats to established revenue streams, especially record sales, have justified increasing involvement in activities that previously would have been classified as selling out, including sponsorship and product placement. This chapter takes a closer look at the activities of 'artist-brands' (Meier 2017). It also considers how big (non-music) corporations are becoming difficult to avoid if a musician is to distribute and promote his or her music through online and offline channels. While a promotional orientation has become normalized for musicians, there are signs it hasn't been entirely naturalized, with artists occasionally breaking the fourth wall to question their non-musical labour. Why would a superstar like Lady Gaga feel compelled to take a step back from promotional activities despite a history of cleverly straddling the line between art and commerce?

In the previous chapters, I have mapped out changing perspectives on selling out, looking at how use of the concept has varied over time and genre, and at how particular activities have gone from stigmatized to normalized, no longer invoking critiques. The construction of authenticity as a key value for popular music culture – and the rockist bias underpinning debates – has served to legitimate certain artists and genres while excluding others. Challenges to the validity of authenticity and its presumed relationship to commercialism introduced more nuanced interpretations of art and commerce. In the 1980s and 1990s, encounters between independent musicians and mainstream music industries ultimately resulted in a re-evaluation of the role of major record labels: once viewed as the corporate enemy interested only in the bottom line, increasing interdependence between indies and majors recast majors as sometimes useful partners. In the same time period, rap stood out for championing consumer brands as potentially better, or at least more transparent, allies than the mainstream music industries. Partnerships with consumer brands were not a sign of commercial compromise or corporate submission for rappers, but evidence of a combined musical and entrepreneurial success that has driven the genre to its current domination of the mainstream music charts and that has provided a template to artists open to sponsorship, endorsement, product placement and licensing opportunities (which is to say, most artists).

At the turn of the twenty-first century, advertising took centre stage for its potential to fill a gap in revenue streams and provide an alternative to radio play. While the promises of big fees and widespread exposure turned out to be fantasy for all but some rare and lucky artists, the standardization of licensing as a revenue stream seemed to be the final nail in the selling out coffin. In previous eras, the concept of selling out was focused around particular themes: popular music as art, commercial success and excess, independence and cultural autonomy, racial authenticity and licensing to advertising. Today, there is no longer a category of activity that, in and of itself, is regarded as selling out in popular music culture. By exploring the broader contexts of the selling out debates in decades past, we can understand how perspectives of artists today have been shaped by cultural and industrial changes chipping away at boundaries between culture and commerce that once helped to define and justify popular music's artistic status. On the one hand, the concept of selling out has always been contentious and open to debate by inauthenticists, poptimists and pragmatists who recognize the impossibility of determining popular music as art solely through its proximity to commerce. On the other hand, there has been a consistent movement away from popular music idealized as art and towards popular music as partner to and province of consumer brands and multinational corporations. Claims that there's 'no such thing as selling out' (McCourt 2005, Berkmann 2010, Corr 2012, Eshun 2012, Molotkow 2012, England-Nelson 2015), that 'selling out no longer exists' (Fiorletta 2011, Richards 2011), and similar sentiments (Stevenson 2005, Hopper 2013) have increased in frequency and volume.

In Chapter 5, I noted the role of regulatory changes and promotional culture in shifting the attitudes of artists towards licensing music to advertising. In this chapter, I take a closer look at the major changes that have shaped the activities and perspectives of artists – including the consequences of digitalization, the rise of promotional culture (the presence of marketing strategies across all areas of life) and market-driven cultural policies – to explain why the last decade has seen an escalation and intensification of commercial activities for popular musicians, with the concept of selling out appearing evermore anachronistic. I look at the range of promotional activities that reflect the music industries in the age of the artist-brand (Meier 2017), and I consider how the quenchless desire of the promotional machine affects the popular musicians and popular music feeding it.

Digitalization: The cause of and solution to the music industries' problems

Digitalization has been a key factor in forcing a reassessment of ideologies that have formed a foundation for popular music culture since its validation as art in the 1960s. The shift in format from analogue to digital and, later and more importantly, the integration of music making and listening into personal computing, have had a transformative effect on the music industries and most everyday music activities. How we make and listen to music now relies largely, if not entirely, on digital technologies, from digital audio workstations to digital music files. The switch to digital may have been at its root technological, but the consequences of the switch have been profoundly cultural, reinventing experiences of owning, collecting and listening to music when no tangible form is required, and shaping the sound of music through digitally enabled techniques and opportunities (see Morris 2015, Strachan 2017). I focus here specifically on perceived threats to the revenue stream of recorded music sales enabled by digitalization, which opened the door to more and varied partnerships between artists and consumer brands.

 The transition to a digital music format for the sale of recorded music resulted in a series of unintended consequences. The introduction of the compact disc in the 1980s was, in a sense, just another point in the chronology of audio format replacement, which asked music fans to invest in new players and, at least in the case of favourites, to purchase the same album repeatedly. But the digital basis of CDs also signalled the end of physical audio formats. As Jeremy Morris points out, music on CDs is digital, but 'the CD commodity as a whole was only musically digital' (2015: 2) given that it was still bought, sold and owned as a physical form. It's the switch to digital music files that required 'a reconfiguration of the industrial models and mechanisms used to make, market, and move music commodities' in a way that earlier format changes did not (Morris 2015: 3).

In combination with the increased spread and speed of the internet in the late 1990s, digital music files obviated the need to purchase any music or music-specific hardware at all. For the music industries, the development of peer-to-peer networks of music distribution was a huge blow, both in terms of lost revenue but, perhaps more significantly, in terms of framing expectations of access and value for consumers. The music industries had confronted fears of widespread consumer piracy before – through the 'home taping is killing music' campaign of the 1980s, for example – but not on this scale, and user attitudes towards sharing online did not align with the criminal frame promoted by anti-piracy campaigns (Klein, Moss and Edwards 2015). While legal streaming platforms like Spotify have offered a model that has lured most consumers from the legally contested peer-to-peer networks, the threat to traditional revenue streams has hardly receded: in 2018, streaming generated the largest portion of the global music revenues pie, but overall revenues are only two-thirds of what they were in 1999, when digital music files began to challenge the dominance of CDs (Savage 2018a). There is less money for the traditional players (musicians, record labels) and the musicians who are benefitting from streaming are, in some cases, not the same as those who continue to see sales of physical formats (Caramanica 2018). Potential diversification through streaming is a minor victory for regions, genres and artists with less support from the traditional music industries. At the same time, the fact that physical sales do not directly map onto the digital music charts can be seen as another threat to the Big Three major labels (Sony, Universal and Warner), despite their enduring dominance across all charts. Revenue generated for the Big Three by artists with high traditional sales, but without a major presence in digital spaces, has a limited lifespan.

The growth of streaming also represents a broader power shift from the consumer electronics sector to the information technology sector (alongside telecommunication companies): non-music corporations have exercised increasing control over the music market, an example of 'the shift in consumer capitalism's frontiers from domestic consumption to networked mobile personalisation' (Hesmondhalgh and Meier 2017: 1562). Whereas the major music companies had strong relationships with consumer electronics companies – both were invested in improvements to sound quality that could lead to sales – for most technology companies, music is just one of many sources of data to be monetized. No longer able to unite around shared goals and aligned strategies, the music industries were faced with the challenge of building a relationship with the major technology companies.

The music industries responded to the threat of illegal downloading by targeting both individuals and platforms. The RIAA filed lawsuits against individual downloaders, which was terrible PR for the music industries, but did manage to freak out many would-be users of peer-to-peer platforms. The RIAA also focused their energy towards the platforms themselves, and the landmark 2001 case that the RIAA filed against Napster was ultimately successful in shutting down the most dominant peer-to-peer operations (see Klein, Moss and Edwards 2015 for an overview of competing positions around these copyright battles). Having built a temporary legal dam against this unintended and unanticipated consequence of the integration of music and computing technologies, the music industries then set out to use and invest in digital technologies to achieve their own objectives. Robert Strachan notes that 'despite the undoubtedly negative effects upon music sales resulting from illegal downloads and the significantly lowered revenue to be garnered from streaming services' music companies have 'successfully exploited Web 2.0 in terms of mediation and marketing' (2017: 35) as through campaigns intended to be perceived as 'viral' or DIY: 'Techniques such as viral marketing, co-creational engagement and social media campaigns tend to be part of highly orchestrated, carefully timed, multipronged campaigns' (Strachan 2017: 37).

Investment by the major music companies in streaming companies is another example of their strategic response to digitalization (Marshall 2015, Strachan 2017). The consolidation of the major music companies into the Big Three has translated into big power when it comes to negotiating with streaming and video-sharing platforms. With control over 80% of the music market, these conglomerates have been able to invest in Spotify (Marshall 2015, Singleton 2015), to exert pressure on YouTube to improve their system of copyright enforcement (Moskvitch 2018) and to secure favourable contracts with both (Moskvitch 2018, Wang 2019). Spotify's direct deals with independent or unsigned artists may make the conglomerates nervous (Sisario 2018) but the platform's reliance on the Big Three keeps the company in check.

The major music companies have also tightened their financial control through the development of multiple rights deals, also known as 360 contracts for their coverage of all potential artist revenue streams (Stahl and Meier 2012, Marshall 2013). Justified through 'the "just desserts" position in which labels emphasise the role that they play in building the artist's career' (Marshall 2013: 86) and the 'active partnership' position which 'asserts that labels will do much more for artists in the future' (Marshall 2013: 87), 360 contracts shift risk onto performers and maximize music companies' control, widening the gap that already existed between the few elite artists and the many (especially new) others (Stahl and Meier 2012). As Leslie Meier highlights, 360-degree monetization and multiple rights contracts reflect the shift towards corporate partnerships as a core music commodity: for example, Lady Gaga's multiple rights deal includes revenue from corporate partnerships with a range of consumer brands, from Polaroid to MAC (2017: 76). (The example of Lady Gaga recurs across this chapter. On the one hand, she's a mega pop star, so it's not surprising that she has lots of corporate partnerships. On the other, she has a declared commitment to music as art, which makes her an interesting case when it comes to balancing and articulating choices (Iddon and Marshall 2014).)

Digitalization has provided a mixed bag of opportunities and challenges for the music industries, and this is no less true of the impact of digitalization on artists. Digitalization has lowered the barriers to entry in terms of production (Strachan 2017), enabled many artists to sell music outside the major label system (Kruse 2010) and increased the potential reach of music to more listeners on a global scale than could previously be imagined. One consequence of the democratization of music-making, however, is that 'countless signed and unsigned artists now compete for audience attention, opportunities, and income' (Klein, Meier and Powers 2017: 227), and it has become more difficult for musicians to make a living. While superstars like the Rolling Stones or Katy Perry can rely on their established fame to sell out tours or to sell records to (increasingly older) customers, even the route to becoming a superstar has changed: the 'Pop 2.0' artists that thrive in the streaming environment mix genres and styles through production, instrumentation and collaboration, and 'are extremely gifted at self-presentation on social media' (Caramanica 2018). Choices that might have once attracted charges of selling out as attempts to reach larger audiences are, from this perspective, typical characteristics of digital music chart-toppers. The 'new, utterly modern, increasingly global pop' is marked by qualities like switching between rapping and singing, or English and non-English, genre hybridity and collaborations (Caramanica 2018).

Digitalization of the music industries encourages a transition for artists from creative producers to content providers and recasts the value of recorded music 'as data, rather than as a commercial form of artistic expression' (Negus 2019:

367). Recorded music acquires value as data not merely by attracting listeners (the source of value for traditional formats) but through its combined ability to convey information about listeners and to attract advertising. The mining of recorded music for its promotional potential has been encouraged by and supported within a broader culture increasingly geared towards promotion.

Promotional culture

The term 'promotional culture' was coined in 1991 by Andrew Wernick, who offered a broad definition to capture the idea that culture had become saturated by promotion to the extent that promotion and the object promoted cannot be separated. Wernick described the effect of the market pervading every aspect of life: 'It is as if we are in a hall of mirrors. Each promotional message refers us to a commodity which is itself the site of another promotion' (1991: 313). In a more recent contribution, Aeron Davis (2013) looks at active promotional practices, often but not always coming from the promotional industries. Promotional practices have been adopted far beyond those industries and 'ordinary individuals, in their day-to-day experiences, have both grown accustomed to a promotion-rich society and come to internalize and reproduce basic promotional practices' (Davis 2013: 3).

Space for promotional practices and discourse was opened by the rise of neoliberalism and its celebration of free-market capitalism across powerful Western democracies, including the US and UK, two major centres of the global music industries. The adoption of market-oriented discourse across public and cultural sectors both reflected and encouraged the pervasiveness of promotional language and ideology beyond their traditional place in promotional industries. As Davis writes,

> The rise of market power and the growth of promotion go hand in hand. Since the economic crises of the 1970s, neo-liberal free-market thinking has driven policy-making in the US, the UK and many leading economies. In turbo-charged Anglo-American-style capitalism, marketization and competition and, therefore, promotion have become more extreme.
>
> Davis 2013: 197

Areas of life that were previously considered public resources, among them schools and hospitals, became available for sale. For commercial cultural products like recorded music, promotional activities were always a feature, but the spread of promotional culture can be viewed as ushering such activities from the music company back offices and hands of promotional professionals to the public view and hands of artists. Partnerships between musicians and consumer brands erode distinctions between promoting popular music and promoting other products or services.

The growth of promotional culture has also served to define the generations of young people, including musicians, who have grown up in its neon glow. For many young people, consumerism and entrepreneurialism are natural approaches to performing one's identity. As Michael Serazio argues, if previous generations 'forged their connections and identities through trauma and political upheaval—perhaps producing a more durable self-consciousness from World War II or the 1960s unrest—commercial interests may well circumscribe millennials in the online worlds they inhabit, limiting any collective sense of self to the consumer marketplace' (2015: 601). And they are not just buying their way to a sense of self, they are also selling their way: 'The millennial affect is the affect of the salesman' and 'The self today is an entrepreneurial self, a self that's packaged to be sold' (Deresiewicz 2011). It makes sense that such an entrepreneurial orientation would come more easily to artists of that generation, and accounts of working musicians illustrate the prominence of entrepreneurial activities (Morris 2014, Haynes and Marshall 2018, Duffy and Pooley 2019), even if some musicians remain hesitant to embrace the term 'entrepreneur' (Haynes and Marshall 2018).

Promotional culture is thus wide-reaching, influencing the language and activities of entire sectors and large organizations, and filtering down to individuals, including musicians and fans. Paradoxically, as promotional practices have become more pervasive, the traditional realm of promotion in the music industries has declined: over time, less money has been invested in traditional strategies of promotion (e.g. magazine advertising, music videos). At the same time, promotion has only increased in importance for the music industries: 'Given the diminishing importance of manufacture and distribution to the recording industry, marketing and promotion occupy a position of increasing centrality as a core function of what major music companies do, and how they control access to the market' (Strachan 2017: 38).

Working with consumer brands and developing artists as brands are standard parts of the promotional strategy. Nicholas Carah (2010) describes the current environment for making popular music: 'Popular musicians are caught up in a branded and commodified social and cultural world ... The bundle of myths, meanings and identities crafted through popular music is attached to corporate brands and spaces' (2010: 64–5). Musicians, writes Carah, 'traverse a line between being reservoirs or conduits for the audience's perception of authentic and meaningful popular culture, and being strategic vehicles for the construction of valuable corporate brands' (2010: 65). The turn to corporate partnerships allows artists to piggyback on the marketing strengths of consumer brands but at a cost: if music's value is reduced to data when it's used by online platforms, then it's reduced to promotion in these relationships. Meier looks at partnerships between recording artists and brands, including licensing and endorsement deals, and argues that, while participation in such practices has 'opened up new opportunities for musicians, it also has engendered overwhelmingly commercial and promotional understandings of and assumptions regarding popular music and its role in society' (2017: 2). Meier's conceptualization captures a collapse of popular music and promotional activity as two separate spheres: from the promotion of popular music to popular music *as* promotion.

The importation of branding techniques from the traditional promotional industries into our everyday lives and the work of musicians has eased the collapse by highlighting the similarities in promotional culture between consumer products, popular music artists and ordinary individuals. As Sarah Banet-Weiser asserts, 'branding is different from commercialization or marketing: it is deeply, profoundly cultural' (2012: 14). 'Within contemporary brand culture', she writes, 'the separation between the authentic self and the commodity self is not only more blurred, but this blurring is more expected and tolerated' (2012: 13). Strategies of self-branding have emerged across mediated spaces, from reality television to social media, affirming the self as commodity and 'promotional object' (Hearn 2008: 214).

Cultural producers like popular musicians may have had a head start in understanding themselves as part of a commodity (for example, the music video age confirmed artist looks as an aspect of the package for sale). However, promotion is now as important, if not more important, than the music recordings it previously supported. In their update to Leo Löwenthal's 'The Triumph of Mass Idols', Brooke Duffy and Jefferson Pooley describe today's 'idols of promotion', whose self-descriptions include 'celebrations of promotional pluck' (2019: 42), which highlight success in a precarious labour market. They write, 'the eruption of self-branding rhetoric among today's idols is linked to the unsettling experience of you're-on-your-own workplace capitalism' (2019: 28). For artists, branding is not only a way to sell your musical product, but a new product to sell. The concept of the 'artist-brand' captures the new reality that the 'recording artist "personality" is the primary hub around which various "ancillary" products and licensing agreements may be forged' (Meier 2017: 4). Branding is occurring earlier and earlier in the careers of musicians. No longer limited to work that major labels will undertake with a signed artist, artists are expected to build their brand to make themselves attractive to major labels (Meier 2017: 78). Recent cases have revealed the promotional tail to be wagging the musical dog: social media influencers are among the media celebrities who have been signed by labels on the basis that they've already achieved the hard part (a brand and a fanbase) and labels can provide the easy part (songwriters) (Leight 2018).

For popular music, promotion has expanded from a set of activities that took place after the product was completed to encompass all dimensions of music's production, distribution and consumption (Powers 2013a). Its reach across time and space, beyond discrete activities, leads Devon Powers to declare a 'state of promotion', 'a condition of continual, habitual push' (2013a: 314) under which musical sound, musical labour and music technologies are marked by promotional qualities and objectives. Influence of the wider promotional culture on the 'state of promotion' for popular music has normalized the treatment of artists as brands and partnership opportunities with other brands.

Popular music and cultural policy

Popular music has been both explicitly and incidentally shaped by cultural policy (Cloonan 2007, Homan, Cloonan and Cattermole 2015): through cultural policy debates and direction, 'the state emerges as a key site for the playing-out of various seeming dichotomies – high versus low culture, music as art versus music as culture, public versus private interest, the right to make noisy art versus the right to a good night's sleep' (Homan, Cloonan and Cattermole 2013: 279). Responding to the challenges presented by digitalization and reflecting the promotional fervour growing in and outside the music industries, cultural policy from the 1990s onward has shored up the power of big conglomerates and positioned artists as entrepreneurs competing in a crowded market. With most artists getting less support from labels than they might have had in an earlier era, and with decreasing opportunities in the public sector and a tougher environment for independent artists unable to self-fund, partnerships with consumer brands are a sought-after source of support and revenue. Cultural policy has helped shift the discourse around music-making and commercialism: we can think of 'culture policy makers' as 'unwitting agents to marketing professionals' (McRobbie 1999: 23) because of the increasing role of industry sponsorship as a result of government cuts to arts, media and culture. This section explores some examples of cultural policy that have shaped not only specific practices of musicians, but the language around and understanding of what it means to be a musician in the twenty-first century.

Cultural policy formulated in response to digitalization challenges has consistently consolidated the strength of the already most powerful players, sometimes at the expense of independent, local or new artists. As noted in Chapter 5, media deregulation in the US, enacted through legislation like the Telecommunications Act of 1996, allowed large corporations to dominate the radio industry and led to low-risk and standardized playlists (Taylor 2007, Klein 2008a). In the US and the UK, industry attention soon turned to the threats posed by peer-to-peer filesharing and piracy: major players in the popular music industries used their lobbying power to ensure that legislators rehearsed copyright debates as mouthpieces for rightsholders. Copyright legislation became a battleground dominated by old powerful voices in the cultural industries and new powerful voices of technology corporations. The US Digital Millennium Copyright Act of 1998 and the EU European Copyright Directive of 2001 attempted to support copyright holders to fight piracy by placing greater responsibility on the online service providers. However, between the safe harbour provision that protects online service providers when they can reasonably deny knowledge of infringing activity, the overuse of takedown notices when no infringement has occurred and the scale and scope of policing the online world, both attracted criticism from those who want a stronger response and those who feel the current response is too strong (Klein, Moss and Edwards 2015). US and EU laws implement treaties agreed by the World Intellectual Property Organization (WIPO) and have thus been influential in shaping the terms of the debate in other member countries. The 2019 update to the EU Copyright Directive again pitted large news and entertainment corporations against online service providers, drowning out the voices of ordinary users or lesser-known working musicians, whose interests are more likely to involve freedom of expression than copyright exploitation.

Much cultural policy has since the 1990s adopted a tone which reflects (and shapes) the wider promotional culture detailed above. Cultural policy has determined how music should and could be funded, with a turn from state support towards free-market competition and sponsorship models. While some European countries still provide *dirigiste* commitments or other income benefits to support artists (Banks 2017), state support in the UK has taken a hit in recent years. David Hesmondhalgh et al. (2015) consider the increased role of sponsorship and philanthropy in cultural policy over the past few decades, pushed under Thatcher as an approach to reducing the public sector, and treated by New Labour as a complement to public spending (2015: 81–85). New Labour advanced the neoliberal notion of the cultural entrepreneur (Hesmondhalgh et al. 2015), cutting or over-structuring sources of state support and treating musicians as small businesses. While New Labour responded to criticisms of its Welfare to Work plans by incorporating a so-called 'rock'n'dole' scheme to support musicians who could prove they were seriously pursuing a music career (Slade 1998), the scheme presented off-putting hurdles to potential beneficiaries who might have relied on benefits previously: many of Britpop's key figures honed their skills while on the dole (Lister 1998). Additional cuts to state support of the arts have been applied by the coalition and Conservative governments that have followed New Labour with a programme of austerity measures. Giana Eckhardt and Alan Bradshaw link the erasure of antagonisms between popular music and advertising to a wider decrease in political or subversive music resulting from neoliberalism and the containment of radicalism under capitalism (2014: 180). To the extent that popular music has ever provided a space for opposition to capitalism, the promotional industries are unlikely to nurture such potential.

While UK musicians can at least (for now) rely on the support of the BBC to put lesser-known acts in the spotlight, in the US, the free market mentality has long challenged the necessity of state-supported media and arts subsidies, and the US government at the time of writing has proposed an end to federal funding of National Public Radio (NPR), the Public Broadcasting Services (PBS) and the National Endowment for the Arts (NEA). Setting aside the invaluable contributions of these services to news and children's programming, it's also the case that public radio provides an outlet for more diverse music offerings than commercial radio does. State subsidies of musicians represent a modest budget and examples like the NYC Women's Fund for Media, Music and Theatre – which offers competitive grants of up to $20,000 for musicians who identify as women to fund the creation of music recordings or videos – are rare. Even countries that have been historically more generous in their arts funding are re-appraising arts funding through an economic lens: while 'webs of financial assistance for music can be complex, and unique from country to country, the overall impression is of a funding landscape increasingly driven by market forces as much as cultural ones' (Hogan 2017).

So, policy that responded to the threat of digitalization has strengthened the power of music companies, and policy that responded to the growth in promotional culture (and the neoliberal and market ideologies feeding it) has worsened conditions for making music and taking risks. Music education in schools has been a recurrent victim of budget cuts in the US and UK, with music teachers forced to resort to fundraising. Banks notes the limited educational and career opportunities available to working class aspiring musicians in the UK, citing the 2013 contribution of pop singer Sandie Shaw to a Culture, Media and Sport Select Committee of the UK government 'that public-school educated, middle-class musicians were crowding out artists from more "challenging backgrounds" – a theory earlier suggested by the journalist Simon Price in his conjectures on the "poshification of pop"' (Banks 2017: 111). The role of cuts is direct and classed:

> as cuts are made to out-of-work benefits, and the opportunity to incubate and practice one's talent while subsisting on other forms of welfare or public subsidy have declined, then the chances of ordinary people making it in arts and culture are further diminished. Most such people are unlikely to be able to rely on their families (the so-called 'Bank of Mum and Dad') to subsidise the now obligatory internship, or low or unpaid work, while they strive to 'make it'.
>
> Banks 2017: 113

Exclusionary conditions for becoming a working musician reflect broader trends regarding opportunity and inequality in cultural production (O'Brien and Oakley 2015) and the over-representation of privately educated individuals in 'top jobs', including as pop stars (Weale 2019). The dominance of rap in the US illustrates the possibility of musical stardom for musicians from less privileged backgrounds but, as indicated in Chapter 4, rap developed out of limited educational and career opportunities for youth in inner cities – and the success of a small number of rappers does not represent the experiences of most young African-Americans, who continue to face social and educational inequalities.

Further, as the findings of *Valuing Live Music: The UK Live Music Census 2017* demonstrate, artists that manage to overcome initial hurdles to build a career may find themselves without suitable performance venues or faced with pressure to perform for exposure alone (Webster et al. 2018). A 2019 Digital, Culture,

Media and Sport Committee report on live music recommends greater government support of grassroots talent, music education and music venues, and identifies particular challenges faced by urban music acts whose gigs have been unfairly targeted by police (DCMS 2019). While even Ed Sheeran, the most successful UK musician of 2018, has highlighted the importance of state subsidies for artists (Cauldwell-French and Lydford 2019), struggling musicians would be advised to not hold their breath.

Popular music and promotional activities

The above account, while not exhaustive, gives a taste of the context that has developed since the 1990s, and intensified more recently, against which artists' own promotional activities and partnerships with consumer brands have become normalized and celebrated. In this section, I consider the activities involved in being a brand and working with brands in order to demonstrate the centrality of promotion for today's artists. As well as the imperative to self-promote in a crowded online market, artists must be open to partnerships with consumer brands, with the most successful going on to develop their own consumer brands. Even the activities of making and distributing music are geared towards promotion. Within the music industries, there is increasing awareness of the types of popular music that are ideally suited to music apps and corporate partnerships. Some superstar musicians have answered the question of how to profit from music by investing in music platforms, a tacit acknowledgement that the big money is in technology, not songs.

Working musicians juggle more activities than ever before, with many centred on promotion. Drawing on data collected through the Future of Music Coalition's Artist Revenue Streams project, Kristin Thomson (2013) highlights the proliferation of roles and responsibilities for working musicians, including opportunities offered by technology, like the possibility of global distribution without selling rights, as well as attendant challenges: musicians have to manage many activities and many income streams that may only produce a very small amount of revenue. Drawing on the same survey results, Peter Dicola notes, for example, that 'merchandising, branding, and licensing of one's persona make up only a tiny fraction of musicians' revenue, despite the increased prevalence of social networking' (2013: 338). The normalization of social media participation for musicians as cultural producers comes with a heavy admin burden (Maclean 2016). Still, for most musicians, even DIY practitioners who may be sensitive to issues of commercialism (Jones 2020), merchandise will be produced, Instagram and Facebook accounts will be curated and hope will be placed in online advertising and streaming revenue. These activities may rarely lead to significant profits, but the work of being a brand is a necessary and constant factor for artists who seek the possibility of rewards.

Elements of branding and self-promotion have always played a part in the work of popular musicians, but where musicians in previous eras relied on the support of those in professional roles to manage their activities and appearances, for all but superstar artists, many or most promotional activities are now down to the musicians themselves. The 'forever on' nature of online media means that performance is no longer cordoned off from everyday life. Artists are expected to spend their 'time off' supporting their brand through visible and regular presentation of their authentic selves.

The technology companies that dominate social media and streaming have been mythologized for the democratized opportunities they offer smaller and independent artists, but the orientation of these companies to popular music is closer to that of consumer brands than record labels. Like consumer brands, 'technology giants' use of content also reflects the specificities of their business models' (Meier 2017: 161): in both cases, companies use music to achieve their own separate goals, rather than profiting from the music content itself, as record labels do (or did) through sales.

The case of Arctic Monkeys demonstrates key aspects of Web 2.0 mythology, while also drawing attention to its over-romanticization and limitations, and in particular the ways in which online platforms are not replacing the work of record labels. Songs from the group's 2004 demo were distributed on MySpace and message boards, building their popularity, which ultimately resulted in signing to Domino Records and a debut single ('I Bet You Look Good on the Dancefloor') that went straight to number 1 on the UK singles chart. In this case, the band has claimed to have not even been aware of MySpace, but the story of Arctic Monkeys remains central to the mythology of Web 2.0 as offering music communities the ability to bypass traditional gatekeepers and methods of distribution. That Arctic Monkeys (and other bands who received attention through social media) still signed to a record label tells us that there remains value attached to traditional methods of distribution. Reinforcing this point, in 2019, audio streaming platform Spotify stopped its programme that allowed independent artists to upload their music directly, instead encouraging unsigned artists to work with their distribution partners (Spotify 2019a).

Some artists have turned to crowdfunding platforms like Kickstarter to finance part or all of the activities involved in making music, releasing music and touring. Alternative rock artist Amanda Palmer is an early success story, having raised over $1 million in 2012 for a new album pre-order campaign on Kickstarter. A great deal of promotional work is involved in drumming up interest and investment. 2018 documentary *Kate Nash: Underestimate the Girl* concludes with the singer-songwriter's crowdfunding campaign for 2017 album *Agenda*: 'Hi, I'm Kate Nash, and I want my fans to be my record label!' The segment illustrates the exhausting work of selling oneself required for a successful crowdfunding campaign: 'You're on the internet constantly. Even then you might not get all the money that you want' (*Kate Nash: Underestimate the Girl* 2018). Combining the popularity of online music services with the renewed interest in vinyl among younger listeners, in 2019, online music company Bandcamp launched a vinyl crowdfunding and pressing service, taking back some of the functions of a record label, though still requiring artists to attract buyer commitment in advance.

What these online services reflect is that the ability to 'Do It Yourself' online enabled by Web 2.0 comes with great promotional responsibility. Artists have to build a brand and build up a fanbase in order to access opportunities to make, release and tour in support of music. Even with label support, artists are expected to perform much of the work of promotion, and particularly online work, intended to lower the risk of investment. Some artists seek and receive support from fans, who shoulder part of the promotional burden. Fan labour is a key element and attached to core values for some music scenes: Nancy Baym and Robert Burnett focus on the role of fan support and labour in the Swedish independent music scene, though argue that 'this kind of voluntary fan effort can be seen throughout the music industry, and speaks to the fundamental changes that global industry is experiencing as the music business increasingly shifts to digital formats' (2009: 434). Bart Cammaerts (2010) similarly discusses new promotional activities for independent labels and artists, and the important role of fans. While fans can potentially fill the gap when it comes to the many sites where bands are expected to have a presence (Baym and Burnett 2009), it is also the case that artists put time and effort into their relationship with fans to propel such supportive behaviour (Baym 2018).

Between the orientation of online platforms as more closely aligned with consumer brands than record labels, the pressures of maintaining a brand and online presence, and the expectation that artists take on the risks and perform the promotional work that was once expected of a label, it is no surprise that partnerships with consumer brands have become ever more attractive as a source of support and revenue. Likewise, it is understandable that versions of selling out that have provided a locus of debate in previous decades, as documented throughout the book, seem less relevant to the current generation of artists (Taylor 2012), who are negotiating their relationship to capitalism by trying to accrue capital without having their work reduced to making money (Baym 2018).

Evolving consumer brand partnerships

Today, partnerships with consumer brands reflect and extend those strategies described in previous chapters: sync licensing, sponsorships, endorsements and product placement remain important tools in the arsenal within the dozens of revenue streams contributing to the incomes of working musicians (Future of Music Coalition n.d.).

Advertising is still a key destination for licensed popular music: according to IFPI's 2019 Global Music Report, synchronization licensing represents 2%, or $400 million, of the $19.1 billion total global recorded music revenues (IFPI 2019). While a comparatively small percentage, a licensing deal can make a significant difference to an independent artist or label. However, as suggested in Chapter 5, fees for sync licenses have decreased in tandem with the stigma of selling out. Further, because of the ubiquity of music placement, artists need to do more than licensing music – which often involves artists chasing the brands, rather than the other way around (Meier 2017: 100). Meier identifies 'a shift from the brand as broker to the brand as creator or curator model' as the next phase in popular music's colonization (2017: 101). These brand-music partnerships involve various strategies underpinned by a convincing fit between the consumer brand and artist-brand, with the latter lending the former authenticity. In the era of ubiquitous licensing, the conferral of authenticity requires a more involved relationship between artist and brand than a sync contract. Thus, the most desirable campaigns for brands (and the most financially lucrative for artists), may include licensing, but go beyond licensing to include endorsement and sponsorship arrangements. For endorsement and sponsorship deals to be perceived as 'authentic', pairings between consumer brand and artist rely on a personal link to an artist's lifestyle or persona (Meier 2017: 105).

In the online environment, we see examples of artist associations with brands over which artists have little or no control. Advertising-supported video platforms and Spotify's curated playlists are two examples of spaces where brands choose which artists suit their needs without the demand for artist consent. Such examples are similar to sync licensing in terms of forging an association between artist and brand, but do not require copyright holder consent beyond the artist's presence on the platforms. An advertisement before a music video allows a brand to borrow the cool of the artist for the price of video ads rather than a sync license. YouTube's 2018 deal with Vevo, the video hosting service owned by the major music companies, allows YouTube to sell music video clips directly to advertisers, enabling brands to advertise on artists' and labels' YouTube channels (Kafka 2018). That said, it's also the case that YouTube intends to increase the number of ads between music videos in automatically generated playlists in order to frustrate users into subscribing to its paid service. As YouTube's Global Head of Music Lyor Cohen puts it, 'You're not going to be happy after you are jamming "Stairway to Heaven" and you get an ad right after that' (Breihan 2018). (Cohen's role since 2016 as YouTube's Global Head of Music underscores the centrality of music to video platforms: Cohen has been a major player in the music industries since the 1980s, including, as mentioned in Chapter 4, as president of Def Jam Recordings.)

Music streaming services offer another space for brands to unilaterally bond themselves to artists. For example, artists who appear on Spotify's brand-curated playlists are not approached for consent, but nor are they likely to protest: in Liz Pelly's outstanding piece on Spotify's worrying model, Deerhoof drummer Greg Saunier describes:

> And so, if some absolutely infamous Sweatshop-Owning Shoe Company decides to include you in their playlist to make them look hip, are you going to complain? No. What a joke ... And if Nike is the one putting the song on their playlist, then well, your lips are now touching their Nike shoes. Because that's your ticket to something other than absolute oblivion.
>
> Pelly 2017

Pelly describes the brand-curated playlists as 'the automation of selling out', a model which conveniently removes the need to pay artists (Pelly 2017).

There may be more opportunities online for brands to create a unilateral association with an artist, but artist buy-in has its benefits. Sponsorship and endorsement deals remain popular, though with new twists and, like licensing to advertising, without the heavy baggage of selling out that informed decision-making in previous eras. Consumer brands continue to sponsor music festivals and tours, but have also found new ways to support and build alliances with artists. A band that has attracted a lot of attention for extending the terms of sponsorship to the funding of music videos is Chicago-based OK Go (Meier 2017). The alternative rock group is known for their clever, viral videos, the first of which (treadmill-based 'Here It Goes Again') attracted brands to sponsor subsequent videos: State Farm, Google and Chevrolet are among the sponsors. As bassist Tim Nordwind explains,

> It's always been a very transparent relationship. They're not trying to be creative necessarily, but they know that lots of people watch our videos and they don't fast forward through them. They want to be connected with something that they feel is cool, and we thank them at the end for making this creative thing happen. It's a win-win for everybody, because we get to make the things that we want to make, and they get to be attached to something that a lot of people like.
>
> Quoted in McIntyre 2015

Few bands will be given the number and type of opportunities that OK Go have taken, but the group's approach represents the new model of sponsorship, enabled in part by changing attitudes towards selling out. Brand partnerships are a source of pride, not shame. A 2018 *Atlantic* article, for instance, documented the Instagram influencers faking sponsored content as brand partnerships have gone from challenging credibility to demonstrating credibility: 'A decade ago, shilling products to your fans may have been seen as selling out. Now it's a sign of success' (Lorenz 2018). The same can be said for many musicians, who are happy to acknowledge brand affiliations alongside other successes.

Endorsement deals, whereby an artist endorses a brand and the brand implicitly endorses the artist, typically require a deeper social investment for both parties. Like sponsorships, such deals have evolved and now signal the depth of the relationship in less direct ways. Where once an artist would be expected to act as spokesperson, now the deal may entail a nominal role and some creative involvement for the artist: 'Simply signing an endorsement deal with a brand is starting to look as passe as having no brand partnerships at all, as artists and corporations become intimately involved in ways that would have been unheard of even a decade ago' (Barker 2013). Artists are named creative directors for the consumer brands they endorse (Lady Gaga for Polaroid, Pharrell Williams for Karmaloop TV and Justin Timberlake for Bud Light, for example) and 'traditional endorsements have evolved' to give brands an investor role in artists (Barker 2013).

Product placement offers brands and artists a lower level of commitment and, once again, the fading relevance of selling out has paved the way for corporate brands to appear on stage and in videos. Clay Craig, Mark Flynn and Kyle Holody's (2017) celebratory assessment of the possibilities for relationships between brands and popular music through product placement highlights the increase in recent years of product mentions in lyrics, particularly in rap. Such mentions are rarely paid – there have been rumours of brands willing to pay, but scant evidence of artists taking up the offer – though product placement in music videos is now commonplace. The omnipresence of Beats products in music videos by artists including TI and Pharrell, Nicki Minaj, Coldplay and Lily Allen is not simply a testament to their quality. Lady Gaga's 'Telephone' is an example that proved particularly fertile for product placement (Meier 2017): the video includes at least nine products, including Virgin Mobile, Miracle Whip, Diet Coke and dating website Plenty of Fish, though 'only a handful were paid placements' (Hampp 2010), an odd detail reminding us that commercial culture is part of popular culture (McAllister 2003), whether or not it actively seeks to colonize popular music.

For musicians, corporate support is defended in part as an alternative to the traditional record label model, with brands cast as benefactors (in the words of OK Go's Nordwind, 'We started finding brands that wanted to sponsor our videos as patrons of the arts' (McIntyre 2015)). It's a defence with precedents, as previous chapters have documented: the relationship of rap to consumer brands emerged in part as a response to unsupportive music industries, and some artists who licensed music to advertisements used the revenue to maintain their creative independence. However, artists who avoid a restrictive label deal by partnering with a 'lifestyle' brand should take note that 'partnering brands are actually less invested in marketing *music* because they have less of an ownership stake in the artist. Instead, music is a device for marketing these brands' (Meier 2017: 80, emphasis in original).

Strategies that locate consumer brands within the music industries can seem more genuine, and no doubt there are individuals employed by consumer brands who really care about music and the musicians with whom the brands work. Converse, Red Bull, Starbucks and Mountain Dew are among the brands that have invested in recording studios or record labels aimed at supporting musicians rather than turning a profit. Indie electronic duo Matt and Kim were one of the first artists to release a single on Mountain Dew's Green Label Sound (2008's 'Daylight') and contributed to Converse's 'Three Artists, One Song' series of recordings in 2012. Matt Johnson explained that the Green Label Sound deal included a marketing campaign and allowed the duo to play $5 shows. Not naïve to the brand's objectives, he acknowledged, 'At the end of the day they're just trying to sell more of their product. But at the same time, they *are* supporting the arts. If you're willing to do it elegantly I think it helps both parties' (Dombal 2009, emphasis in original). Most labels launched by consumer brands at the height of the trend in the late 2000s have slowed their activities or ceased operating: brands can get the value they desire from music without putting in so much work. Shorter-term music-related projects provide material for social media advertising campaigns, a useful strategy for encouraging engagement with online advertising and cementing a reputation for supporting music at the same time. For example, the 2019 ad campaign for Levi's Music Project documents the brand's six month mentorship scheme for 13 Liverpool-based musicians, a time-limited, relatively low risk and low investment strategy for the brand to get involved in music making.

The indirect influence of brands

The above section explored the promotional strategies that bring together brands and artists and highlight the influence of consumer brands on popular music. Promotional culture also exerts a more subtle influence on the shape of music and the work of musicians. Musicians are aware of what themes and sounds are likely to open up opportunities; streaming platforms reduce the value of music to monetizable content; and even superstar artists turn to investments in consumer brands as a more reliable source of income.

While brands and artists reference an authentic fit as key to a productive partnership, it is also the case that certain sounds and messages are disproportionately sought after by advertisers. What Meier writes of sync licensing practices is reflective of a more general tendency in partnerships between brands and artists:

> Although a wide range of music may circulate within popular media as a result of sync licensing practices, they are characterized by a homogeneity or sameness in terms of the range of feelings that advertisers in particular attempt to evoke. While niche-specific sad, aggressive or sexy songs may be used in advertisements to a certain degree, there is an overriding bias toward music perceived as happy.
>
> Meier 2017: 120

If brand-artist partnerships privilege certain sounds and messages, we can also think of promotional culture as privileging music that makes money, with no particular aesthetic preference.

Keith Negus writes about promotional forces shaping content in terms of the reliance of digital conglomerates on generating revenue through advertising and the relatively insignificant role of recorded music in the digital economy. Through the reduction of music to content or data, 'The artistic qualities and effort that has gone into the composition, production and performance of music are irrelevant to how digital conglomerates make money' (2019: 376). Take the example of Spotify, the fastest growing music-listening platform and, with YouTube, largely responsible for the increase in music streaming revenue (despite the minimal benefits going into artists' pockets). Branding is an important part of the Spotify model (Morris and Powers 2015), not only through brand-curated playlists (mentioned above), but through Spotify-branded content (featuring a formulaic Spotify sound) (Pelly 2018), and advertising and branding opportunities leveraged across the platform through 'videos, audio, commercial breaks, clickable image pop-ups, overlays, the sponsoring of (extremely popular) Spotify-owned playlists, the sponsoring of live session videos, home page takeovers, and standalone advertisements' (Pelly 2017).

Spotify is in the business of making money from content; that the content happens to be music is almost incidental. Almost, because it is clear that Spotify understands the unique value of music to brands, apparent in the way the company describes the opportunity to reach Gen Zs and millennials through music: 'Our audience turns to Spotify to enhance their moods and moments, and the "happy" mood is something we're inviting advertisers into. Our "Level Up" package uses Spotify's streaming intelligence to target listeners during good vibes playlists, and serves an ad that matches the same upbeat mood' (Spotify 2019b). The negative response of Spotify premium users to the Drake promotion that placed the artist's photo on unrelated playlists (Savage 2018b) suggests that Spotify and its users are not necessarily on the same page in terms of the place of promotion in music consumption. The most dystopian visions of algorithmically organized music consumption point to the role of 'fake artists' on Spotify: composed tracks given prominent placement on playlists, credited to artists with no public profile, and, presumably, earning a lower royalty rate than actual artists (Ingham 2019). A recent 'mood' playlist suggests Sony is exploring a similar strategy (Ingham 2019) and the 2019 distribution deal between AI-generated music company Endel and Warner Music gestures towards future possibilities (Hu 2019).

Of course, AI music would hardly change the experience of streaming for artists, most of whom already cannot rely on streaming for significant income: the number of plays required to meet the monthly minimum wage in the US ($1,472) is out of reach for all but the most successful artists (Sanchez 2019). It's telling that even superstar artists are turning to investments in consumer brands, sometimes music- or technology-related, often beyond, and a far cry from bands making money on t-shirt sales.

Leslie Meier and Vincent Manzerolle (2019) demonstrate how online music platforms use partnerships with celebrity artists to generate interest and celebrity artists use partnerships with online music platforms to generate revenue through (sometimes ethically dubious) promotions. For example, Tidal teamed up with Kanye West in 2016 for the exclusive release of *The Life of Pablo*, though subscribers were later frustrated to see updated versions of the album released widely. Further, although Tidal positioned itself as a 'majority artist-owned company' with a commitment to paying artists a higher royalty rate than competitors, the artists who potentially stood to benefit the most were its investors, which included Jay-Z, Beyoncé, Rihanna, Kanye West, Nicki Minaj, Daft Punk, Jack White, Madonna, Arcade Fire and Coldplay's Chris Martin. The attractiveness of commercial partnerships (in this case with technology companies) for the most high profile and successful artists reveals the normalization of the commercial partnership-based model.

Artists with a combination of capital, connections and concept may choose to invest in their own brands, products and businesses, a practice with a long and successful history for rappers, as explored in Chapter 4. While the success of Dr Dre's Beats Electronics company, sold in 2014 to Apple for $3 billion, is an extreme unlikely to be replicated, it does provide an aspirational template for musicians with entrepreneurial flair. What was accepted and celebrated for rappers from the 1980s has in more recent years become more common for rock or pop artists who may have previously been accused of selling out for such ventures: Neil Young has been an outspoken critic of endorsement deals (explicitly through 1988 single 'This Note's for You'), but open to business ventures like establishing his PonoMusic company, which in 2014 launched a (now discontinued) PonoPlayer portable music player. From Gwen Stefani's L.A.M.B. clothing line to Liam Gallagher's Pretty Green fashion brand (now sold to a large sports retailer), from Lady Gaga's Joanne Trattoria to Moby's Little Pine vegan restaurant, not all ventures are successful but the movement of musicians into various business sectors is simply unremarkable. It is no coincidence that many of the richest musicians in 2019 count among their revenue streams successful non-music brands. In 2019, Rihanna was named the richest female musician in the world, with most of her revenue generated from brand partnerships and her Fenty Beauty brand (Pagano and Kim 2019).

Promotional fatigue

If the above account suggests a new normal in which brands drive the activities, sounds and value of popular music, then there is some evidence of cracks in this model. Promotional fatigue, a term sometimes used by retailers to describe shoppers overwhelmed by offers into inaction, is also an apt description of artists who find their work and lives centred on promotional rather than musical activities to the extent that a break from or stop to such commitments is desirable. Ed Sheeran has quit social media on more than one occasion, a decision that takes on additional meaning for artists whose marketing relies on and loyal fan base expects a social media presence (Kennedy 2015, *Telegraph* 2017). Some artists have quit social media to improve their mental health (for example, Selena Gomez), some have quit to concentrate on making music (Taylor Swift), and still others have quit as an objection to the privacy and data policies of the technology companies (R.E.M.'s Michael Stipe, new age musician Lorena McKennitt).

Social media influencers like Essena O'Neill (Hunt 2015) and Andy Jordan (Petter 2019) have expressed misgivings about marketing products through Instagram, especially those they don't actually use or support, underlining the emotional demands of constant public performance and brand partnership commitments. Social influencers, whose income may be entirely reliant on promotional activities like sponsored posts, risk the discomfort of disingenuous shilling; as promotional activities move from the periphery to the centre for musicians, a similar experience can be expected. As Meier notes, some big stars 'have started to redraw the eroded boundary between culture and promotion' (2017: 150), giving the example of Lady Gaga, whose increasing commitments to self-promotion and brand partnerships had the singer considering whether to quit making music altogether. Lady Gaga explained her perspective in a 2015 talk at the Yale Center for Emotional Intelligence:

> I have had to make decisions like, why am I unhappy? Okay, Stefani/Gaga hybrid person, why are you unhappy? Why is it that you want to quit music, a couple years ago? I was like, well I really don't like selling these fragrances, perfumes. I

don't like wasting my time spending days just shaking people's hands and smiling and taking selfies. It feels shallow to my existence. I have a lot more to offer than my image. I don't like being used to make people money. I feel sad when I'm overworked and that I just become a moneymaking machine and that my passion and creativity take a backseat. That makes me unhappy.

So what did I do? I started to say no. I'm not doing that. I don't want to do that. I'm not taking that picture. I'm not going to that event. I'm not standing by that because that's not what I stand for. And slowly but surely, I remembered who I am, and then you go home, and you look in the mirror, and you're like, 'Yes, I can go to bed with you every night.' Because that person, I know that person. That person has balls, that person has integrity, that person has an opinion.

Yale University 2015

I've included a lengthy excerpt here because such candour about the emotional effects of promotion-centred work on musicians is rare, no doubt in part because most musicians cannot afford to risk losing such opportunities. Lady Gaga is exceptional in this regard, but the feeling that making music is being crowded out by promotional activities is present in other gestures and statements, such as the ambivalence of DIY bands towards Facebook (DiBlasi 2018, Jones 2020).

In the end, most artists who quit social media return to the platforms, and in 2019 Lady Gaga, now an acclaimed actor as well as successful singer, launched her Haus Laboratories beauty brand exclusively on Amazon: 'I have a platform in the world. God gave me this voice for a reason, I don't know why, I ask myself that question all the time, but I'm sure as hell not going to put out a beauty brand that is going to drive insecurity and fear into people. This is about liberation' (quoted in Strugatz 2019). Even if moments of promotional fatigue are only temporary, they offer a prompt for important discussions about working conditions for musicians, the beneficiaries of promotional labour and the influence of promotional culture on the sound and meaning of popular music. Unfortunately, as this book charts, the language of selling out has been dismissed as irrelevant at precisely the moment that we seem to need it most. Discussions of popular music and the music industries have traded selling out discourse for promotional and entrepreneurial discourse, limiting our ability to resist or imagine alternatives.

Popular music culture and promotional culture have been dancing partners throughout the history of commercial popular music. This chapter has explored how the challenges of digitalization for the popular music industries have opened the door to a greater role for promotional culture, underpinned by the development of cultural policy increasingly entrepreneurial in spirit and economically minded in intention. I have looked at how these changes have encouraged the evolution of promotional activities and demanded more and more promotional labour of musicians. A key concern of the shift documented is that consumer brand partnerships and advertising-supported platforms only care about the aesthetics of popular music insofar as they can be monetized. As Meier argues, 'The music branding trend threatens to drown out more oppositional musics, not because critical or dissenting musics do not exist (they do), but because they may be crowded out by the sounds of upbeat music that permeate media and seep into commercial spaces' (2017: 143). The relationship of claims about selling out's irrelevance to the promotional state of popular music is circular: 'It turns out that the stigma associated with selling out actually had a market value insofar as it served to limit the number of artists interested in such opportunities' (Meier 2017: 160).

The loss of selling out discourse, its broader causes and implications, is not limited to popular music culture. Across the cultural industries, as well as in politics, journalism and education, we are witnessing a creeping acceptance of commercialism as the glue holding sectors together and the benefactor rewarding individual actors. In the concluding chapter, I draw out the themes that have emerged throughout the book and consider some revealing parallels from non-music worlds. Dismissal of the concept and language of selling out should be heeded as a warning sign that promotional culture is displacing ideas and activities that used to exist outside it.

7

Popular music and beyond

This book has focused on the commercialization of popular music culture through the lens of selling out, a discourse which since the 1960s has provided a route for policing the role of commerce in popular music. In recent years, attitudes towards selling out have relaxed amidst multiplying relationships between artists and consumer brands; the adoption of an increasingly promotional orientation by artists; and changing loci of money and power towards the technology sector.

The evolution of popular music culture's relationship to commerce is a symptom of broader patterns of commercialization. Decades of neoliberal and entrepreneurial ideology have encouraged us to look to the market to guide, support and advance the public and cultural sectors. Privatization has been put forth as a solution for stretched or ailing government services: explicitly, as when assets are sold off or industries deregulated, and implicitly, as when language and strategies of the private sector are imported to the public sector. Promotional culture has spread its wings to encompass both how we experience the world around us and how we present ourselves within it. In this concluding chapter, I look beyond the popular music world to offer snapshots of other areas of life that have had to make peace with processes of commercialization: journalism, education and healthcare. We could argue that the stakes involved in popular music culture are comparatively lower, and the loss of selling out for popular music simply a reflection of a world that can no longer accommodate idealistic divisions between culture and commerce. Instead, I propose the possibility that what has happened in popular music culture can be seen as driving change, rather than only reflecting it. I look at the values that the discourse of selling out has served to protect, possible effects of its loss, and where we might go from here.

Beyond popular music

As this account suggests, the commercialization of popular music culture was joined by critiques of commercialization only to a point. Commercialization and critique seemed to grow apace from the 1960s through the 1990s. Around the turn of the twenty-first century, whereas commercial opportunities continued to proliferate, critiques became muted, a change symbolized by the advancement of 'no such thing as selling out' arguments. Across other sectors, a similar pattern has taken hold: cultural sectors and formerly public sectors are re-conceived as markets open to investment by advertisers and private capital, changes that provoked concerns which eventually gave way to resignation, acceptance and celebration. In this section, I consider the commercialization of journalism, education and healthcare, sectors with arguably higher stakes than popular music, but which can also be seen as linked in important ways to the loss of selling out in popular music culture. As activists and academics continue to fight for spaces free from commercial control across affected sectors, the normalization of commercialization erects a challenging barrier to action.

The cultural industries have been continually shaped by waves of marketization since the 1980s (Hesmondhalgh 2013b). Convergence, enabled by digitalization, encouraged a proliferation of sales, mergers and arrangements with advertisers, models of which had already been set in motion through previous waves of privatization and deregulation. None of the cultural industries has been untouched by these changes. Like independent music, independent television has undergone major structural changes as a result of commercial pressures. For production staff in the sector, the space to create meaningful or serious programming has become limited, and many face a choice between selling out their values to work on programmes they don't believe in or leaving the industry (Lee 2018). Even the less 'popular' music industries have felt the forces of commercialization: both jazz (Chapman 2018) and classical music (Ritchey 2019) have been adopted as symbols of the success of neoliberalism, an assertion underlined by partnerships between musicians and powerful corporations. Of all the cultural industries, it is journalism that has attracted the most hand-wringing in terms of the potential impact of commercialization on democratic ideals.

For print journalism, digitalization presented a double whammy to advertising and subscriptions, the standard funding strands for most news organizations throughout the twentieth century. The reliance of newspapers on advertising was shaken up by the new world of digital advertising, where old rates didn't apply and other web-based companies offered advertisers target audiences by detailed demographics and preferences. Facebook and Google together enjoy over half of the digital advertising market in the US (Dang 2019). Subscriptions took a major hit from the introduction of online versions of publications: why would readers subscribe when they could get the same content for free? Over time, paper versions of major publications have taken a backseat to web versions, with online subscription models slow to translate into profits (though emboldened by successful subscription models in other areas like music, film and television).

For advertisers, journalism's crisis has been an opportunity. Aeron Davis (2013) describes a range of now standard promotional influences on news production, from the power of big corporate advertisers to the reliance on sources produced by public relations (PR) professionals. In recent years, advertisers have wielded significantly more control, abetted by digital technology. The result is what Mara Einstein (2016) calls 'black ops advertising': native advertising and content marketing, strategies which blur the line between advertising and editorial and which would have been viewed as outrageous in earlier eras, have managed to remake advertising into news-like stories and videos that we willingly share with friends and family.

The growth of news conglomerates in the 1990s raised concerns about newspapers increasingly serving the needs of advertisers and 'breaching separations that were said in the past to be essential for journalistic integrity' (Glaberson 1995). By the mid-2000s, the involvement of journalists in PR, a symbolic collapse of editorial-advertising boundaries, became more common: 'Under the old-school values, PR meant "selling out" and sacrificing honour for the corporate shilling. To some extent, this outdated opinion persists today, but clearly the profession is becoming more acceptable, as so many journalists are increasingly crossing over to the "other side"' (McCormack 2007). What is required in the competitive world of online journalism is illustrated by a founder of *Vice* dismissing the term 'sell out' as 'juvenile and naïve' (Grigoriadis 2003), and a profile of the *Huffington Post* quoting Andrew Breitbart's declaration that 'there is really no such thing as selling out' in the battle to be noticed online (Carr and Peters 2011).

The pressure on journalism to accommodate corporate sponsors and private investors has parallels in other areas of life that were previously considered public resources, but are now for sale, among them schools and hospitals (Davis 2013). From the early school years through to university, corporate sponsors have since the 1990s had a more visible and influential role in education. A 2001 news story on two US college students who agreed to be spokespeople for a credit card company in exchange for the company footing their education bill provides the context for why such an arrangement is celebrated rather than scorned:

> In a world where kindergartners learn to count with books created by Cheerios, where Channel One beams commercials into classrooms and where Coke and Pepsi compete for turf alongside hall lockers, this is the latest frontier, a perfect synergy between media- and marketing-savvy teenagers and companies desperate to capture the lucrative, yet elusive, youth market.
>
> Critics bemoan creeping commercialism in education, but Mr. Barrett and Mr. McCabe show how far it has already encroached. Students are not just surrounded by marketing tactics; they are adopting them. Among their peers, and First USA's competitors, there is neither shock nor accusations of selling out, but only, 'Why didn't I think of that first?'
>
> Zernike 2001

While the US can be seen as the global frontrunner and gross extreme in the commercialization of everything, other countries are often not far behind, as documented by Deborah Philips and Gary Whannel's (2013) account of how for-profit companies were enabled to enter into educational provision in Britain. In addition to funding educational institutions, companies have been invited to use schools as an advertising space and exercise sponsorship opportunities across a range of resources and activities. Some of the contributions of sponsors (for example, teaching packs and television programmes) even influence the shape of the curriculum.

The opening for the encroachment of commercial sponsors around the world has been the withdrawal of state support. Reduction in US government support for universities in the 1970s led to commercialization of higher education, from athletics to academics (Bok 2003). The 'promotional university' critiqued by Andrew Wernick in 1991 has embraced its commercial destiny, prompting important scholarly interventions into the marketization and corporatization of universities (Giroux 2009), from the branding of universities (Hearn 2010, Banet-Weiser 2013) to the 'assault on universities' which has resulted in an emphasis on vocational subjects and 'value for money' (Bailey and Freedman 2011). The feeling within the sector is, unfortunately, one of a horse bolted.

The role of commercial sponsors in British education is mirrored in healthcare, where sponsor support is leveraged across a wide range of activities and resources, including nursing posts, research, symposia and beds (Philips and Whannel 2013). Development of ethical guidelines has not slowed movement in the direction of private and commercial sponsorship. Again, the US provides a model of private sector healthcare for other countries to follow, despite the many problems it presents. In *America's Bitter Pill* (2015), Steven Brill explores the passage of the Affordable Care Act under Obama as an attempt to resolve inequalities and fix America's healthcare industry, highlighting endemic problems, from the profit-seeking deals of drug companies to outrageous charges for basic medical supplies and procedures. In order to remain profitable, private insurance companies charge different premiums for different customers, with coverage varying dramatically. It's no surprise that insurance companies have a bad reputation. One solution is for insurers to meet with Hollywood executives to try to control their image in film and television (Petersen 2002), a sad indictment of the promotional vacuum we find ourselves in.

If anything, the US should be a cautionary tale, but public systems like the UK's National Health Service (NHS) are increasingly incorporating the products and services of for-profit companies (often US-based) into their models. A lovely tradition like Finland's baby box – a starter kit provided by the government to expectant mothers (and symbolizing an equal start in life) (Lee 2013) – is re-imagined in the US as an opportunity to collect information for and distribute the products of advertisers, and to sell the concept back to countries with public systems. Canadian hospitals and NHS trusts in England and Wales have partnered with the US-based Baby Box Co. to provide the 'free' boxes to women. The entry of private companies into the baby box 'market' opens the door for commercial sponsorship and monetized data collection.

Reliance on philanthropists to fill funding holes in sectors like education and healthcare may seem less nefarious than the turn to for-profit companies and consumer brands, but philanthropic arrangements present similar issues and dynamics. Linsey McGoey (2015) considers the problems with philanthrocapitalism, using the Gates Foundation as a case study and highlighting impacts on education and healthcare. She argues that there is little oversight in how foundations choose to distribute their funds; some small organizations rely entirely on the large foundations for income, leaving them open to non-expert influence and uncertain futures; and the assumption that what benefits the philanthropist will benefit the community is simplistic and reductive. If we think of corporate sponsors or consumer brands as providing an almost philanthropic service to ailing sectors – whether music, journalism, education or healthcare – we must keep in mind that even actual philanthropists are driven by financial interests and are able to exert their power to shape sectors in ways that run contrary to the advice of experts. Global health issues prioritized by the Gates Foundation are often not aligned with the areas doctors and researchers have identified as having critical need and the greatest potential impact (McGoey 2015).

Popular music culture as both reflection and force

While examples of the commercialization of journalism, education and healthcare have at times attracted charges of selling out, as with popular music, such claims have become rare now that commercial companies are woven across the sectors. The most straightforward interpretation of the loss of selling out in popular music culture is that we're simply witnessing the reflection of broader cultural change: the commercialization of cultural and public sectors has normalized a market orientation and, for popular music culture, as elsewhere, the role of commerce, private companies and consumer brands is so commonplace that it is unlikely to cause outrage. However, we can also see the acceptance of commercialization in popular music culture as validating broader change and, indeed, as indirectly driving broader change.

In the introduction to this book, I described selling out discourse in popular music culture as an evocative and ordinary example of language used to police the commercial influence in culture. While many people may view the commercialization of journalism, education and healthcare as concerning, few would feel they have the necessary expertise to weigh in on the circumstances that have led to the current situation, the potential consequences for democracy and society, and the tools required to repair broken systems. Likewise, policy debates, including public consultations, that relate to issues of commercialization (for example, debates about the concentration of media ownership or the role of competition in drug pricing) are largely out of most people's conversational comfort zone, despite earnest attempts by policymakers to involve the public and encourage deliberation. At the same time, the impulse to challenge artists for selling out in popular music culture, and the debates that follow such charges, highlight values that matter to us and that we see as threatened by the role of commerce in society. 'Discourse is a practice not just of representing the world, but of signifying the world, constituting and constructing the world in meaning' (Fairclough 1992: 64), and selling out discourse works to monitor and protect values that are important to us.

While some of the values at the centre of selling out debates are relevant primarily to cultural sectors, others are clearly applicable to a wide range of goods and services that, depending on where and when you are in the world, have been, are or could be conceived as public, including journalism, education and healthcare. Revisiting the values traced throughout the book underlines the heavy lifting performed by selling out discourse across time and genre.

Chapter 1 explored how the introduction of selling out to the vocabulary of popular music culture communicated our belief in popular music as art, and our expectation that artistic integrity and authentic artistic expression rely in part on distance from commercial influence. While it is right that we interrogate notions of integrity and authenticity that aim to divide and exclude, they are values that respect popular music as art. Crucially, and mirroring debates in other art worlds, the role of selling out discourse is evidence that neither the commercial setting of popular music production and consumption, nor the commodity status of popular music, prevents us from experiencing or treating popular music as art. This is a lesson worth remembering when concerns of commercial influence are dismissed as irrelevant or too little, too late. There must be space for distinctions between commercial contexts that allow for artistic values to thrive versus those that potentially constrain them. Selling out in the arena rock era, the focus of Chapter 2, demonstrates that commercial and artistic success can co-exist; however, the scaling up associated with 'going commercial' – and the consequent distance of stars from fans, and distance of fans from each other – may challenge the sense of community that popular music, at its best, can forge. In the same era, artists who played with notions of authenticity and selling out reminded us not to take popular music *too* seriously and risk losing the value of pop.

The place of independent labels in popular music culture highlights the value of cultural autonomy and the belief among some musicians that such autonomy is unlikely to be achieved under the corporate and controlling approach of major record labels. Chapter 3 considered how the incorporation of independent labels into the major music companies (whether amicably or aggressively) has left little space for independence, though musicians continue to express the value of independence as important for supporting unconventional sounds and radical messages. As David Hesmondhalgh and Leslie Meier explain, 'what happened to indie and alternative music is arguably symptomatic of some broader changes in the relationship between business on the one hand and political, cultural and aesthetic opposition on the other, in a way that has significant implications for the very concept of "media independence"' (2014: 100).

Chapter 4's focus on the case of selling out in rap reinforces the importance of authenticity and community as meaningful values in popular music culture, though the threat here is not corporations or consumer brands – at least not directly. Rap's seemingly easier relationship with commercialism is a result of racism in the music industries and the experiences of the communities in which rap developed. The meaning of selling out in popular music culture does not exist in a bubble and forces outside of popular music culture will influence values inside it. The racial context of selling out has shaped the values of authenticity and community for rap, with powerful agents, including consumer brands and major recording companies, able to support or suppress such values through their influence.

Power is also central to understanding the use of popular music in advertising, one of the most visible examples of partnerships between musicians and consumer brands. Chapter 5 drew attention to the power dynamics inherent to such relationships. The normalization of popular music in advertising increases the power of marketers as gatekeepers, and the likelihood that advertising-friendly sounds and messages will be privileged. Popular music's use in advertising is designed to support the advertiser, not the other way around: 'Achieving brands' goals and building brand value is what popular music is *for* under this approach – a far cry from the language of "collaboration", "partnership" and "patronage" routinely used in relation to these arrangements' (Meier 2017: 86, emphasis in original).

As Chapter 6 indicated, we now find ourselves in an era of 'no such thing as selling out', which might suggest that values of artistry, integrity, authenticity, community, autonomy and power are no longer held by musicians and fans, or that activities previously regarded as selling out are no longer viewed as compromising those values. Cases of promotional fatigue among musicians can be seen as a crack in the veneer of supposedly happy partnerships and point to a different possibility: values of artistry, integrity, authenticity, community, autonomy and power continue to matter to musicians and fans, but the ability to express these values has been hindered.

Putting selling out back to work

The role of selling out discourse for monitoring and maintaining values makes it critical to challenge claims that activities previously regarded as selling out have been assimilated seamlessly into popular music culture. On the contrary, the loss of selling out and the proliferation of previously contentious activities have real and deleterious consequences.

The loss of selling out is bad for musicians. Celebrations of the role of consumer brands in popular music insist that companies are supporting musicians, but they can also be seen as working against the interests of artists. The centrality of promotion and branding linked to the commercialization of popular music culture justifies changes to areas of cultural policy that once offered support for musicians. It's difficult to challenge the tendency of cultural policy to privilege measurable financial benefits over the social benefits of music when similar promotional values have been adopted within popular music culture. A serious risk of stressing the economic benefits of public investment in the arts (over the social good) is that such a justification suggests 'no aspect of the welfare state is invulnerable' to the same expectation (Philips and Whannel 2013: 103). The growing reliance on consumer brand partnerships also magnifies the gap between superstars and everybody else. Although commercial opportunities like licensing to advertising or sponsorship are often celebrated as potential revenue streams for artists, in reality it is the superstars who least need the revenue who are offered the most lucrative opportunities.

The loss of selling out is bad for music listeners (or, that is to say, almost all of us). The commercialization of popular music culture normalizes a promotional orientation that we carry with us through everyday life. Although critiques of capitalism and commercialism persist in popular culture, these views do not seem to translate into consumer action. Popular television can critique big technology companies (see the *Doctor Who* episode 'Kerblam!' for a not-so-subtle satire of Amazon) or cynical merchandising (*The Boys*, for example, reimagines superheroes as public-image obsessed and merchandise crazy) with no discernible effect on behaviour or public debate. Without the language of selling out, we are hindered in our ability to transpose critiques of commercialism in popular culture to other marketized, privatized and commercialized areas of life.

The loss of selling out is bad for music. As observed in Chapter 6, partnerships with consumer brands favour happy music and happy lyrics, because they are the sounds and messages that most brands want associated with their products and services. As Leslie Meier (2017) explains, music that does not fit this mould continues to exist, but risks being excluded from commercial spaces. If we count Spotify's own and brand-curated playlists among those spaces, then the impact on what has become a normal mode of listening to and discovering new music is clear. Further, by privileging a narrow range of sounds and messages, the commercialization of popular music culture limits the potential of music to contribute to human flourishing and well-being. While aesthetic judgement has been (rightly) challenged by critics as oppressive or elitist, the danger of consumer brands and big technology companies is that they are in a sense aesthetically neutral: while there is evidence that they privilege happy sounds and happy messages, the more accurate charge is that they privilege whatever is believed to sell. As Mark Banks argues, '*politically*, we need to hang on to the idea that there is more to cultural objects than the commercial values they can expediently generate – evidenced not least in their capacities to objectively shape peoples' efforts to understand and live their own lives, and to live with others' (2017: 23, emphasis in original).

Although this book does not promise to solve the problems faced by musicians or to offer an alternative to the underlying structures that have produced the current conditions for making and listening to music, the story of selling out – its role in policing boundaries between culture and commerce, its declared irrelevance – reinforces the need to support musicians and protect their resources. The fight for better conditions for musicians should take into consideration the consequences of consumer brand partnerships, both on those artists who take up such opportunities and on those who choose to not take that path (but who are left with fewer commercial-free opportunities). Collective action is key to rectifying the revenue problems that have led to a reliance on brands: Meier recommends collaborations with artist organizations on guidelines for fair remuneration and treatment, and urges artists to consider a 'collective "no"' which 'packs a much bigger punch than a more individualistic approach' (2017: 150).

Greater opportunities for public deliberation of cultural policy would help to ensure that the voices of artists and fans are not drowned out by old powerful voices in the cultural industries and new powerful voices of technology corporations. As the case of copyright demonstrates, parties disagree about the form and function of cultural policy, and ordinary users or lesser-known working musicians are unlikely to share the same concerns about protecting revenue as those that stand to profit the most (Klein, Moss and Edwards 2015). In *What Money Can't Buy: The Moral Limits of Markets*, Michael Sandel submits, 'Our only hope of keeping markets in their place is to deliberate openly and publicly about the meaning of the goods and social practices we prize' (2012: 202). The work of organizations like the Washington DC-based Future of Music

Coalition, which communicates issues that working musicians face, identifies solutions and advocates for change, is indispensable to the deliberative process.

As well as the fight for change, we face a fight to defend and promote those spaces that can challenge commercialism. Public service broadcasting and quality music journalism remain valuable boosters of artists who go against the commercial tide. The demise of traditional gatekeepers heralded by the internet can be seen in a new light, given the powerful gatekeeping role of technology companies. As noted in Chapter 6, government reports have acknowledged the need to support grassroots talent, music education and music venues, but unless real action is taken, opportunities will continue to dwindle. David Hesmondhalgh's (2013) analysis of singing together as an ordinary form of musical participation broadens the scope of activities that may forge musical sociality and extends the idea of communality we attach to music; both formal and informal chances to participate in music must be valued and preserved.

What I hope this book has accomplished towards these ambitious ends is to illustrate the work that selling out discourse does to communicate and protect values that matter to us and to highlight the threat that commercialism poses to those values. The impulse to charge a musician with selling out should not be dismissed as naïve, unrealistic or unfair, but should be redirected to the real culprits. The choices of individual artists are guided by the circumstances they find themselves in as a result of corporations (music or otherwise) that put profits above all else. Do the corporations involved in the production, distribution and consumption of popular music treat it as art? Are values of integrity, authenticity, autonomy and community supported? Where is power located and how is it wielded? We must ask these questions in defence of popular music culture. As the tendrils of commercialism expand their reach and tighten their grip across diverse sectors, saving popular music culture might just help save the world.

References

Adorno, Theodor (1990), 'On Popular Music', in Simon Frith and Andrew Goodwin (eds), *On Record: Rock, Pop, and the Written Word*, 301–14, London: Routledge.
Adorno, Theodor and Max Horkheimer (1999), 'The Culture Industry: Enlightenment as Mass Deception', in Simon During (ed.), *The Cultural Studies Reader*, 31–41, London: Routledge.
Allan, David (2008), 'A Content Analysis of Music Placement in Prime-Time Television Advertising', *Journal of Advertising Research,* 48(3): 404–17.
Ardery, Julia S. (1997), '"Loser Wins": Outsider Art and the Salvaging of Disinterestedness', *Poetics,* 24(5): 329–46. https://doi.org/10.1016/S0304-422X(96)00015-0.
Arnold, Gina (1993), *Route 666: On the Road to Nirvana*, New York: St. Martin's Press.
Aronczyk, Melissa (2013), *Branding the Nation: The Global Business of National Identity*, Oxford: Oxford University Press.
Aronczyk, Melissa and Devon Powers (eds) (2010), *Blowing Up the Brand: Critical Perspectives on Promotional Culture*, New York: Peter Lang.
Austerlitz, Saul (2014), 'The Pernicious Rise of Poptimism', *New York Times Sunday Magazine*, 6 April: 48–9. Available online: www.nytimes.com/2014/04/06/magazine/the-pernicious-rise-of-poptimism.html.
Azerrad, Michael (2001), *Our Band Could Be Your Life: Scenes from the American Indie Underground 1981–1991*, New York: Bay Back Books.
Bailey, Michael and Des Freedman (eds) (2011), *The Assault on Universities: A Manifesto for Resistance*, London: Pluto Press.
Banet-Weiser, Sarah (2012), *Authentic™: The Politics of Ambivalence in a Brand Culture*, New York: New York University Press.
Banet-Weiser, Sarah (2013), 'Rate Your Knowledge: The Branded University', in Matthew P. McAllister and Emily West (eds), *The Routledge Companion to Advertising and Promotional Culture*, 298–312, New York: Routledge.
Banks, Mark (2006), 'Moral Economy and Cultural Work', *Sociology*, 40(3): 455–72.
Banks, Mark (2010), 'Autonomy Guaranteed? Cultural Work and the "Art–Commerce Relation"', *Journal for Cultural Research,* 14(3): 251–69. https://doi.org/10.1080/14797581003791487.
Banks, Mark (2017), *Creative Justice: Cultural Industries, Work and Inequality*, London: Rowman and Littlefield.
Baraka, Rhonda (2001), 'The Billboard/BET R&B Hip-Hop Conference Awards: Profit by Association, Mainstream Marketers Step Up Their Courtship of Black Pop', *Billboard*, 1 September.

Barker, Andrew (2013), 'Branding Deals with Pop Stars Go Beyond the Casual Endorsement', *Variety*, 16 April. Available online: https://variety.com/2013/music/features/endorsement-deals-1200334594/.

Barnhard, Rachel and Jack Rutledge (2009), 'Music + Ads: Advertising Is the New Radio', *Adweek*, 4 June. Available online: www.adweek.com/brand-marketing/music-ads-advertising-new-radio-99496/.

Battersby, Christine (1989), *Gender and Genius – Towards a Feminist Aesthetics*, London: Women's Press.

Baumann, Shyon (2001), 'Intellectualization and Art World Development: Film in the United States', *American Sociological Review*, 66: 404–26.

Baym, Nancy K. (2018), *Playing to the Crowd: Musicians, Audiences, and the Intimate Work of Connection*, New York: NYU Press.

Baym, Nancy K. and Robert Burnett (2009), 'Amateur Experts: International Fan Labor in Swedish Independent Music', *International Journal of Cultural Studies*, 12(5): 433–49.

BBC (2017), 'Waterstones under Fire for Secret Shops', *BBC News*. Available online: www.bbc.co.uk/news/business-39101186.

The Beatles (2000), *The Beatles Anthology*, San Francisco, CA: Chronicle Books.

Becker, Howard S. (1984), *Art Worlds*, Berkeley, CA: University of California Press.

Behr, Adam, Matt Brennan and Martin Cloonan (2016), 'Cultural Value and Cultural Policy: Some Evidence from the World of Live Music', *International Journal of Cultural Policy*, 22(3): 403–18.

Belfiore, Eleonora (2015), '"Impact", "Value" and "Bad Economics": Making Sense of the Problem of Value in the Arts and Humanities', *Arts and Humanities in Higher Education*, 14(1): 95–110.

Belfiore, Eleonora (2018), 'Whose Cultural Value? Representation, Power and Creative Industries', *International Journal of Cultural Policy*, https://doi.org/10.1080/10286632.2018.1495713.

Berkmann, Marcus (2010), 'No Such Thing as Selling Out', *Independent*, 21 October. Available online: www.independent.co.uk/voices/commentators/marcus-berkmann-no-such-thing-as-selling-out-2112070.html.

Blanco, Alvin (2011), 'Run-DMC Recall "My Adidas" Impact, 25 Years Later', *MTV*, 11 November. Available online: www.mtv.com/news/1674282/run-dmc-my-adidas/.

Bok, Derek (2003), *Universities in the Marketplace: The Commercialization of Higher Education*, Princeton, NJ: Princeton University Press.

Boltanski, Luc and Eve Chiapello (2005), *The New Spirit of Capitalism*, trans. G. Elliott, London: Verso.

Bourdieu, Pierre (1996), *The Rules of Art*, Cambridge: Polity Press.

boyd, danah (2014), '"Selling Out" Is Meaningless: Teens Live in the Commercial World We Created', *Medium*, 27 May. Available online: https://medium.com/message/selling-out-is-meaningless-3450a5bc98d2.

Brackett, David (1999), 'Music', in Bruce Horner and Thomas Swiss (eds), *Key Terms in Popular Music and Culture*, 124–40, Oxford: Blackwell.

Brackett, David (2016), *Categorizing Sound: Genre and Twentieth-century Popular Music*, Oakland, CA: University of California Press.

Branigan, Tania (2001), 'Courtney Lashes Out at Music Industry for "Destroying Cobain"', *Guardian*, 11 September. Available online: www.theguardian.com/culture/2001/sep/11/artsfeatures.

Breihan, Tom (2018), 'YouTube to "Frustrate" Users With Ads So They Pay for Music', *Stereogum*, 22 March. Available online: www.stereogum.com/1988077/youtube-to-frustrate-users-with-ads-so-they-pay-for-music/news/.

Brill, Steven (2015), *America's Bitter Pill: Money, Politics, Backroom Deals, and the Fight to Fix Our Broken Healthcare System*, New York: Random House.

Brown, Jane D. and Kenneth Campbell (1986), 'Race and Gender in Music Videos: The Same Beat but a Different Drummer', *Journal of Communication*, 36(1): 94–106.

Bruno, Antony (2009), 'Synch Placement in a TV Ad for Apple: Spots Still Deliver Boost, but to Fewer Songs', *Billboard*, 26 September: 14.

Burston, Paul (1999), 'Lightning Strikes Twice', *Guardian*, 23 January. Available online: www.theguardian.com/theguardian/1999/jan/23/weekend7.weekend4.

Cagle, Van M. (1995), *Reconstructing Pop/Subculture: Art, Rock, and Andy Warhol*, London: Sage.

Cammaerts, Bart (2010), 'From Vinyl to One/Zero and Back to Scratch: Independent Belgian Micro Labels in Search of an Ever More Elusive Fan Base', Media@LSE Electronic Working Papers, No. 20. Available online: www2.lse.ac.uk/media@lse/research/mediaWorkingPapers/ewpNumber20.aspx.

Carah, Nicholas (2010), *Pop Brands: Branding, Popular Music, and Young People*, New York: Peter Lang.

Caramanica, Jon (2018), 'How a New Kind of Pop Star Stormed 2018', *New York Times*, 20 December. Available online: www.nytimes.com/interactive/2018/12/20/arts/music/new-pop-music.html.

Carr, David and Jeremy W. Peters (2011), 'Big Personality and Behind-the-Scenes Executive Prove a Top Media Team', *New York Times*, 8 February: Section B.

Cartwright, Joanna, Helen McCormick and Gary Warnaby (2016), 'Consumers' Emotional Responses to the Christmas TV Advertising of Four Retail Brands', *Journal of Retailing and Consumer Services*, 29: 82–91. https://doi.org/10.1016/j.jretconser.2015.11.001.

Cauldwell-French, Evy and Annie Lydford (2019), *Public Investment, Public Gain: How Public Investment in the Arts Generates Economic Value Across the Creative Industries and Beyond*, Creative Industries Federation and Arts Council England. Available online: www.creativeindustriesfederation.com/news/report-launched-public-investment-public-gain.

Century, Douglas (2006), 'Jay-Z Puts a Cap on Cristal', *New York Times*, 2 July. Available online: www.nytimes.com/2006/07/02/fashion/02cris.html.

Chapman, Dale (2018), *The Jazz Bubble: Neoclassical Jazz in Neoliberal Culture*. Oakland, CA: University of California Press.

Chapple, Steve and Reebee Garofalo (1977), *Rock'n'Roll is Here to Pay: The History and Politics of the Music Industry*. Chicago: Nelson-Hall.

Chiapello, Eve and Norman Fairclough (2002), 'Understanding the New Management Ideology: A Transdisciplinary Contribution from Critical Discourse Analysis and New Sociology of Capitalism', *Discourse & Society*, 13(2): 185–208.

Cloonan, Martin (2007) *Popular Music and the State: Culture, Trade, or Industry?*, Aldershot: Ashgate.

Coates, Norma (1997), '(R)evolution Now? Rock and the Political Potential of Gender', in Sheila Whiteley (ed.), *Sexing the Groove: Popular Music and Gender*, 50–64, New York: Routledge.

Cohen, Jonathan (2008), 'Morning Glory: My Morning Jacket', *Billboard*, 17 May. Available online: www.billboard.com/biz/articles/news/1308180/morning-glory-my-morning-jacket.

Cook, Nicholas (1994), 'Music and Meaning in the Commercials', *Popular Music*, 13(1): 27–40. https://doi.org/10.1017/S0261143000006826.

Corr, Alan (2012), 'The Business of Selling Out', *RTÉ.ie*, 10 July. Available online: www.rte.ie/entertainment/2012/0710/438690-1/.

Coward, Kyle (2015), 'When Hip-Hop First Went Corporate', *Atlantic*, 21 April. Available online: www.theatlantic.com/business/archive/2015/04/breaking-ad-when-hip-hop-first-went-corporate/390930/.

Coyle, Michael and Jon Dolan (1999), 'Modeling Authenticity, Authenticating Commercial Models', in Kevin J. Dettmar and William Richey (eds), *Reading Rock and Roll: Authenticity, Appropriation, Aesthetics*, 17–35, New York: Columbia University Press.

Craig, Clay, Mark A. Flynn and Kyle J. Holody (2017), 'Name Dropping and Product Mentions: Branding in Popular Music Lyrics', *Journal of Promotion Management*, 23(2): 258–76.

Cross, Gary (2000), *An All-Consuming Century: Why Commercialism Won in Modern America*, New York: Columbia University Press.

Crossick, Geoffrey and Patrycja Kaszynska (2016), *Understanding the Value of Arts & Culture: The AHRC Cultural Value Project*. Swindon: Arts and Humanities Research Council. Available online: www.ahrc.ac.uk/documents/publications/ cultural-value-project-final-report/.

Crow, Thomas (2014), *The Long March of Pop: Art, Music, and Design, 1930–1995*, New Haven, CT: Yale University Press.

Dale, Pete (2008), 'It Was Easy, It Was Cheap, So What?: Reconsidering the DIY Principle of Punk and Indie Music', *Popular Music History*, 3(2): 171–93.

Damian, Jacqueline (1968), 'Poetry in Today's Pop Music', *Music Journal*, 26(6): 49.
Dang, Sheila (2019), 'Google, Facebook Have Tight Grip on Growing U.S. Online Ad Market: Report', *Reuters*, 5 June. Available online: www.reuters.com/article/us-alphabet-facebook-advertising/google-facebook-have-tight-grip-on-growing-u-s-online-ad-market-report-idUSKCN1T61IV.
Davies, Helen (2001), 'All Rock and Roll Is Homosocial: The Representation of Women in the British Rock Music Press', *Popular Music*, 20(3): 301–19.
Davis, Aeron (2013), *Promotional Cultures: The Rise and Spread of Advertising, Public Relations, Marketing and Branding*, Cambridge: Polity.
DCMS (2019) *Live Music: Ninth Report of Session 2017–19*. Available online: https://publications.parliament.uk/pa/cm201719/cmselect/cmcumeds/733/733.pdf.
Deresiewicz, William (2011) 'The Entrepreneurial Generation', *New York Times*, 12 November. Available online: www.nytimes.com/2011/11/13/opinion/sunday/the-entrepreneurial-generation.html.
Diamond, Jason (2016), 'How Bob Seger's "Like a Rock" Defined a Generation of American Sports', *Rolling Stone*, 6 September. Available online: www.rollingstone.com/sports/bob-segers-like-a-rock-commercial-and-american-sports-w438146.
DiBlasi, Loren (2018), 'DIY Bands Can't Quit Facebook Even If They Want To', *Paste*, 7 May. Available online: www.pastemagazine.com/articles/2018/05/diy-bands-cant-quit-facebook-even-if-they-want-to.html.
Dicola, Peter (2013), 'Money from Music: Survey Evidence on Musicians' Revenue and Lessons about Copyright Incentives', *Arizona Law Journal*, 55: 301–70.
Dombal, Ryan (2009), 'Matt & Kim's Matt Talks Selling Out, Joy, Rick Rubin', *Pitchfork*, 19 January. Available online: https://pitchfork.com/news/34412-matt-kims-matt-talks-selling-out-joy-rick-rubin/.
Dougan, John (2006), *The Who Sell Out*, New York: Bloomsbury.
Duffy, Brooke Erin and Jefferson Pooley (2019), 'Idols of Promotion: The Triumph of Self-Branding in an Age of Precarity', *Journal of Communication*, 69 (1): 26–48.
Eckhardt, Giana M. and Alan Bradshaw (2014), 'The Erasure of Antagonisms between Popular Music and Advertising', *Marketing Theory*, 14(2): 167–83. https://doi.org/10.1177/1470593114521452.
Einstein, Mara (2016), *Black Ops Advertising*, New York: OR Books.
Elan, Priya (2016), 'Skepta's New Air Max: Why Grime and R&B Stars Can't Wait to Sign Up with Nike', *Guardian*, 8 March. Available online: www.theguardian.com/fashion/2016/mar/08/skepta-air-max-grime-rihanna-drake-manolo-blahnik.
Elliott, Stuart (2009), 'Commercials and Musicians Share the Need to be Heard', *New York Times*, 6 February: B6.
England-Nelson, Jordan (2015), 'New Breed of Artists Emerges in Digital Era', *Pasadena Star-News*, 7 March.
Eshun, Ekow (2012), 'From Here to Here So Now What?', *Esquire*, January: 108–13.

Esposito, Jim (1974), 'Wet Willie: Keep On Smilin'', *Creem*, September. Available online: www.rocksbackpages.com/Library/Article/wet-willie-keep-on-smilin.

Fairclough, Norman (1992), *Discourse and Social Change*, Cambridge: Polity.

Fairclough, Norman (2003), *Analysing Discourse: Textual Analysis for Social Research*, London: Routledge.

Fine, Gary Alan (2003), 'Crafting Authenticity: The Validation of Identity in Self-Taught Art', *Theory and Society*, 32(2), 153–80. https://doi.org/10.1023/A:1023943503531.

Fiorletta, Alicia (2011), 'Interview with Alan Day from Four Year Strong: Aging To Perfection', *The Aquarian*, 16 November. Available online: www.theaquarian.com/2011/11/16/interview-with-alan-day-from-four-year-strong-aging-to-perfection/.

Foege, Alec (1998), 'Walking the Line between Selling and Selling Out', *New York Times*, 10 May: Section 2, 46.

Fonarow, Wendy (2006), *Empire of Dirt: The Aesthetics and Rituals of British Indie Music*, Middletown, CT: Wesleyan University Press.

Fong-Torres, Ben (1986), 'Lou Reed: The Prince of Darkness Lightens Up', *GQ*, September. Available online: www.rocksbackpages.com/Library/Article/lou-reed-the-prince-of-darkness-lightens-up.

Forman, Murray (2000), '"Represent": Race, Space and Place in Rap Music', *Popular Music*, 19(1): 65–90.

Forman, Murray (2002), *The 'Hood Comes First: Race, Space, and Place in Rap and Hip-Hop*, Middletown, CT: Wesleyan University Press.

Frank, Thomas (1997), *The Conquest of Cool: Business Culture, Counterculture, and the Rise of Hip Consumerism*. Chicago: The University of Chicago Press.

Frith, Simon (1981a), '"The Magic That Can Set You Free": The Ideology of Folk and the Myth of the Rock Community', *Popular Music*, 1: 159–68.

Frith, Simon (1981b), *Sound Effects: Youth, Leisure, and the Politics of Rock'n'roll*, New York: Pantheon Books.

Frith, Simon (1986), 'Art versus Technology: The Strange Case of Popular Music', *Media, Culture & Society*, 8(3): 263–79.

Frith, Simon (2004), 'Why Does Music Make People So Cross?', *Nordic Journal of Music Therapy*, 13(1): 64–69. http://dx.doi.org/10.1080/08098130409478098.

Frith, Simon and Howard Horne (1987), *Art into Pop*, London: Methuen and Co.

Future of Music Coalition (n.d.), '42 Revenue Streams', *Future of Music Coalition*. Available online: http://money.futureofmusic.org/40-revenue-streams/.

Gendron, Bernard (2002), *Between Montmartre and the Mudd Club: Popular Music and the Avant-Garde*, Chicago: University of Chicago Press.

Genius (2017), 'Rappers Talk about What "Selling Out" Means in Hip-Hop Today', *Genius*, 13 Oct. Available online: https://genius.com/a/white-famous-six-rappers-talk-about-what-selling-out-means-in-hip-hop-today.

Gennari, John (2006), *Blowin' Hot and Cool: Jazz and Its Critics*. Chicago: University of Chicago Press.

Gilroy, Paul (2010), *Darker than Blue: On the Moral Economies of Black Atlantic Culture*. Cambridge, MA: The Belknap Press of Harvard University Press.

Giroux, Henry A. (2009), 'Democracy's Nemesis: The Rise of the Corporate University', *Cultural Studies ↔ Critical Methodologies*, 9(5): 669–95.

Glaberson, William (1995), 'News Gathering; The Press: Bought and Sold and Gray All Over', *New York Times*, 30 July: Section 4, Page 1.

Goldberg, Michael (1978), 'Flamin' Groovies' Cyril Jordan Isn't Angry', *Trouser Press*, July. Available online: www.rocksbackpages.com/Library/Article/flamin-groovies-cyril-jordan-isnt-angry-.

Goldberg, Michael (1983), 'Take the Money and Run', *Rolling Stone*, 7 July. Available online: www.rocksbackpages.com/Library/Article/take-the-money-and-run.

Goldie, Anna (2008), 'A New Syncing Feeling'. *Music Week*, 10 May: 8.

Goldstein, Richard (1967), 'The Children of Rock Belt the Blues', *New York Times*, 30 July: 84.

Goodman, Fred (1997), *The Mansion on the Hill: Dylan, Young, Geffen, Springsteen and the Head-on Collision of Rock and Commerce*, New York: Vintage Books.

Graakjær, Nicolai Jørgensgaard (2014), 'The Bonding of a Band and a Brand: On Music Placement in Television Commercials from a Text Analytical Perspective', *Popular Music and Society*, 37(5): 517–37. http://dx.doi.org/10.1080/03007766.2013.861242.

Graakjær, Nicolai Jørgensgaard (2015), *Analyzing Music in Advertising: Television Commercials and Consumer Choice*, New York: Routledge.

Grazian, David (2003), *Blue Chicago: The Search for Authenticity in Urban Blues Clubs*, Chicago: University of Chicago Press.

Greenburg, Zach O'Malley (2015), *Empire State of Mind: How Jay-Z Went From Street Corner to Corner Office*, New York: Penguin.

Greenburg, Zach O'Malley (2018), *3 KINGS: Diddy, Dr. Dre, Jay-Z and Hip-Hop's Multibillion-Dollar Rise*, New York: Little, Brown.

Grewal, Sam (2003), 'The Mythology of Selling Out', *Toronto Star*, 13 May: E03.

Grigoriadis, Vanessa (2003), 'The Edge of Hip: Vice, the Brand', *New York Times*, 28 September: Section 9.

Guardian (2017), 'Grace Slick Takes Fast Food Company's Money to Fund Causes it Opposes', *Guardian*, 23 February. Available online: www.theguardian.com/music/2017/feb/23/grace-slick-money-chick-fil-a-starship-nothings-gonna-stop-us-now-lgbtq-causes.

Hagan, Geo (2014), 'The 10 Biggest Sellout Moments in Hip-Hop', *The Richest*, 19 December. Available online: www.therichest.com/expensive-lifestyle/the-10-biggest-sellout-moments-in-hip-hop/.

Hall, James (2015), 'And the Brands Played On: How EDM Can Sell Almost Anything', *Guardian*, 28 December. Available online: www.theguardian.com/music/2015/dec/28/how-edm-can-sell-almost-anything-brands-marketing.

Hamilton, Jack (2016), *Just around Midnight: Rock and Roll and the Racial Imagination*, Cambridge, MA: Harvard University Press.

Hampp, Andrew (2010), 'How Miracle Whip, Plenty of Fish Tapped Lady Gaga's "Telephone"', *AdAge*, 13 March. Available online: https://adage.com/article/madisonvine-news/miracle-whip-plenty-fish-tap-lady-gaga-s-telephone/142794.

Harrison, Anthony Kwame (2009), *Hip Hop Underground: The Integrity and Ethics of Racial Identification*, Philadelphia: Temple University Press.

Harron, Mary (1979), 'The Mekons: Blows against Individuation', *Melody Maker*, 3 February. Available online: www.rocksbackpages.com/Library/Article/the-mekons-blows-against-individuation.

Harvey, Mark (2016), 'Politics and Power in the Record Industry: The Beatles, the Beach Boys, and the Album as Art Form', *Musicology Australia*, 38(2): 153–71.

Haynes, Jo and Lee Marshall (2018), 'Reluctant Entrepreneurs: Musicians and Entrepreneurship in the "New" Music Industry', *The British Journal of Sociology*, 69(2): 459–82.

Hearn, Alison (2008), '"Meat, Mask, Burden": Probing the Contours of the Branded "Self"', *Journal of Consumer Culture*, 8(2): 197–217.

Hearn, Alison (2010), '"Through the Looking Glass": The Promotional University 2.0', in Melissa Aronczyk and Devon Powers (eds), *Blowing Up the Brand: Critical Perspectives on Promotional Culture*, 195–217, New York: Peter Lang.

Hesmondhalgh, David (1997), 'Post-Punk's Attempt to Democratise the Music Industry: The Success and Failure of Rough Trade', *Popular Music*, 16(3): 255–74. https://doi.org/10.1017/S0261143000008400.

Hesmondhalgh, David (1999), 'Indie: The Institutional Politics and Aesthetics of a Popular Music Genre', *Cultural Studies*, 13(1): 34–61. http://dx.doi.org/10.1080/095023899335365.

Hesmondhalgh, David (2006), 'Bourdieu, the Media and Cultural Production', *Media, Culture & Society*, 28(2): 211–31.

Hesmondhalgh, David (2013a), *Why Music Matters*, Malden: Wiley-Blackwell.

Hesmondhalgh, David (2013b), *The Cultural Industries* (3rd edition), London: Sage.

Hesmondhalgh, David (2017), 'Capitalism and the Media: Moral Economy, Well-Being and Capabilities', *Media, Culture & Society*, 39(2): 202–18.

Hesmondhalgh, David and Sarah Baker (2011), *Creative Labour: Media Work in Three Cultural Industries*, Abingdon: Routledge.

Hesmondhalgh, David and Leslie M. Meier (2014), 'Popular Music, Independence and the Concept of the Alternative in Contemporary Capitalism', in James Bennett and Niki Strange (eds), *Media Independence: Working with Freedom or Working for Free?* 94–116, New York: Routledge.

Hesmondhalgh, David and Leslie M. Meier (2017), 'What the Digitalisation of Music Tells Us about Capitalism, Culture and the Power of the Information Technology Sector', *Information, Communication & Society*, 21(11): 1555–70.

Hesmondhalgh, David, Kate Oakley, David Lee and Melissa Nisbett (2015), *Culture, Economy and Politics: The Case of New Labour*, Basingstoke: Palgrave Macmillan.

Hess, Mickey (2005a), 'Hip-Hop Realness and the White Performer', *Critical Studies in Media Communication*, 22(5): 372–89.

Hess, Mickey (2005b), 'Metal Faces, Rap Masks: Identity and Resistance in Hip Hop's Persona Artist', *Popular Music and Society*, 28(3): 297–311.

Hibbett, Ryan (2005), 'What is Indie Rock?', *Popular Music and Society*, 28(1): 55–77.

Hines, Candace G. (2005), 'Black Musical Traditions and Copyright Law: Historical Tensions', *Michigan Journal of Race and Law*, 10(2): 463–93.

Hip-Hop Evolution (2018), [TV programme] Netflix, 19 October.

Hogan, Marc (2017), 'How Countries around the World Fund Music—and Why It Matters', *Pitchfork*, 26 June. Available online: https://pitchfork.com/features/article/how-countries-around-the-world-fund-musicand-why-it-matters/.

Homan, Shane, Martin Cloonan and Jen Cattermole (2013), 'Introduction: popular music and policy', *International Journal of Cultural Policy*, 19(3): 275–80.

Homan, Shane, Martin Cloonan and Jen Cattermole (eds) (2015), *Popular Music and Cultural Policy*. London: Routledge.

Hopper, Jessica (2013), 'How Selling Out Saved Indie Rock', *Buzzfeed*, 10 November. Available online: www.buzzfeed.com/jessicahopper/how-selling-out-saved-indie-rock.

Hu, Cherie (2019), 'Slave to the 'Rithm? Not So Fast: Everything You Need to Know about the Deal between Endel and Warner Music', *Water & Music*, 25 March. Available online: www.getrevue.co/profile/cheriehu42/issues/slave-to-the-rithm-not-so-fast-everything-you-need-to-know-about-the-deal-between-endel-and-warner-music-168092.

Hunt, Elle (2015), 'Essena O'Neill Quits Instagram Claiming Social Media "Is Not Real Life"', *Guardian*, 3 November. Available online: www.theguardian.com/media/2015/nov/03/instagram-star-essena-oneill-quits-2d-life-to-reveal-true-story-behind-images.

Huron, David (1989), 'Music in Advertising: An Analytic Paradigm', *The Musical Quarterly*, 73(4): 557–74. https://doi.org/10.1093/mq/73.4.557.

Iddon, Martin and Melanie L. Marshall (eds) (2014), *Lady Gaga and Popular Music: Performing Gender, Fashion, and Culture*, London: Routledge.

IFPI (International Federation of the Phonographic Industry) (2018), *Global Music Report 2018: Annual State of the Industry*. Available online: www.ifpi.org/downloads/GMR2018.pdf.

IFPI (International Federation of the Phonographic Industry) (2019), *Global Music Report 2019: Annual State of the Industry*. Available online: www.ifpi.org/downloads/GMR2019.pdf.

Indvik, Lauren (2017), 'Tommy Hilfiger's On-Again, Off-Again Relationship with Hip-Hop Is Back in Full Swing', *Billboard*, 8 February. Available online: www.billboard.com/articles/news/magazine-feature/7677920/tommy-hilfiger-hip-hop-relationship.

Ingham, Tim (2019), '"Fake Artists" Have Billions of Streams on Spotify. Is Sony Now Playing the Service at Its Own Game?', *Rolling Stone*, 15 May. Available online: www.rollingstone.com/music/music-features/fake-artists-have-billions-of-streams-on-spotify-is-sony-now-playing-the-service-at-its-own-game-834746/.

Jackson Jr, John L. (2005), *Real Black: Adventures in Racial Sincerity*, Chicago: University of Chicago Press.

James, Martin (2001), *Moby: Replay – his Life and Times*, Chicago, IL: Olmstead Press.

Jameson, Frederic (1998), *The Cultural Turn: Selected Writings on the Postmodern 1983–1998*, London: Verso.

Jeffries, Michael P. (2011), *Thug Life: Race, Gender, and the Meaning of Hip-Hop*, Chicago: University of Chicago Press.

Jian, Miaoju (2018), 'The Survival Struggle and Resistant Politics of a DIY Music Career in East Asia: Case Studies of China and Taiwan', *Cultural Sociology*, 12(2): 224–40.

Jones, Ellis (2020), 'What Does Facebook "Afford" Do-It-Yourself Musicians? Considering Social Media Affordances as Sites of Contestation', *Media, Culture & Society*, 42(2): 277–292. https://doi.org/10.1177/0163443719853498.

Kafka, Peter (2018), 'YouTube Is Using a New Deal with Vevo, the Music Labels' Video Venture, to Boost Ad Sales', *Vox*, 7 May. Available online: www.vox.com/2018/5/7/17325618/youtube-vevo-music-video-ad-sales-deal-ariana-grande.

Kate Nash: Underestimate the Girl (2018), [Film] Dir. Amy Goldstein, USA: Span Productions.

Keightley, Keir (2001), 'Reconsidering Rock', in Simon Frith, Will Straw and John Street (eds), *The Cambridge Companion to Pop and Rock*, 109–42, Cambridge: Cambridge University Press.

Keightley, Keir (2011), 'The Historical Consciousness of Sunshine Pop', *Journal of Popular Music Studies*, 23(3): 343–61. https://doi.org/10.1111/j.1533-1598.2011.01297.x.

Kennedy, Maev (2015), 'Ed Sheeran Quits Social Media – for Now', *Guardian*, 13 December. Available online: www.theguardian.com/music/2015/dec/13/ed-sheeran-quits-social-media-instagram-world-tour.

Kennedy, Randall (2008), *Sellout: The Politics of Racial Betrayal*, New York: Vintage.

Khalili-Tari, Daniel (2017), 'How Independent Artists Have Changed the Music Industry', *Independent*, 15 December. Available online: www.independent.co.uk/arts-entertainment/music/features/independent-artists-music-industry-stormzy-aj-tracey-stefflon-don-hardy-caprio-major-label-streaming-a8110936.html.

Kim, Hank (2002), 'Def Jam, H-P Explore Branded Music Alliance; Product-Placement Deal Could Alter Custom of Hip-Hop Endorsements', *Advertising Age*, 9 September: 4.

King, Aliya S. (1999), 'More Rappers Hop into the Apparel Business', *Billboard*, 8 May: 49–50.

Klein, Bethany (2008a), '"The New Radio": Music Licensing as a Response to Industry Woe', *Media, Culture & Society*, 30(4): 463–78. https://doi.org/10.1177/0163443708091177.

Klein, Bethany (2008b), 'In Perfect Harmony: Popular Music and Cola Advertising', *Popular Music and Society,* 31(1): 1–20. https://doi.org/10.1080/03007760601061290.

Klein, Bethany (2009), *As Heard on TV: Popular Music in Advertising*, Aldershot: Ashgate.

Klein, Bethany, Giles Moss and Lee Edwards (2015), *Understanding Copyright: Intellectual Property in the Digital Age*, London: Sage.

Klein, Bethany and Leslie M. Meier (2017), 'In Sync? Music Supervisors, Music Placement Practices, and Industrial Change', in Miguel Mera, Ronald Sadoff and Ben Winters (eds), *The Routledge Companion to Screen Music and Sound*, 281–90, New York: Routledge.

Klein, Bethany, Leslie M. Meier and Devon Powers (2017), 'Selling Out: Musicians, Autonomy, and Compromise in the Digital Age', *Popular Music and Society*, 40(2): 222–38. http://dx.doi.org/10.1080/03007766.2015.1120101.

Klein, Naomi (2000), *No Logo*, New York: Picador.

Knopper, Steve (2018), 'The Grunge Gold Rush: Is There a Lesson Here?', *NPR*, January 12. Available online: www.npr.org/sections/therecord/2018/01/12/577063077/the-grunge-gold-rush?t=1557325379108.

Kruse, Holly (2003), *Site and Sound: Understanding Independent Music Scenes*, New York: Peter Lang.

Kruse, Holly (2010), 'Local Identity and Independent Music Scenes, Online and Off', *Popular Music and Society*, 33(5): 625–639.

Kumanyika, Chenjerai (2015), '"We Demand Justice. We Just Getting Started": The Constitutive Rhetoric of 1Hood Media's Hip-Hop Activism', *Popular Music* 34(3): 432–51.

Laing, Dave (2015), *One Chord Wonders: Power and Meaning in Punk Rock*, Oakland, CA: PM Press.

Lee, David (2018), *Independent Television Production in the UK: From Cottage Industry to Big Business*, London: Palgrave Macmillan.

Lee, Helena (2013), 'Why Finnish Babies Sleep in Cardboard Boxes', *BBC News*, 4 June. Available online: www.bbc.co.uk/news/magazine-22751415.

Leight, Elias (2018), 'You Don't Need to Be a Musician to Get a Record Deal in 2018', *Rolling Stone*, 25 July. Available online: www.rollingstone.com/music/music-features/you-dont-need-to-be-a-musician-to-get-a-record-deal-in-2018-702710/.

Leonard, Marion (2007), *Gender in the Music Industry: Rock, Discourse, and Girl Power*, Aldershot: Ashgate.

Lewis, Justin (2013), *Beyond Consumer Capitalism: Media and the Limits to Imagination*, Cambridge: Polity.

Lister, David (1998), 'Dole-Queue Blues that Gave Britpop Its Soul', *Independent*, 18 February. Available online: www.independent.co.uk/news/dole-queue-blues-that-gave-britpop-its-soul-1145415.html.

Lorenz, Taylor (2018), 'Rising Instagram Stars Are Posting Fake Sponsored Content', *Atlantic*, 18 December. Available online: www.theatlantic.com/technology/archive/2018/12/influencers-are-faking-brand-deals/578401/.

Loss, Robert (2015), 'No Apologies: A Critique of the Rockist v. Poptimist Paradigm', *PopMatters*, 9 August. Available online: www.popmatters.com/no-apologies-a-critique-of-the-rockist-v-poptimist-paradigm-2495499446.html.

Love, Joanna K. (2019), *Soda Goes Pop: Pepsi-Cola Advertising and Popular Music*, Ann Arbor, MI: University of Michigan Press.

Lynskey, Dorian (2011), 'The Great Rock'n'roll Sellout', *Guardian*, 30 June. Available online: www.theguardian.com/music/2011/jun/30/rocknroll-sellout.

Maclean, Gavin (2016), 'Art versus Commerce?: The Work of Musicians in the Field of Cultural Production', PhD diss., Heriot-Watt University.

Marriott, Michel (1992), 'Hip-Hop's Hostile Takeover', *New York Times*, 20 September. Available online: www.nytimes.com/1992/09/20/style/hip-hop-s-hostile-takeover.html.

Marshall, Lee (2013), 'The 360 Deal and the "New" Music Industry', *European Journal of Cultural Studies*, 16(1): 77–99. https://doi.org/10.1177/1367549412457478.

Marshall, Lee (2015), '"Let's Keep Music Special. F--- Spotify": On-Demand Streaming and the Controversy Over Artist Royalties', *Creative Industries Journal*, 8(2): 177–89.

McAllister, Matthew P. (1996), *The Commercialization of American Culture: New Advertising, Control, and Democracy*, New York: Sage.

McAllister, Matthew P. (2003), 'Is Commercial Culture Popular Culture?: A Question for Popular Communication Scholars', *Popular Communication* 1(1): 41–49.

McAllister, Matthew P. and Emily West (eds) (2013), *The Routledge Companion to Advertising and Promotional Culture*, New York: Routledge.

McAvoy, Linda (2002), 'Auto Ads: Are Musicians Selling Out or Cashing In?', *Toronto Star*, 27 April: G25.

McCormack, David (2007), 'The Pulling Power of the "Dark Side"', *Guardian*, 22 January. Available online: www.theguardian.com/media/2007/jan/22/mondaymediasection3.

McGoey, Linsey (2015), *No Such Thing as a Free Gift: The Gates Foundation and the Price of Philanthropy*, New York: Verso Books.

McGuigan, Jim (2009), *Cool Capitalism*, London: Pluto Press.

McRobbie, Angela (1999), *In the Culture Society: Art, Fashion and Popular Music*, London: Routledge.

McIntyre, Hugh (2015), 'If Your Brand Wants A Cool Music Video, Call OK Go', *Forbes*, 5 July. Available online: www.forbes.com/sites/hughmcintyre/2015/07/05/if-your-brand-wants-a-cool-music-video-call-ok-go/.

McLeod, Kembrew (1999), 'Authenticity within Hip-Hop and Other Cultures Threatened with Assimilation', *Journal of Communication*, 49(4): 134–50.

McLeod, Kembrew (2016), *Parallel Lines*, New York: Bloomsbury.

Meier, Leslie M. (2017), *Popular Music as Promotion: Music and Branding in the Digital Age*, Cambridge: Polity.

Meier, Leslie M. and Vincent R. Manzerolle (2019), 'Rising Tides? Data Capture, Platform Accumulation, and New Monopolies in the Digital Music Economy', *New Media & Society*, 21(3): 543–61.

Mellery-Pratt, Robin (2014), 'Run-D.M.C.'s "My Adidas" and the Birth of Hip Hop Sneaker Culture', *Business of Fashion*, 18 July. Available online: www.businessoffashion.com/articles/video/run-d-m-c-s-adidas-birth-hip-hop-sneaker-culture.

Melody Maker (1965), 'Every So Often a Group is Poised on the Brink of a Breakthrough. Word Has It It's . . . The Who', *Melody Maker*, 5 June: 7.

Mitchell, Gail (2009), 'Boom Boom Wow', *Billboard*, 30 May. Available online: www.billboard.com/articles/news/268553/black-eyed-peas-boom-boom-wow.

Mitchell, Gail (2018), 'Why Hasn't the Hip-Hop Boom Pushed More Black Executives to the Top?', *Billboard*, 13 April. Available online: www.billboard.com/articles/business/8313035/hip-hop-boom-black-executives-music-business-labels.

McCourt, Tom (2005), 'The Cost of Not Selling Out', *Flow Journal*, 18 November. Available online: www.flowjournal.org/2005/11/the-cost-of-not-selling-out/.

Molotkow, Alexandra (2012), 'Why the Old-School Music Snob Is the Least Cool Kid on Twitter', *New York Times Magazine*, 8 April: 52.

Morris, Chris (1992), 'New Acts Catch Up with Punk's Past: Grunge-Rockers Reignite Interest in Genre', *Billboard*, 18 April: 1.

Morris, Jeremy Wade (2014), 'Artists as Entrepreneurs, Fans as Workers', *Popular Music and Society*, 37(3): 273–90

Morris, Jeremy Wade (2015), *Selling Digital Music, Formatting Culture*, Oakland, CA: University of California Press.

Morris, Jeremy Wade and Devon Powers (2015), 'Control, Curation and Musical Experience in Streaming Music Services', *Creative Industries Journal*, 8(2): 106–22.

Moore, Allan (2002), 'Authenticity as Authentication', *Popular Music*, 21(2): 209–23.

Moore, Ryan (2004), 'Postmodernism and Punk subculture: Cultures of Authenticity and Deconstruction', *The Communication Review*, 7(3): 305–27.

Moore, Ryan (2005), 'Alternative to What? Subcultural Capital and the Commercialization of a Music Scene', *Deviant Behavior*, 26(3): 229–52. http://dx.doi.org/10.1080/01639620590905618.

Moore, Ryan (2007), 'Friends Don't Let Friends Listen to Corporate Rock: Punk as a Field of Cultural Production', *Journal of Contemporary Ethnography*, 36(4): 438–74.

Moore, Ryan (2009), *Sells Like Teen Spirit: Music, Youth Culture, and Social Crisis*, New York: NYU Press.

Moran, Charles (2008), 'Indie Act Seeks Backup Brand; In Today's World, "Selling Out" Is the Only Way to Cash In', *Advertising Age*, 10 March: 3.

Morley, Paul (2006), 'Rockism – It's the New Rockism', *Guardian*, 26 May. Available online: www.theguardian.com/music/2006/may/26/popandrock.coldplay.

Moskvitch, Katie (2018), 'YouTube Music is Great for Record Labels, but Bad for Music Lovers', *Wired*, 23 May. Available online: www.wired.co.uk/article/youtube-music-premium-originals.

MTV (1996), 'Moby Song in Car Commercial for Good Cause', *MTV*, 26 March. Available online: www.mtv.com/news/507274/moby-song-in-car-commercial-for-good-cause/.

Music Week (1999), 'Pure Genius as Leftfield Opt for Guinness Ad', *Music Week*, 5 June: 24.

Music Week (2013), 'Ad Syncs: Are Television Commercials the New Radio?', *Music Week*, 10 May: 25.

Neal, Mark Anthony (1997), 'Sold Out on Soul: The Corporate Annexation of Black Popular Music', *Popular Music & Society*, 21(3): 117–35, https://doi.org/10.1080/03007769708591682.

Neal, Mark Anthony (1999), *What the Music Said: Black Popular Music and Black Popular Culture*, New York: Routledge.

Negus, Keith (1999), *Music Genres and Corporate Cultures*, London: Routledge.

Negus, Keith (2019), 'From Creator to Data: The Post-record Music Industry and the Digital Conglomerates', *Media, Culture & Society*, 41(3): 367–84.

Nelson, Havelock (1991), 'Tone Loc Expands Vision on New Set', *Billboard*, 2 November: 22.

Newman, Melinda (2006), 'Doors Songs in Ads? Well, Maybe . . .', *Billboard*, 15 April: 24.

O'Brien, David (2010), *Measuring the Value of Culture: A Report to the Department for Culture Media and Sport*. Available online: www.gov.uk/government/publications/measuring-the-value-of-culture-a-report-to-the-department-for-culture-media-and-sport.

O'Brien, David and Kate Oakley (2015), *Cultural Value and Inequality: A Critical Literature Review*. A Report commissioned by the Arts and Humanities Research Council's Cultural Value Project. Available online: https://ahrc.ukri.org/documents/project-reports-and-reviews/cultural-value-and-inequality-a-critical-literature-review/

O'Connor, Alan (2008), *Punk Record Labels and the Struggle for Autonomy: The Emergence of DIY*, Plymouth: Lexington.

Ogbar, Jeffrey O.G. (1999), 'Slouching Toward Bork: The Culture Wars and Self-criticism in Hip-Hop Music', *Journal of Black Studies*, 30(2): 164–83.

Orejuela, Fernando and Stephanie Shonekan (eds) (2018), *Black Lives Matter and Music: Protest, Intervention, Reflection*, Bloomington, IN: Indiana University Press.

Ozzi, Dan (2015), 'Major Label Debut: Punk's "Sell Out" Albums Revisited', *Vice*, 2 April. Available online: https://noisey.vice.com/en_au/article/rkqwqy/major-label-debut-punks-sell-out-albums-revisited.

Pagano, Alyssa and Irene Kim (2019), 'Rihanna is the Richest Female Musician in the World. Here's How She Makes and Spends Her $600 Million', *Business Insider*, 6 June. Available online: www.businessinsider.com/rihanna-richest-female-musician-net-worth-makes-spends-millions-2019-6.

Pakinkis, Tom (2013), 'PJ Bloom on Changing Sync Revenues and Opportunities for Rights-holders', *Music Week*, 15 March. Available online: www.musicweek.com/news/read/pj-bloom-on-changing-sync-revenues-and-opportunities-for-rights-holders/054069.

Paoletta, Michael (2006), 'Inside Pitch: Ad Agency Opens Its Doors to Recording Artists—with Results', *Billboard*, 6 May: 20–22.

Pelly, Liz (2017), 'The Problem with Muzak', *The Baffler*, December: No. 37. Available online: https://thebaffler.com/salvos/the-problem-with-muzak-pelly.

Pelly, Liz (2018), 'Streambait Pop', *The Baffler*, 11 December. Available online: https://thebaffler.com/downstream/streambait-pop-pelly.

Petter, Olivia (2019), '"I'd Lost Who I Was": *Made in Chelsea* Star Says Being an Influencer Made Him Feel Like a Puppet', *Independent*, 15 February. Available online: www.independent.co.uk/life-style/made-in-chelsea-andy-jordan-instagram-influencer-socialmedia-bbc-puppet-downsides-a8780476.html.

Pequeno, Ze (2009), 'Selling Out to Survive', *Pop Matters*, 29 November. Available online: www.popmatters.com/feature/116256-selling-out-to-survive/P1/.

Petersen, Melody (2002), 'Heartfelt Advice, Hefty Fees', *New York Times*, 11 August: Section 3.

Peterson, Richard A. (1997), *Creating Country Music: Fabricating Authenticity*, Chicago: University of Chicago Press.

Philips, Deborah and Gary Whannel (2013), *The Trojan Horse: The Growth of Commercial Sponsorship*, New York: Bloomsbury.

Phillips, Yoh (2016), 'Power of Influence: Hip-Hop's Rocky Relationship with Brands and Product', *djbooth.net*, 30 June. Available online: https://djbooth.net/features/2016-06-30-hip-hop-history-with-brands-and-products.

Pilkington, Ed (2006), 'A History of Violence', *Guardian*, 6 October. Available online: www.theguardian.com/film/2006/oct/06/awardsandprizes.martinscorsese.

Pillsbury, Glenn T. (2006), *Damage Incorporated: Metallica and the Production of Musical Identity*, New York: Routledge.

Powell, Kevin (1996), 'Live from Death Row', *Vibe*, February. Available online: www.vibe.com/2012/12/dr-dre-vibe-cover-story-live-death-row-feb-96.

Powers, Devon (2013a), 'Now Hear This: The State of Promotion and Popular Music', in Matthew P. McAllister and Emily West (eds), *The Routledge Companion to Advertising and Promotional Culture*, 313–25, New York: Routledge.

Powers, Devon (2013b), *Writing the Record: The Village Voice and the Birth of Rock Criticism*, Amherst, MA: University of Massachusetts Press.

Prior, Nick (2013), 'Bourdieu and the Sociology of Music Consumption: A Critical Assessment of Recent Developments', *Sociology Compass,* 7(3): 181–93.

Quinn, Eithne (2005), *Nuthin' But A 'G' Thang: The Culture and Commerce of Gangsta Rap*, New York: Columbia University Press.

Rabin, Nathan (2012), 'In 1990, Hammer, Vanilla Ice, A Tribe Called Quest, and Ice Cube Reflected the Splintering of the Hip-Hop Nation', *The AV Club*, 31 July. Available online: https://music.avclub.com/in-1990-hammer-vanilla-ice-a-tribe-called-quest-and-1798232852.

Reynolds, Simon (2005), *Rip It Up and Start Again: Postpunk 1978–1984*, London: Faber and Faber.

Richards, Chris (2011), 'Music Review: Best Coast and Wavves at 9:30 Club', *Washington Post*, February 1. Available online: www.washingtonpost.com/lifestyle/style/music-review-best-coast-and-wavves-at-930-club/2011/02/01/ABS05tO_story.html.

Ricks, Christopher (2003), *Dylan's Visions of Sin*, Edinburgh: Canongate.

Ritchey, Marianna (2019), *Composing Capital: Classical Music in the Neoliberal Era*. Chicago: University of Chicago Press.

Robehmed, Natalie (2013), 'How Rapper Dom Kennedy Made It without a Record Deal', *Forbes*, 30 October. Available online: www.forbes.com/sites/natalierobehmed/2013/10/30/how-rapper-dom-kennedy-made-it-without-a-record-deal/.

Rorem, Ned (1968), 'The Music of the Beatles', *Music Educators Journal*, 55(4): 33–83. https://doi.org/10.2307/3392348.

Rose, Tricia (1994), *Black Noise: Rap Music and Black Culture in Contemporary America*, Middletown, CT: Wesleyan University Press.

Rose, Tricia (2008), *The Hip Hop Wars: What We Talk about When We Talk about Hip Hop – and Why It Matters*, New York: Basic Books.

Rosen, Jody (2006), 'The Perils of Poptimism', *Slate*, 9 May. Available online: www.slate.com/articles/arts/music_box/2006/05/the_perils_of_poptimism.html.

Ryan, Bill (1991), *Making Capital From Culture*, Berlin: Walter de Gruyter.

Saha, Anamik (2018), *Race and the Cultural Industries*, Cambridge: Polity.

Sanchez, Daniel (2019), 'Streaming Music Royalties are Even Worse Than We Thought — At Least According to This Indie Label', *Digital Music News*, 30 January. Available online: www.digitalmusicnews.com/2019/01/30/2018-streaming-music-price-bible/.

Sandel, Michael J. (2012), *What Money Can't Buy: The Moral Limits of Markets*, London: Penguin Books.

Sanneh, Kelefa (2004), 'The Rap against Rockism', *New York Times*, 31 October: AR1, 32. Available online: www.nytimes.com/2004/10/31/arts/music/the-rap-against-rockism.html.

Savage, Jon (1991), *England's Dreaming: Sex Pistols and Punk Rock*, London: Faber and Faber.

Savage, Mark (2018a), 'Streaming Is Music's Biggest Money-maker', *BBC News*, 24 April. Available online: www.bbc.co.uk/news/entertainment-arts-43877494.

Savage, Mark (2018b), 'Spotify Users Demand Refunds over Drake Promotion', *BBC News*, 3 July. Available online: www.bbc.co.uk/news/entertainment-arts-44695062.

Sayer, Andrew (1999), 'Valuing Culture and Economy', in Larry Ray and Andrew Sayer (eds), *Culture and Economy after the Cultural Turn*, 53–75, London: Sage.

Sayer, Andrew (2000), 'Moral Economy and Political Economy', *Studies in Political Economy*, 61(1): 79–103.

Sayer, Andrew (2007), 'Moral Economy as Critique', *New Political Economy*, 12(2): 261–70.

Scherzinger, Martin Rudolph (2005), 'Music, Corporate Power, and Unending War', *Cultural Critique*, 60(1): 23–67.
Seiler, Cotten (2000), 'The Commodification of Rebellion: Rock Culture and Consumer Capitalism', in Mark Gottdiener (ed), *New Forms of Consumption: Consumers, Culture and Commodification*, 203–26, Oxford: Rowman & Littlefield.
Sennett, Richard (1998), *The Corrosion of Character. The Personal Consequences of Work in the New Capitalism*, New York: Norton.
Serazio, Michael (2015), 'Selling (Digital) Millennials: The Social Construction and Technological Bias of a Consumer Generation', *Television & New Media*, 16(7): 599–615.
Shuker, Roy (2016), *Understanding Popular Music Culture* (5th edition), London: Routledge.
Shumway, David R. (2007), 'Authenticity: Modernity, Stardom, and Rock & Roll', *Modernism/modernity*, 14(3): 527–33.
Singleton, Micah (2015), 'This Was Sony Music's Contract with Spotify: The Details the Major Labels Don't Want You to See', *The Verge*, 19 May. Available online: www.theverge.com/2015/5/19/8621581/sony-music-spotify-contract.
Sisario, Ben (2018), 'A New Spotify Initiative Makes the Big Record Labels Nervous', *New York Times*, 6 September. Available online: www.nytimes.com/2018/09/06/business/media/spotify-music-industry-record-labels.html.
Slade, Paul (1998), 'Money: Are You Ready to Rock 'n' Dole?', *Independent*, 24 June. Available online: www.independent.co.uk/arts-entertainment/money-are-you-ready-to-rock-n-dole-1167173.html.
Small, Christopher (1998), *Musicking: The Meanings of Performing and Listening*, Middletown, CT: Wesleyan University Press.
Spotify (2019a), 'We're Closing the Upload Beta Program. Here's What Artists Need to Know', *Spotify*, 1 July. Available online: https://artists.spotify.com/blog/we're-closing-the-upload-beta-program.
Spotify (2019b), *Culture Next: The Trends Defining Gen Zs and Millennials*, *Spotify*, Volume 1. Available online: www.spotifyforbrands.com/en-GB/culturenext/.
Stahl, Matt (2015), 'Tactical Destabilization for Economic Justice: The First Phase of the 1984-2004 Rhythm & Blues Royalty Reform Movement', *Queen Mary Journal of Intellectual Property*, 5(3): 344–63.
Stahl, Matt and Leslie M. Meier (2012), 'The Firm Foundation of Organizational Flexibility: The 360 Contract in the Digitalizing Music Industry', *Canadian Journal of Communication*, 37(3): 441–58. https://doi.org/10.22230/cjc.2012v37n3a2544.
Stevenson, Seth (2005), 'Paul McCartney? Is That You? What He's Doing in That Fidelity Ad', *Slate*, 19 September. Available online: https://slate.com/business/2005/09/why-is-paul-mccartney-doing-ads.html.
Strachan, Robert (2007), 'Micro-Independent Record Labels in the UK: Discourse, DIY Cultural Production and the Music Industry', *European Journal of Cultural Studies*, 10(2): 245–65.

Strachan, Robert (2017), *Sonic Technologies: Popular Music, Digital Culture and the Creative Process*, New York: Bloomsbury.

Stratton, Jon (1983), 'Capitalism and Romantic Ideology in the Record Business', *Popular Music*, 3: 143–56. https://doi.org/10.1017/S0261143000001604.

Strugatz, Rachel (2019), 'Revealed: Lady Gaga's New Beauty Line', *Business of Fashion*, 9 July. Available online: www.businessoffashion.com/articles/bof-exclusive/lady-gaga-haus-laboratories-beauty-brand-details.

Suisman, David (2009), *Selling Sounds: The Commercial Revolution in American Music*, Cambridge, MA: Harvard University Press.

Sullivan, Caroline (2008), 'Slaves to Synth', *Guardian*, 17 December. Available online: www.theguardian.com/music/2008/dec/17/electro-pop-female-artists.

Taylor, Timothy D. (2000), 'World Music in Television Ads', *American Music*, 18(2): 162–92. https://doi.org/10.2307/3052482.

Taylor, Timothy D. (2007), 'The Changing Shape of the Culture Industry; or, How Did Electronica Music Get into Television Commercials?', *Television & New Media*, 8(3): 235–58. https://doi.org/10.1177/1527476407301837.

Taylor, Timothy D. (2012), *The Sounds of Capitalism: Advertising, Music, and the Conquest of Culture*, Chicago: University of Chicago Press.

Telegraph (2017), 'Ed Sheeran Quits Twitter after Trolls Leave Him "Trying to Work Out Why People Dislike Me So Much"', *Telegraph*, 4 July. Available online: www.telegraph.co.uk/music/news/ed-sheeran-quits-twitter-trolls-leave-trying-work-people-dislike/.

Tetzlaff, David (1994), 'Music for Meaning: Reading the Discourse of Authenticity in Rock', *Journal of Communication Inquiry*, 18(1): 95–117. https://doi.org/10.1177/019685999401800106.

Thomson, Kristin (2013), 'Roles, Revenue, and Responsibilities: The Changing Nature of Being a Working Musician', *Work and Occupations*, 40(4): 514–525.

Toronto Star (2002), 'Shabby Genesis: Conceived for Jingle Hell', *Toronto Star*, 9 November: J06.

Toronto Star (2006), 'Yorke Atop Toronto', *Toronto Star*, 23 July: C02.

Tota, Anna Lisa (2001), '"When Orff Meets Guiness": Music in Advertising as a Form of Cultural Hybrid', *Poetics*, 29: 109–23. https://doi.org/10.1016/S0304-422X(01)00030-4.

Toynbee, Jason (2000), *Making Popular Music: Musicians, Creativity and Institutions*, London: Arnold.

Toynbee, Jason (2002), 'Mainstreaming, from Hegemonic Centre to Global Networks', in David Hesmondhalgh and Keith Negus (eds), *Popular Music Studies*, 149–63, London: Hodder Arnold.

Turow, Joseph (2011), *The Daily You: How the New Advertising Industry Is Defining Your Identity and Your Worth*, New Haven, CT: Yale University Press.

Ugwu, Reggie (2014), 'Backstage with St. Vincent: New Style, New Label and a Bold New Album', *Billboard*, 24 February. Available online: www.billboard.com/articles/news/5915666/backstage-with-st-vincent-new-style-new-label-and-a-bold-new-album.

Valentine, Penny (1977), 'Peter Frampton: The Rise And Rise', *Creem*, October. Available online:http://www.rocksbackpages.com/Library/Article/peter-frampton-the-rise-and-rise-

Victor, Daniel (2017), 'Pepsi Pulls Ad Accused of Trivializing Black Lives Matter', *New York Times*, 5 April. Available online: https://www.nytimes.com/2017/04/05/business/kendall-jenner-pepsi-ad.html

Waksman, Steve (2009), *This Ain't the Summer of Love: Conflict and Crossover in Heavy Metal and Punk*, Berkeley: University of California Press.

Wald, Elijah (2015), *Dylan Goes Electric!: Newport, Seeger, Dylan, and the Night that Split the Sixties*, New York: Harper Collins.

Wang, Amy X (2019), 'Music's Big Three Labels Make $19 Million a Day From Streaming', *Rolling Stone*. Available online: www.rollingstone.com/music/music-news/musics-big-three-labels-19-million-a-day-from-streaming-798749/.

Weale, Sally (2019), 'Britain's Top Jobs Still in Hands of Private School Elite, Study Finds', *Guardian*, 25 June. Available online: www.theguardian.com/society/2019/jun/25/britains-top-jobs-still-in-hands-of-private-school-elite-study-finds.

Webster, Emma, Matt Brennan, Adam Behr, Martin Cloonan and Jake Ansell (2018), *Valuing Live Music: The UK Live Music Census 2017 Report*. Available online: http://livemusicexchange.org/resources/valuing-live-music-uk-live-music-census-report-2017-emma-webster-matt-brennan-adam-behr-and-martin-cloonan-with-jake-ansell-2018/.

Wernick, Andrew (1991), *Promotional Culture: Advertising, Ideology and Symbolic Expression*, Thousand Oaks, CA: Sage.

Williams, Krissah (2005), 'In Hip-Hop, Making Name-Dropping Pay', *Washington Post*, 29 August. Available online: www.washingtonpost.com/archive/business/2005/08/29/in-hip-hop-making-name-dropping-pay/cc04fdcd-4e3e-4d99-80dd-915286b2fcf4/?utm_term=.2eddaad1ca79.

Williams, Richard (1969), 'John & Yoko (part 1)', *Melody Maker*, 6 December. Available online: www.rocksbackpages.com/Library/Article/john--yoko-part-1.

Yale University (2015), 'Emotion Revolution Closing Session', *YouYube*, 24 October. Available online: www.youtube.com/watch?v=P5Xus-Y0biQ.

Zernike, Kate (2001), 'And Now a Word from Their Cool College Sponsor', *New York Times*, 19 July: Section B.

Index

'1 Million Bottlebags' (Public Enemy) 95
360 contracts 81, 123, 131–2

A$AP Ferg 86
A&M 68
academia 25
'active partnership' position 131–2
Adidas 93–4
Adorno, Theodor 10, 43, 64
advertising 5, 6, 36, 111–16, 128
    antagonisms between music and 138
    country music 110
    creative revolution 11
    digital 154–5
    licensing 116–23, 143
    online environment 144
    rap artists 95, 98, 99
    selling out 123–6
    television commercials 15–16
aesthetics 28, 54, 162
Affordable Care Act, US 157
African-Americans 2, 15, 88, 89, 106, 107
Aftermath Entertainment 102
Agenda (Kate Nash) 142
AI music 148–9
album covers 34–5, 48
alternative music 75, 76. *See also* independent music
alternative production. *See* independent record labels
'(Always Be My) Sunshine' (Jay-Z) 104
Amazon 151
American Idiot 80
America's Bitter Pill (Brill) 157
anti-commercialism 56–9, 109
Aoki, Steve 118
Apple 121, 123, 149
Arcade Fire 149
Arctic Monkeys 141
arena rock 14, 39, 48–52, 54, 57
Arnold, Gina 75, 76–7

art
    authenticity 21–3
    and capitalism 1 (*see also* selling out)
    and commercialism 32–7, 44
    folk tradition 19–20
    music as 18–19
    rock as 23–6, 54
art education 24–5
Artic Monkeys 5
artist-brands 136
artistic genius 31
artistic v. commercial success 42–5, 56, 57, 58
Atlantic 110, 145
audiences 39, 91, 92
authenticity 9, 36, 55–6, 127
    black artists 30–1
    black music 91
    Bob Dylan 29–30
    folk music 20
    glitter rock 52–3
    hip-hop 86–7
    metal 82
    and popular music as art 21–3
    rap music 87, 104–6, 108
    rock music 54
    rock'n'roll 85, 86
    and technology 25
    women 31–2
autonomy. *See* cultural autonomy
AZ 98
Azerrad, Michael 27, 75, 76, 77, 78, 79, 80

Babes in Toyland 79
baby boxes 157
Bandcamp 142
Banet-Weiser, Sarah 22, 36, 115, 135
Banks, Mark 13, 62, 64–5, 139, 162
Barbie 99
Baumann, Shyon 23
Baym, Nancy 142
BBC 138

beach music 92
Beatles, The 26–8
　arena concerts 51
　as indie predecessors 75
　mohair suits 4
　Pop Art 34
　'Revolution' 113, 116
　Sergeant Pepper 25, 26, 27, 34, 47–8
Beats Electronics 149
Bee Gees, The 46
beverage companies 97–8
Beyoncé 55, 149
Bieber, Justin 92
Billboard 75, 76, 98, 99
black artists 15, 85–6. *See also* race
　authenticity 30–1
　Black Swan 67
　MTV 91–2
　music production 89–90
　royalties 91
　segregation 92
Black Eyed Peas 35
Black Lives Matter 109
black music 88, 91, 92
black ops advertising 155
Black Swan Records 67, 90
Blanco, Alvin 93–4
Bleach (Nirvana) 78
Blondie 4, 15, 53–4
Bloom, PJ 122–3
Blow, Kurtis 86, 98
blues musicians 21
Bomp! 70
bookshops 82–3
Born to Run (Springsteen) 57
Bourdieu, Pierre 25, 63–4, 65
boutique labels 96, 102
Bowie, David 35, 52, 54
boyd, danah 6
Brackett, David 88
Bradshaw, Alan 115, 138
brand alignment 117–18
branding 134–6, 141
brands. *See* consumer brands
Breitbart, Andrew 155
Brill, Steven 157
Brown, Jane 92
Burke, Clem 53–4

Burnett, Robert 142
Buzzcocks 70

Cagle, Van M. 35, 52
Cale, John 24
Cammaerts, Bart 142
Campbell, Kenneth 92
capabilities approach 13
capitalism 1, 8, 44, 133
　cool capitalism 11
Capitol 26–7
Carah, Nicholas 115, 134–5
Cardi B 98
CBS 68–9
CDs 129–30
censorship 45
Centre for Contemporary Cultural
　　Studies, Birmingham 25
Chapple, Steve 39, 44, 45, 51
chart success and corporate interest
　96–100
Chevrolet 118
Chicago 53
Chick-fil-A 122
Chiswick 69, 70
Chronic, The (Dr Dre) 102
Chuck D 95
Chumbawamba 122
Citibank 119
Clash, The 5, 68–9, 71
class 28, 139
CMJ New Music Report 76
Cobain, Kurt 79, 86
Coca-Cola (Coke) 98, 112, 117
Cohen, Lyor 144
college radio 75–6
college rock 75
commercial success 39–41, 52–6
　and artistic success 42–5, 56, 57, 58
commercialism 10, 11, 22, 32–7, 44. *See
　also* anti-commercialism
　going commercial 45–8
　rap music 92–106
commercialization 59, 153, 154, 161–2
　education 155–6
　healthcare 156–8
　journalism 154–5
commercials. *See* advertising

commodification 87
commodification of discourse 8
commoditization 48
'Complete Control' (The Clash) 69
consumer brand partnerships 128, 135, 136, 140, 143–7, 161
consumer brands. *See also* branding
   brand alignment 117–18
   indirect influence 147–50
   sportswear brand 97
consumerism 6–7, 11
Converse 97, 146
cool capitalism 11
Coors Aspen Edge 119
Coppola, Roman 119
copyright 91, 137. *See also* licensing
corporate interest 96–100
corporate rock. *See* arena rock
corporate sponsorship 94
counterculture 45
counterculture values 41
country music 21, 88, 109–10
Coward, Kyle 96
Crass 69
Crawdaddy! 24
Creation Records 73
creative revolution 11
creativity 10, 64, 118–20
Creedence Clearwater Revival 116
Cristal 100
Crow, Thomas 19–20, 33–4, 35
crowdfunding 142
crowd-pleasing 4
cultural autonomy 5, 15, 61, 62–6, 81–2
cultural entrepreneurs 13
cultural policy 2, 136–40
cultural production 63–4
cultural value 12–13
culture industry 10, 42, 43
Curry, Denzel 86

Daft Punk 149
Dale, Pete 80
Damned, The 69
Dangerhouse 70
Davey D 109
Davies, Helen 32, 48
Davis, Aeron 10, 133, 155

Defiant Ones, The 102
Densmore, John 118
Desperate Bicycles, The 70
Dicola, Peter 140
Diddy 101
Digital Millennium Copyright Act 1998, US 137
Digital Underground 97
digitalization 81, 82, 127, 129–33, 154–5
Dinosaur Jr 79
discourse 8, 158
discourse analysis 8
distribution 91
Dodos, The 122
Domino Records 141
Donnas, The 117
Doors, The 118
Dougan, John 34
Downbeat 24
Dr Dre 92, 96, 102, 149
Drake 98
Duffy, Brooke 135
Dylan, Bob 17, 27, 28–30, 36, 75

East Asia 82
Eazy-E 101
Eckhardt, Giana 115, 138
Ed Sullivan Show 111
education 24–5, 139, 155–6
educational discourse 8
Einstein, Mara 155
Electric Mud (Muddy Waters) 30–1
electronic groups 52–3
EMI 27, 68
Eminem 92
Endel 148
endorsement deals 145
entrepreneurialism 100–4
European Copyright Directive 2001 137
exchange value 42
Exploding Plastic Inevitable 34

Facebook 155
Fairclough, Norman 8
fake artists 148
fan labour 142
film 42
financial success. *See* commercial success

Fine, Gary 25
Flamin' Groovies 47, 70
folk art 19–20, 22
folk movement 75
folk music 19, 20, 28–30
folk rock 20, 30
Forbes 102
Forman, Murray 101
'Fortunate Son' (Creedence Clearwater Revival) 116
Foucault, Michel 64
Frampton, Peter 47–8
Frank, Thomas 11
Frith, Simon
    art school 25, 36
    authenticity 29
    folk rock 20
    Pop Art 35
    punk 67
    rock community 57–8
    rock music 43–4
    Sound Effects 40
    technology 25
    'Why Does Music Make People So Cross?' 4
    Woodstock Festival 49
Fruity Pebbles' Barney Rubble 99
funding 10
Future of Music Coalition 162–3

Gallagher, Liam 149
gangsta rap 95, 96–7, 100
Garofalo, Reebee 39, 44, 45, 51
Gates Foundation 157–8
Geffen, David 44, 78
gender 28, 31–2
Gendron, Bernard 24, 26, 27, 28, 53
Genius 86
Gennari, John 18
genres 88, 91–2
Gilroy, Paul 103
glam rock 52
glitter rock 52, 54, 58
going commercial 45–8
Goldberg, Michael 112–13
Goldstein, Richard 46
Gomez, Selena 150
Goodman, Fred 40, 42, 44, 56, 57, 58

Google 155
Gordon, Kim 35, 78
Graakjær, Nicolai 115
Graham, Bill 51
Grazian, David 55
Green Day 5, 80–1
Green Label Sound 146, 147
grime artists 82, 110
Grundy, Bill 68
Guardian 122

Hamilton, Jack 31, 85–6, 89
Hammond, John 18
Hard Day's Night, A (The Beatles) 28
hardcore punk 71–2
Harvey, Mark 27
healthcare 156–8
Heavy D 98
Hendrix, Jimmy 107
Hesmondhalgh, David
    independent record labels 65, 67
    indie music 74
    moral economy 13
    philanthropy 138
    post-punk 71
    prestige and popularity 64
    publishing 65
    punk v. rock 58
    selling out 73
higher education 156
hillbilly music 88
hip-hop 21–2, 55–6, 86–7, 98, 101, 103, 110
Hip-Hop Evolution 109
hippies 67
Honda 120
Hopper, Jessica 6
Horkheimer, Max 10, 43
Horne, Howard 25, 35, 36
Huffington Post 155
Hüsker Dü 77–8

Ice Cube 103, 108
'I'd Like to Teach the World to Sing (in Perfect Harmony)' 112
In It for the Money (Supergrass) 5
Independent Group, Institute of Contemporary Art, London 33

independent bookshops 82–3
independent charts 72
independent music 63. *See also* indie music
independent record labels 15, 61–2, 65–6, 81–2
   boutique model 96, 102
   history 66–72
   and major labels 64, 72–8
   promotional activities 142
independent record shops 82
indie music 74–5, 76, 82
indie values 81–3
Instagram influencers 145, 150
Institute of Contemporary Art, London 33
institutional autonomy 65
insurance companies 157
Interscope Records 102
Isle of Wight festival 49

Jackson, Michael 112
Jackson Jr, John L. 101, 105
James, Jim 119
Jawbreaker 81
Jay-Z 96, 100, 101–2, 104, 109, 149
jazz criticism 18
Jenner, Kendall 109
John, Elton 53
Johnson, Matt 147
Jordan, Andy 150
journalism 154–5
Jovan 112–13
Just around Midnight (Hamilton) 31
'just desserts' position 131–2

K Records 79
Kate Nash: Underestimate the Girl 142
Keep On Smilin' (Wet Willie) 47
Keightley, Keir 18, 21, 27, 33, 55
Kennedy, Randall 2–3, 107
Kickstarter 142
Kraftwerk 53
KRS-One 98
Kruse, Holly 76, 79

Lady Gaga 16, 35, 132, 145, 146, 149, 150–1
Ladybug Transistor 119
Laing, David 66, 67, 68, 69, 70

Lambda Legal 122
Landau, Jon 56, 57
language 8
Lennon, John 4, 24, 26, 28, 51
Levi's 119, 147
Lewis, Justin 6
LGBTQ organizations 122
licensing 116–23, 143, 147
'Like a Rock' (Bob Seger) 118
Lilys 119
LL Cool J 98
Lollapalooza concert tour 79
Long, Meric 122
Long March to Pop (Crow) 33
Lookout Records 80, 81
Love, Courtney 79
'Love Me Do' (The Beatles) 26
Ludacris 99
Lynskey, Dorian 5
lyrics 27–8

Macy's 99
Madonna 112, 149
magnetic tape 25
'Mahgeetah' (My Morning Jacket) 119
malt liquor 95–6
Mann, Aimee 121
Mann, Manfred 44
Manzerolle, Vincent 149
Mark P 69
Martin, Chris 149
mass culture 43–4
Master P 97
master rights 116
Maximum Rock'n'Roll 80
MC Hammer 97, 98, 106, 109
MC Shan 98
McCartney, Paul 26
McGoey, Linsey 157–8
McGuigan, Jim 11
McKennitt, Lorena 150
McKenzie River Corporation 95
McLaren, Malcolm 68
McLeod, Kembrew 53, 54, 104
media deregulation 114, 137
Meier, Leslie
   360 deal contracts 132
   aesthetics 152

artist-brands 136
commercialization 161
consumer brand partnerships 143
culture industry 10
independent record labels 65
online music platforms 149
promotional activities 126
support for artists 162
sync licensing 147
technology companies 141
Mekons, The 46
Mellery-Pratt, Robin 94
Melody Maker 24, 34, 46
Mensa, Vic 86
metal 82
Michael, George 5
middle-class 28
Millennials 134
Minaj, Nicki 149
Moby 120, 122, 149
Modernism 20, 33
Molotkow, Alexandra 6
Monterey Pop Festival 1967 49
Moore, Alan 23
Moore, Ryan 79
moral economy 13
Morris, Errol 119
Morris, Jeremy 129–30
Motown 90
Mould, Bob 77–8
Mountain Dew 146
MTV 91–2
Muddy Waters 30–1
music charts 72, 73, 76, 96–100, 112
music criticism 24, 25
music education 139
music festivals 49, 79
music industry
    commercial success 39–41
    impact of digitalization on 129–33
    incorporation of independent music 72–8
    professionalization 40, 46–7, 65
    and race 87–9
    roots 43
music journalism 24
music production 46–7, 63–4, 89–90
music videos 5

Music Week 119
'My Adidas' (Run-DMC) 93–4
My Morning Jacket 119
MySpace 141

Napster 131
Nas 98
Nash, Kate 142
National Health Service (NHS) 157
Neal, Mark Anthony 90, 105, 108
negotiated autonomy 64
Negus, Keith 13–14, 88, 89, 92–3, 132, 148
neoliberalism 133, 138, 154
Nevermind (Nirvana) 75, 78, 79
New Labour 73, 138
new wave 53, 54, 55, 58
New York Times 55, 78
New York Times Magazine 6
Newport Folk Festival 1965 28–30, 75
Nike 97, 113, 116
Nirvana 4, 75, 78–80
Nordwind, Tim 145, 146
Norton, Greg 77
'Nothing's Gonna Stop Us Now' (Starship) 122
Nussbaum, Martha 13
NYC Women's Fund for Media, Music and Theatre 138
Nyro, Laura 44

Oasis 73
Ochs, Phil 29, 49
OK Go 145
'On Popular Music' (Adorno) 43
One Chord Wonders (Laing) 66
O'Neill, Essena 150
online journalism 155
O'Reilly, Bill 99
Our Band Could Be Your Life (Azerrad) 27, 75

Pace, Harry 67
Page, Jimmy 24
Palmer, Amanda 142
Parallel Lines (Blondie) 53, 54
Paramount 67, 90
Pearl Jam 5

peer-to-peer networks 130, 131, 137
Pelly, Liz 144, 148
Pepsi 98, 99, 109, 112
Perry, Katy 132
Peterson, Richard 23
philanthrocapitalism 157–8
philanthropy 108
Philips, Deborah 156
Pillsbury, Glenn T. 3, 9–10
Pillsbury Doughboy 99
Play (Moby) 120
poetry 27–8
PonoMusic 149
Pooley, Jefferson 135
pop 31
Pop 2.0 artists 132
Pop Art 19, 32, 33–7
popism 55, 56
popular music 3
    as art 18–19, 21–3
postmodernism 33
post-punk 71
Powell, Kevin 100
Powers, Devon 24, 115, 136
Presley, Elvis 111–12
Price, Simon 139
private healthcare 157
privatization 153
product placement 146
production 46–7, 63–4, 89–90
professionalization 40, 46–7, 65
promotion 10
promotional activities 140–3
promotional culture 11–12, 127, 133–6, 147–50, 153
promotional fatigue 16, 150–2
promotional universities 156
pseudo-individuality 43
Public Enemy 95
publishing 65
publishing rights 116
punk 35, 53, 58, 66, 67–9, 82. *See also* hardcore punk; post-punk
    and college radio 75
    Top of the Pops 73
punk community 80
'Punk Is Dead' (Crass) 69
punk labels 69–70

Quinn, Eithne 95, 100–1, 106, 110

race 28, 31, 87–9, 106–9. *See also* black artists; black music
racial indictments 2
radical autonomy 64
radio 75–6, 113, 114, 121, 137, 138
Radiohead 57
Ramones, The 68, 71
rap artists 15
rap music 88, 91, 128
    authenticity 87, 104–6, 108
    chart success and corporate interest 96–100
    commerce and entrepreneurialism 100–4
    commercial opportunities 92–6
    selling out 86, 106
    social class 139
Record Business 72
record labels/record companies 10. *See also* independent record labels
    commercialism 44
    rap music 96–7
Record Store Day 82
recorded music market 6–7
Red Bull 146
Reebok 99
Reed, Lou 120
'Remote Control' (The Clash) 69
Reprise 80
'Revolution' (The Beatles) 113, 116
RIAA 131
Richards, Keith 24
Rihanna 150
rock community 57–8
rock culture 18, 49
rock music 22. *See also* arena rock; glitter rock
    anti-commercialism 109
    as art 23–6, 54
    audiences 39
    authenticity 52–3, 54
    commercial success 39–40, 44
    commoditization 48
    as counterculture 45
    and gender 31–2
    going commercial 45–6, 47

as mass culture 43–4
and race 31
selling out 85
rock myth 54–5
rock superstars 58
rockism 41, 54, 55, 56
rock'n'dole scheme 73, 138
rock'n'roll 85–6, 91, 111–12
Rock'n'Roll Is Here to Pay (Chapple and Garofalo) 39–40
Rolling Stone 48
Rolling Stones, The 4, 34, 49, 51, 112–13, 132
Romanticism 1, 3, 9, 17, 20, 27, 35–6, 62
Rose, Tricia 92, 97, 98, 101, 102, 103, 108
Rosen, Jody. 55
Ross, Rick 99
Rough Trade Records 68, 71
royalties 91
Run-DMC 93–4, 98
Ryan, Bill 42

Saha, Anamik 87, 88, 97
San Diego 79
Sandel, Michael 162
Sanneh, Kelefa 55
Saunier, Greg 144
Savage, Jon 67, 68, 69, 70
Scorsese, Martin 42
Seattle 79
Seeger, Peter 20, 112
Seger, Bob 118
segregation 92
Seiler, Cotten 49, 58, 76
self-branding 135–6
self-censorship 45
selling out 1, 2–7, 42, 61. *See also* going commercial
advertising 123–6
Blondie 54
discourse and debates 7–14
independent record labels 73
and race 106–9
rap music 86, 106
rock music 85
selling out discourse 158, 160–3

Sen, Amartya 13
Serazio, Michael 134
Sergeant Pepper (The Beatles) 25, 26, 27, 34, 47–8
Sermon, Erick 86
Sex Pistols 68, 71
Shaw, Sandie 139
Sheeran, Ed 16, 140, 150
Shock G 97
Shumway, David 21, 22
Sideburns 46
Simmons, Russell 101, 106
Slate 55
Slick, Grace 122
'Smells Like Teen Spirit' (Nirvana) 78
Smith, Patti 70
Sniffin' Glue 69
Snoop Dogg 96
social class 28, 139
social media 132, 140–1, 150
social media influencers 136, 145, 150
sociology of music 25, 63
soft drinks companies 97–8
Sonic Youth 35, 78
Sony 73, 130, 148
soul music 31, 85–6, 92
Soulja Boy 86
Sound Effects (Frith) 40
Spiral Scratch (Buzzcocks) 70
sponsorship 94. *See also* advertising; corporate interest; promotion
sportswear brands 97. *See also* Adidas; Nike
Spotify 81, 131, 141–2, 144, 148
Springsteen, Bruce 14–15, 55, 56–7, 58
Sprite 98
SST 77
St. Ides liquor 95–6
Stahl, Matt 91
Starbucks 146
Starship 122
state support 10, 137–40, 163
Stefani, Gwen 149
Stein, Chris 53
Stiff 69, 70

Stipe, Michael 150
Strachan, Robert 131, 134
Stratton, Jon 44
streaming 130–1, 132, 144, 149
Sub Pop 78, 79, 81
success. *See* chart success and corporate interest; commercial success
Super Furry Animals 117
Supergrass 5
superstars 161
sync licensing 116, 122–3, 143, 147

Taylor, Timothy 6, 115
technology 25–6
technology companies 141
'Telephone' (Lady Gaga) 146
Television 70
television 154
television appearances 5
television commercials 15–16, 114
'Things Go Better with Coke' 112
'This Note's for You' (Neil Young) 5
Thomson, Kristin 140
Tidal 149
Timberlake, Justin 145
Tommy Hilfiger 100
Tone Loc 106
Top of the Pops 5, 73
Toronto Star 57, 121, 122
Townshend, Pete 35
Toynbee, Jason 65
Travis, Geoff 68
Tribe Called Quest, A 98
Trouser Press 47
'True to the Game' (Ice Cube) 108
'Turn Off the Radio' (Ice Cube) 103–4
Tyler, Steven 50

unemployment 73
Universal 130
universities 156
US Digital Millennium Copyright Act 1998 137
Usher 92

Valuing Live Music: The UK Live Music Census 2017 139
Velvet Underground 34
Vevo 144
Vice 80, 155
Village Voice 24
vinyl 142
Virgin 68

Waksman, Steve 50, 71, 76
Wald, Elijah 29
'Walk on the Wild Side' (Lou Reed) 120
Warhol, Andy 33, 34, 35
Warner 77–8, 130, 148
Waterstones 82–3
Wayne, Lily 99
Web 2.0 mythology 141
Wernick, Andrew 133, 156
West, Kanye 149
Wet Willie 47
Whannel, Gary 156
What Money Can't Buy (Sandel) 162
White, Jack 149
Who, The 34, 49
  The Who Sell Out 5, 17, 34–5
Why Music Matters (Hesmondhalgh) 13
Wickham, Andy 49
Williams, Pharrell 145
women 31–2
Wonder, Stevie 27, 75
Woodstock Festival 1969 49
Wrangler 116
Writing the Record (Powers) 24
Wu-Tang Clan 97, 101

Year Punk Broke, The 78–9
Yo! MTV Raps 92
Young, Neil 5, 149
Young MC 98
young people 134
YouTube 81, 131, 144, 148

Zen Arcade (Hüsker Dü) 77, 78
Zeppelin, Led 53